The Spanish American Roots of William Carlos Williams

The Spanish American Roots of

WILLIAM CARLOS WILLIAMS

by Julio Marzán

Foreword by David Ignatow

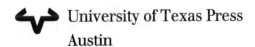 University of Texas Press
Austin

Requests for permission to reproduce material from this work should be
sent to Permissions, University of Texas Press, Box 7819, Austin, TX
78713-7819.

⊗ The paper used in this publication meets the minimum requirements
of American National Standard for Information Sciences—Permanence
of Paper for Printed Library Materials, ANSI Z39, 48-1984.

Library of Congress Cataloging-in-Publication Data
Marzán, Julio, date
      The Spanish American roots of William Carlos Williams /
by Julio Marzán.
            p.   cm.
      Includes bibliographical references and index.
      ISBN 0-292-75160-5
      1. Williams, William Carlos, 1883-1963—Knowledge—Latin America.
      2. American poetry—Latin American influences.
      3. American poetry—Spanish influences.
      4. Latin America—In literature.
      I. Title.
      PS3545.I544Z6293 1994
      811'.52—dc20
                                                    93-38636

Contents

For my wife, Janeth

Foreword

Once again, William Carlos Williams shows the way. In the sixties, his portrayal of American life as lived and spoken became for the vast majority of American poets the mode to which they dedicated their talents and commitment, establishing for the future the liberation of American poetry from its subservience to forms of poetry and writing alien to American life.

Today, as the poetry of our increasingly multicultural society develops its own subjects and invented forms, each growing out of the example established by Williams, it is important to realize that he too came of a mixed heritage, part Latin, part English, with emphasis in his upbringing on the Spanish language. It was a heritage he never denied or hid from himself or from others. Today, he can be read not only as the liberator of contemporary American poetry into its natural elements of speech and style but also as one who stands as the guarantor of all that is relevant and fine emerging in the poetry of our multicultural society.

The Spanish American Roots of William Carlos Williams is as fascinating as was the man himself. He is brought fully to life in its pages, with his problems, conscious and unconscious, in making himself felt and respected as a poet in the English language. That he succeeded, even beyond his dreams, is vividly and faithfully demonstrated in this seminal book.

—David Ignatow

I always knew that I was I, precisely where I stood and that nothing could make me accept anything that had no counterpart in myself by which to recognize it. I always said to myself that I did not speak English, for one thing, and that should be the basis for a beginning, . . .

("The Basis of Faith in Art")

But they have no access to my sources
Let them write them as they may and
perfect it as they can they will never
come to the secret of that form

("The Cure")

Introduction
In Search of William Carlos Williams

The chronology of the making of this book begins in the late 1970's, at the celebration of the restoration of the Passaic Falls, a poetry reading by Allen Ginsberg and David Ignatow. Williams, of course, was present in spirit for the ceremonies, the lunch break, and especially the tour of the falls, during which I imagined him walking through the predominantly Latin neighborhood. It occurred to me then that Passaic had probably started to receive Latins in the nineteenth century, when New York City had. Williams' mother, I knew, was one of them, a thought that prompted my wondering how, as their numbers grew over the years, Williams looked upon those symbols of his mother's origins. And my curiosity came as a surprise to me because until that moment I hadn't given that half of Williams' background any significant thought. The day's events had apparently set off questions I had been harboring unconsciously.

I recalled reading that Williams' father, English by birth, grew up in the Caribbean and that his mother was born and raised in Mayagüez. Coming to New Jersey in the nineteenth century, they belonged to a trickle of northbound immigrants from the Caribbean, part of a modest wave of assorted Latin Americans and Spaniards who settled in the New York area. Williams—the fact had failed to make a real impression on me—was half-Puerto Rican, no minor realization for an emergent writer who was born in Puerto Rico and who suddenly remembered reading an interview in which, after being told that Denise Levertov was from Russian and Jewish stock, Williams had answered that her background had "probably influenced her work."

A book, however, was not what I had in mind when I started to reread Williams in this new context. That day in Passaic had left me as engrossed in trying to understand my own mental workings as in the relevance to American literature of Williams' Puerto Rican background: how, despite what I knew about his mother's being from Mayagüez, nothing I had read or been taught about Williams had motivated me to associate him with anything other than mainstream Anglo America. I was familiar with his reference to Puerto Rico in "All the Fancy Things" and his dismissing Latins as romantics in "Adam" and "The Desert Music." But when I read those poems as a sixties English major, they simply reinforced stereotypes about Latins that I too had assimilated with English-speaking culture. Actually, my undergraduate interest in Williams was filtered through Ginsberg and the Beats, who excited me back then but whom I ultimately didn't follow. I'll never forget hearing Ginsberg read "The pure products of America / go crazy . . ."[1] And while my good education extracurricularly exposed me to that new writing, it formally defined with razor-edged fence borders that terrain understood to be the genuine article in literature, which meant the great male writers from Anglo America and Europe. So when I first read somewhere that Williams' mother was Puerto Rican, I followed the example of my education: I thought nothing of it.

A late sixties and early seventies consciousness heightened my awareness of my own cultural roots, a process whose added reward was, as it was for the world, my discovering the new Latin American writers. Even though I wrote in English and was struggling to overcome many stale expectations, whether fraternal or inimical, of the minority writer, I identified with the writers from Latin America. But my psyche remained contradictory. Concerning Williams, I continued to carry on like a dutiful English major. After coming across his name as a translator from the Spanish, for example, I still was not provoked to pursue any connection to his Spanish-language background. Needless to say, I also kept Williams in a province of my mind protected from updated usages of "minority" and "ethnic," modifiers that in Williams' time primarily existed in the glossaries of social scientists and that today still cause a growl in the stomach of many a critic. I knew better than to associate Williams with modifiers that would have stamped him as a writer of extra-literary significance. Like his critics, as I later learned, I too had pardoned Williams for writing well.

But merely establishing an ethnic connection wasn't my objective in returning to Williams. I was motivated by self-interest. Being from a Spanish-speaking culture and writing in English produced a range of challenges, and I wanted to investigate to what extent Williams' work showed any signs of having grappled with those challenges and what lessons there were for me. Additionally, the questions that hatched that day in New Jersey also hinted at the possibility of discovering in Williams a major Latin literary root in Anglo American letters. If Williams was a product of his Spanish-language background, then he would be an antecedent to a nascent writing that appears to have no roots in this country's literature. This was an intriguing hypothesis, although a fearsome one; I anticipated the need for some extensive biographical sleuthing. Once my reading started in earnest, however, I found out that, while there were secret passageways to Williams, there were really no secrets to unearth; he flaunted details of his Latin background incessantly, but stylized in a manner that gives them the veneer of being of decorative, quaint, or simply secondary importance.

But the opposite proved to be true. Williams' Latin *half* revealed itself as his spiritual center. His major creative achievement was his translating the exotic voice of that core into the voice of an Anglo persona amenable to a reading public that conventionally held in low regard that most important component of his historical person. By means of his literary persona, Williams succeeded in elevating to a higher plane, on the proscenium of the reader's imagination, the very thing that his country had historically demonstrated a penchant for trivializing: his dramatic cultural dilemma as an American, the same inner drama of all those "others" who possessed two irreconcilable cultures and were assumed "nonentities."

Williams' mission was therefore dual, to make his country rethink its myths and to find the balance between his person and his persona—which in secret comprised two personae. To accomplish his dual mission, Williams often resorted to a stylistic code, a system of ciphers that became evident once I began mapping the triangular bridge between his two cultures and his writings. By codifying, in images and structures that simultaneously spoke for his person and his personae, Williams transformed obstacles that would have undermined his writings and turned them into the advantage of a unique style. Thus, in devising ways to manage his loyalty to his selves and his uncooperative country, Williams discovered the virtues of the imagination and his powers as an artist.

In *A Life of Picasso* John Richardson describes Picasso as a painter who came "to be regarded as a French artist . . . However, . . . remained a Spaniard at heart, a man of the Mediterranean." Richardson argues that, despite Picasso's French reputation, the key to his work is to be found in his Andalusian roots:

> For Picasso this demonic Andalusian birthright would be
> a lifelong source of anguish, also a lifelong source of power.[2]

A similar anguish produced Williams. From growing up in Rutherford, he had inherited Anglo American culture, which was modern and industrial and socially correct but which belittled his Spanish American half, inherited from his mother and partly from his father. But even though born in Rutherford, by growing up among foreigner parents, Williams also developed the insecurity of being defective as an American. Anglo America offered Williams what France represented to Picasso: a culture to claim and possess. By contrast, his Caribbean background was, in Williams' words, "meager" and "romantic." Nevertheless, as Richardson tells us of Picasso, whose unprestigious Andalusia was a lifelong source of anguish, Williams' own Latin American roots and anguished sense of foreignness also became his "lifelong source of power."

The source of Williams' anguish and power is the focus of this book. While not a biography, it is predicated on a new, as yet unwritten biography, one extrapolated from his works and a revision of the criticism. Williams' critics have uniformly failed Williams in refusing to pursue avenues of investigation that he constantly challenged them to take. Given the glaring evidence in his works of an inner cultural conflict, the critics' failure to examine the source of that drama is itself glaring. It can be said that, blindsided by the mainstream culture's perception of biculturalism as marginal to the American experience, the critics have been incapable of seeing any connection between Williams' Latin American (usually referred to as "Spanish") background and his contributions to the nation's literature. Nevertheless, that connection exists, and as this book demonstrates, *had* to be in the work, even if only Williams himself could identify it, in order for Williams to feel that he existed in his writings. Unfortunately his critics, consciously or not, have collaborated in the preservation of Williams' Anglo persona, remote from the total picture of his background. The purpose here is not to dismiss the body of Williams criticism; this book simply intends to be complementary. To brush aside all the previous criticism would be to lose sight of Williams' impact on contemporary poetry, as well as to forget that Williams' Anglo persona was also indeed genuine because he was literally, not nominally, bicultural.

Having described Williams as bicultural, however, I beg the reader to approach this book without preconceptions about my critical approach. While Williams' particular ethnic background is the most perspicuous novel ingredient in this appreciation of his work, this study is not an "ethnic interpretation." The new cultural context introduced and the continental American history applied form part of the cosmos of a lost Williams, the bicultural one who has been customized (with his help) to fit into the mainstream and its "catalogue." On the written page Williams translated his biculturalism into symbols and structures, and these demanded a scrupulous analysis both of his poems, which he wrote as an artist whose medium was language, as well as of his "conceptualist" prose. Deciphering his imagery required that, after factoring in autobiographical details that were heretofore left out, one put aside any penchant for performing exercises in social science and appreciate to the maximum Williams' understanding of poetry as art.

For Williams, *art* signified therapy, liberation, and stratagem. He believed in the therapeutic power of *art* to "cure" many ills, including both Anglo American Euro-mindedness and the stress it caused him. Harboring that prognosis, he saw the need to set free his country's bound imagination, a malady for which he saw a "cure" in the new nonrepresentational art of his day, especially cubism. By breaking with traditional ways of seeing, that revolutionary art afforded the opportunity to beneficially shake up his rigid "townspeople" while allowing him to render his full self in his work. But performing *art* also signified for Williams having a stratagem, a covert way in which to remain true to himself and to the possibility of having a writer's career. In summary, his secret life of polar public and private selves was the material for a fractured, contradictory autobiography that only held together in the illogical, enciphered, musical balance of art. In other words, Williams' soul, divided and conflictive in life, on the canvas of his work became a harmonizing composite of components and simultaneous opposing viewpoints best captured in the style of a cubist portrait.

The Spanish American Roots of William Carlos Williams

Chapter 1
A Cubist Portrait

*I had a great time making up my mind what my literary
signature should be—something of profound importance,
obviously. An advertising friend of my father's spoke up
strongly for plain W. Williams. "It's a common name," he
said, "but think of the advantage of being the W. Williams."
To me the full name seemed the most revealing and therefore better.*

(*The Autobiography of William Carlos Williams* 108)

In his painting "I Saw the Figure Five in Gold," intended as a portrait of
William Carlos Williams, Charles Demuth turned the poet's names into
visual images. Along the top edge to the left hang the solid, horizontally
cropped upper-case letters of "BILL." In the cavity between the knife-
shaped top and the pregnant-belly bottom of the largest figure "5," in a
black background plane, with part of the "o" and all the "s" covered over
by a ray of color, floats "Carlo." Williams' complete identity is given only
in initials centered on the bottom edge, "WCW," an encoding that reiterates a cipher motif of this painting. What is the number "5" if not a cipher?
And while the outstanding "BILL" grabs our attention in the foreground,
its letters as solid as the figure "5," "Carlo" is in weak marquis lights,
white dots with no counterpart in this painting except that the dots also
suggest code: "Carlo" is a ghostly encoded presence.

Demuth apparently felt closest to Williams as Carlos. In 1907, responding to a letter in which Williams announced his intention to become a
writer, Demuth wrote back to "Carlos":

*Carlos, Carlos, how good your letter did sound—you have no idea
how your letter affects me. I have always felt that it would happen to
you someday—that you simply* have *to write. However, hearing that it
would happen this winter was grand news . . .*

I will not be able to see you before I go—Yes it is too bad. Still, Carlos when I come back—when I come back, we may both have a start in a small way then . . .

And Carlos even though nothing happens after your six months' work up in Boston, don't give up, will you?[1]

Williams ascribed Demuth's calling him Carlos to the painter's affection for the name: "Charlie always called me Carlos—the only person in my life to do so. He liked the name."[2] But Demuth, whose given name is the English equivalent of Carlos, was also subtly celebrating a side to Williams in which he identified himself:

Demuth's life involved a vital inner existence dependent upon intuition and feeling while the surface of his life was comparatively uneventful.

(Farnham 4)

Williams too, as we shall see, was someone whose exterior camouflaged a different inner self. And he too gravitated to those in whom he saw himself, which made for a friendship bonded by a mutual appreciation of the hidden parts of the other. In *The Autobiography,* Williams confirms this mutual appreciation in a scene that describes his walks with Demuth in West Philadelphia:

There was a high brick wall along the south side of Locust Street, just west of Thirty-sixth, inside of which there must have been an old garden, long neglected. The thought of it fascinated me. Charlie laughed when I spoke of it. "Not many could enjoy such a thing as that," he said, "by merely looking at the outside of the wall."

(*A* 53)

Demuth, then, generated the contrasting imagery of the two names from his mode of relating to Williams, from his close identification with Williams' having outer and inner identities. To Demuth, as his painting affirms, Carlos was a real person and a vital contribution to the poet. Demuth's incorporating "Carlos" completes the portrait with that essential component less visible to the world amidst the clang and noise of "BILL." Thus that quieter "Carlo[s]" is in dots or distant lights, which Demuth certainly knew would evoke either code, imperceptibility, or both. The artist lights up the name in our consciousness by rendering it in a style that is unique in the painting. In summary, Demuth's imagery offers a visual model of the Williams on which this study is based, of Bill and Carlos as distinct and interacting selves.

Williams' possessing a Carlos self is not a new thesis. On occasion Carlos has been acknowledged in several contexts of Williams' life, primarily as a figurative element to highlight references to Williams' connection to Spanish or as an imagistic thread to his mother's Hispanic background. Where Carlos has yet to figure is in any serious exegesis of Williams' *work*, in which his Hispanic background has routinely been perceived as being of secondary or marginal interest. Nevertheless, as in the symbolism of Williams' complete name, Carlos holds a central position even in the work, a presence not readily visible because Williams most often invoked Carlos in code.

In the poem "El Hombre," to illustrate, the Spanish title translates as both literally "The Man,' and "Man" as in Everyman, which more immediately appears to suit this contemplative poem:

> It is a strange courage
> you give me ancient star.
>
> (The Collected Poems, Vol. I 76)

Below the surface of those lines, however, something more dramatic is taking place: a game of origins and etymologies that Williams often played, at times so subtly that it would appear he intended for no one else to participate. Here "courage" can be read for its face value as well as its Latin root, *cor,* also the root of the Spanish *corazón,* "heart." The modifier "strange" harkens back to its root, the Latin *extra,* meaning "foreign," but probably also came to Williams from the Spanish *extraño.* (In both examples, French derivatives are linguistically possible, but Spanish and English were the actors in Williams' intimate drama.) Similarly, "ancient" plays on the Spanish for "old," *anciano,* from the Latin *ante,* "before." This was one of Williams' favorite hyperboles: in both his discarded *Endymion*-like poem and his synopsis of it in *The Autobiography,* he refers to his hero's being saved by an "ancient nurse." Finally, "star" is a variant of the Greek root for Helen ("bright one"). One of his mother's three given names was Helene, which was why she was called Elena. Translated back to its etymological roots, the couplet tells us that what "old Helen" gave Williams was a "foreign heart": "It is a foreign heart / you give me old Helen."

Elena's courage was strange because she did not *encourage* his career as a poet:

> Shine alone in the sunrise
> Toward which you lend no part!

(CPI 76)

His "ancient star" shines in the background, giving her "strange courage" but not playing a part in the rise of the sun/son. Williams' penchant for that pun is confirmed by its more overt play in the title of his poem "Brilliant Sad Sun."

Another Carlos presence can be discerned from an alternate interpretation of this poem, one based on Williams' admiration of the Spanish poet Luis de Góngora (1561–1627), whom in the essay "Federico García Lorca" Williams singles out as *el hombre:* "Góngora was the man!" (*Selected Essays* 224). Through "El Hombre," Williams received the inspiriting influence of Góngora, a different kind of "ancient star" in his "line." This antecedent shines in Williams' dark past, made invisible by the blond brilliance of Bill, in which Góngora plays no visible role and yet continues to impart his "strange courage." (For this interpretation to sound less far-fetched, see Chapter 5.) But indeed "El Hombre" is also about Everyman, like Quixote, strangely inspirited by the light of a remote star; two poems, possibly three, one contemplative and the other(s) autobiographical, co-existing in a single conceit. The public, contemplative poem speaks in the persona of Bill while the autobiographical poems speak in the ghostly voice of Carlos.

The Spanish title, then, was more than decorative; the use of Spanish called attention to an encoding, in a secret style that gravitated to the conceit, the pun, the enciphering that obliged Williams' reader, as Góngora expected of his, to "remove its bark." This claim, of course, contradicts Williams' reputation as the poet who spoke "straight ahead," the genius of the spontaneous, spoken idiom—a legacy that fits neatly into his busy biography divided between doctoring and writing. That legacy is indeed quite remote from the deliberation implicit in the semantic layering being ascribed to "El Hombre," but the Williams this study is introducing evokes an even more crowded image: Williams as a doctor-poet divided into two poetic personae, with a Metaphysical poet's imagination.

Williams inherited his Carlos identity from his Puerto Rican mother, Elena, who indeed lent an important part to her son's rise. Although near the end of his life Williams confirmed her importance to him, until recently critics have interpreted his claim as tributary and largely symbolic. The criticism broadly assumed that, while Elena was key to him, owing to her being disconnected from his English-speaking world she really had little to do with the formation of the *poet,* an assumption that implicitly discounted any contributions from her background. Williams himself also contributed to this distortion because, writing as the Anglo Bill, he habitually distracted the reader from establishing any umbilical connections from his works to his mother or her culture; those were his sources, secrets for him to keep. In several works he even reinvents Bill as the child of European immigrants, as in the Stecher Trilogy. (*White Mule, In the Money,* and *The Build-up*).

Among Williams' alter identities perhaps his most misleading (and contradictory to his other writings) was of himself as the scion of European immigrants. He did of course partake of the immigrant *mythos* that is part of U.S. cultural history. But the symbols of that immigration have little meaning when used to explain the experience of immigrants from Latin America, like Williams' parents. On the other hand, his application of the European immigrant model is also wholly comprehensible. His parents immigrated to this country long before Latin Americans came in great numbers. Anglo Americans of his day were most likely to personally know few Latin Americans and to harbor many stereotypes—the Mexican peon and wetback, the movie Don Juans, the dancing female bombshells—that obviously discouraged anybody from identifying themselves with any immigration presumed to be entirely of that lot. Indicative of the general tenor of the times and society's ignorance of Latins, until 1930 the census classified "Hispanic" as a racial subgroup.[3] Moreover, Williams' parents landed here in the earliest stages of an immigration whose unique character did not begin to define itself until its numbers began to surge after World War II.

Puerto Ricans came first, contrasting with the less visible earlier islanders by being rural and poor. Different from the Europeans, who had also faced rejection, Puerto Ricans were additionally unwelcome for being racially mixed. Over the years, however, Puerto Rican political gains, civil rights triumphs, and even corpses paved over many social potholes for subsequent Latin immigrants. In 1959 Cubans populated Miami and the Northeast. Dominicans later settled both in Miami and New York, followed by Central and South Americans in several parts of the United States. Collectively, this population opened a new chapter in U.S. immigration history, a shift of Americans from one part of America to another, never crossing a demarcation between the Old World and the New. Their remote European ties were Spanish, if not literally then linguistically or simply mythically, a culture that, as Williams argues in *In the American Grain,* literally burned its ships and committed itself to fusing with America. As the heterogeneous postwar immigration settled in, the uniqueness of Latin Americans as U.S. immigrants became clear: this new population descended from nowhere other than America: the Old World of the American immigrant is the roots of America itself.

In this broader American context is framed the specific arrival of Williams' parents to New Jersey. Elena Hoheb was one of a few Latin Americans who came to the United States in the nineteenth century, and specifically one of a handful of Puerto Ricans who arrived before the Spanish-American War in 1898, as a result of which their homeland passed from Spanish to Yankee hands. Williams' English-born father, William George, grew up in the Spanish-speaking Caribbean from the age of five. He was, according to Williams, a bilingual who preferred to speak Spanish to his wife. The household, at least during Williams' childhood, was predominantly Spanish-speaking, a setting that created a backdrop to a very common upbringing in this society: William Carlos grew up bicultural. This implicitly signified that, like any child of immigrants or from a minority culture in the United States, Williams grew up aware of living in a society that devalued the foreign culture he received at home, imposing on him the life-informing quest to reconcile his cultures.

Historically in the United States, children of white immigrants have reconciled their biculturalism by purging their foreign half and assimilating. According to this convention, as a child Williams had to choose between being an ostracized foreigner or an American. And Williams went through that rite of passage, but not wholeheartedly, eventually questioning the convention in earnest (*In the American Grain, The Great American Novel*), an inner division that he became most keenly aware of when he confronted his circumstance as a writer. For Williams' time, being a writer meant a mainstream writer, the alternative being invisibility. African American culture, as Williams himself knew and the Beats later underscored, was the only true alternative to Anglo American culture, and Williams obviously didn't belong to it. Although he was aware that he was different from friends such as Ezra Pound and Hilda Doolittle in important ways, Williams' reflex identity was nevertheless white Anglo American, inherited from his language, his surroundings, and his father's English roots.

His having grown up being called Bill, of course, became a conscious asset when Williams began to write. Bill was heard and listened to, not being a foreigner to this society. Nevertheless, Williams lived troubled that Bill was actually a capitulation to a tradition that stifled his true person. This preoccupation led to his heightened cognizance that his completely unforeign Bill identity was a creation of language, a condition that kept him ever conscious of how language affects perception and perception, language. Language was impure and unreliable, he viscerally realized better than most others; language was easily adulterated by the listener's prejudices and preconceptions. His serious contemplation of this phenomenon gave rise to a style built around the treacherous possibilities of language, a sense of what was semantically predictable and unpredictable in different contexts:

> That which is heard from the lips of those to whom we are talking in our day's affairs mingles with what we see in the streets and everywhere about us as it mingles also with our imaginations. By this chemistry is fabricated a language of the day which shifts and reveals its meaning as clouds shift and turn in the sky and sometimes send down rain or snow or hail.
>
> (*Imaginations* 59)

Language was subject to this "chemistry," what he also called a formula of "time and place and enforcement," a chemistry of climate that constituted an artist's particular "weather," and if the artist was to contribute anything of value, then succumbing to it was unthinkable. In this Williams emulated the Spaniard Juan Ruiz, the Archpriest of Hita, writer of *The Book of Good Love,* and Dante. On the surface, these two seem to be opposites. Ruiz defied the Church's narrow teachings on love; Dante strove to remain faithful to them. "Dante restricts; the archpriest expands" ("Against the Weather," *SE* 204). And yet both works were alike in that in each case the poet remained true to his artist's vision, which is invariably more giving than his "weather." Dante duly condemned the unblessed lovers, and yet "by the grace with which he has portrayed" (*SE* 205) Paolo and Francesca, he also appeared to pity them. Thus, however differently each writer appeared to respond to his peculiar "weather," each graced his poem with the more generous vision of the artist himself, who always speaks in the language of the work's structure: "In the structure the artist speaks as an artist purely. There he cannot lie" (*SE* 204).

Although both models paralleled Williams' struggle with his own "weather," Dante's alliance with the Church, which Williams described as "unnatural" (*SE* 205), seemed to best address his own cultural circumstance. Reflecting his own experience, he deduced that the inner conflict Dante experienced in order to remain true to himself as an artist was something that the "struggle of the work must reveal" (*SE* 205). This struggle was one between the artist and his material, with the objective "to wrestle his content out of the narrow into the greater meaning" (*SE* 205), allowing the reader to see more than the "weather" would like:

> *Dante was the agent of art facing a time and place and enforcement which were his "weather." Taking this weather as his starting point, as an artist, he had to deal with it to affirm that which to him was greater than it. By his structure he shows this struggle.*

> (*SE* 205)

Williams confronted his "weather," then, *as an artist* because in that way he would affirm "that which to him was greater than" the social pettiness that would reduce him. Thus, as an artist, Williams' answer to his "weather" shows up in the "structure" of his work. Confronting his "weather" called for him to become a "creature of the weather":

> My whole life
> has hung too long upon a partial victory.

> But, creature of the weather, I
> don't want to go any faster than
> I have to go to win.

> (*Paterson* 30)

This weatherman's consciousness made him keen to the kinds of writings empowered to claim an audience in his society, sensitive to who was in and who was out of the "catalogue" that was discussed "At Kenneth Burke's Place":

> And "the earth under our feet,"
> we say glibly, hating
> the "Esoteric," which is not
> to be included in our anthologies, the
> unthinkable: the younger generation
> the colored (unless marketable)
> and—Plato was no different—the
> "private language."
>
> (*The Collected Poems, Vol. II* 106–107)

Even as a mature poet, Williams was tainted by at least two of those "unthinkables." He was Bill but also of a different cultural color, Carlos, a foreigner, a liability. In reconciling those two halves, he spoke a private language, although it may have sounded to all the world like English. So Bill's solidarity in Burke's presence ("we say glibly, hating") was contradicted by another consciousness, which on reflection cannot agree with what was so glibly said. The earth, that secret voice quickly adds, "also is a 'private language'" and "Catalogues are not its business." The two perspectives in that poem are what in today's parlance are labeled as "mainstream" and "minority." Williams possessed both inharmoniously. He was, in other words, no different from any other "Latino," or "minority" or "non-mainstream" writer who must reconcile that dichotomy today.

Fortunately, Williams was blessed with the absence of such labels, as well as the attending pressures, from either friendly or antagonistic labelers, that assuredly would have befallen him today. And Bill would have managed to survive on his own, unadulterated by others' foreignizing preconceptions, succeeding as the poet inducted into the canon of American literature. But when Williams looked into his "core," it was he, not others, who always encountered his other half, the ghostly reflection in "A Portrait in Greys":

> Must I be always
> moving counter to you? Is there no place
> where we can be at peace together
> and the motion of our drawing apart
> be altogether taken up?
> I see myself
> standing upon your shoulders touching
> a grey, broken sky—

but you, weighted down with me,
yet gripping my ankles,—move
                    laboriously on,
where it is level and undisturbed by colors.

(*CPI* 99)

The relation between his selves wasn't always clear to Williams; that's why the portrait is in "greys"—a tribute to the painter Juan Gris (*gris* being the color "grey" in Spanish) and a bilingual pun: in Spanish *grey* can figuratively signify a group with common characteristics, like a race or nation. What is clear is that his other self is inevitably Carlos. The Anglo American Bill stands on the shoulders of the Spanish American Carlos, who is always "moving counter" to where the poet aspires to go. Only death will end the search for a spiritual place where they can be at peace together, where metaphysically time and spatial distances are inseparable, so the motion of their separation will be "altogether taken up," a place "where it is level and undisturbed by colors."

The sense of social fragmentation becomes the motif of the poem "XXV," from *Spring and All*, which consists mainly of catch phrases, slogans, and found lines from signs in New York State:

What the hell do you know about it?

AXIOMS

Do not get killed

Careful Crossing Campaign
Cross Crossings Cautiously

THE HORSES   black
                            &
PRANCED   white

(*I* 146–147)

The question "What the hell do you know about it?" came from Ezra Pound's pointed challenge to what a "bloomin' foreigner" like Williams knew about America to talk about it. Deeply hurt by Pound's jab, Williams also responded satirically in *The Great American Novel* (*I* 158), and quoted from and got even with Pound in his "Prologue" to *Kora in Hell* (*I* 11–12). (Both reactions will be discussed at length in Chapter 7.) In the above

lines, he answered Pound with axioms that evoke warnings about the per-
ils of the prejudices in the America that he purportedly knew nothing
about. Even more explicit evidence of Williams' subtle social consciousness in this poem is offered by the stanza that followed in the version of
Spring and All in *Imaginations* published in 1970, but that is absent from
the version found in the 1986 *The Collected Poems of William Carlos Williams, Vol. I:*

> What's the use of sweating over
> this sort of thing, Carl, here
> it is all set up—

> *(I 147)*

The editors' note on this poem observes that the stanza was omitted,
"probably deliberately" from the "corrected typescript (Yale Za 49)" (by
Williams, we must assume). They also interpret that "Carl" may be "Carl
Van Doren, who had recently published in *The New Republic* (March
1922) an academic essay on 'American Realism.'" If anything, Van Doren
serves as an ambiguous cover that also semantically enriches the stanza.
The elitist national character exhibited by Pound is the thread sustained
in the lines that follow:

> Outings in New York City

> Ho for the open country

> *(I 147)*

As Williams' emphasis was on the *closedness* of the society, evident in the
aforementioned images in "XXV," the desire to head for "the open country" refers both to the countryside away from the city and the *open*
country as opposed to the one ruled by the *catalogue* of axioms, a subdued image that years later will rise to the surface text in the "catalogue"
discussed "At Kenneth Burke's Place." Understanding how things are "set
up," then, "Carl" understood that to become a writer called for his making
several compromises with his inner self.

Compromise, of course, was a leitmotif of Williams' life. He had wanted
to become an artist, but succumbed to his parents' wishes to emulate his
namesake Uncle Carlos and become a physician. He lusted after dark
women, but married the white flower Florence. On the other hand, Williams refused to resign himself to having to actually compromise any-

thing. After he became a doctor, he spread his time between his family, his patients, and his writing; even though married, he appeared to satisfy his lusts surreptitiously—or at least vicariously. Consistent with that determination, he accepted the challenge of being an American writer as he responded to the other pressures that demanded that he compromise: without sacrificing his real objective. Only by appreciating this existential determination to have it both ways can we comprehend the struggle he successfully translated into structure. The account of Williams' selecting a pen name, for example, while treated in *The Autobiography* in a tone that makes light of the matter, emblematically plays out this determination. "To me," he concluded, "the full name seemed the most revealing and therefore better" (*A* 108). He never concedes to the reader an explanation of what the full name revealed, and yet reveals that there was a fullness in the name, allowing the language to work by itself in the imagination of the reader, who would be reading a writer named Williams while William Carlos feels satisfied that he completed his intended act of identifying himself fully.

Until recently the criticism on Williams had fallen short by leaving these cryptic lacunae unexplored, in part because critics were unaware of them. But this incognizance was also owing to their reluctance to investigate Williams' bicultural background as an element significant to his work. Even when critics have acknowledged that "Carlos" played a role, to the point of contradicting themselves they have resisted concluding that it was more than a cameo. In *The Early Poetry of William Carlos Williams,* for example, Rod Townley discerned the dualism in Williams' personality, a secret and a public side, and referred to the "Spanish influence" in *The Tempers* (*CPI* 1)

> *Yet this Spanish influence helped at the same time to make* The Tempers *a secret and devious book.*[4]

Townley also grasped the importance that Williams attached to his bicultural name:

> *Between the two bland Williams' of his name there lurks a Carlos, a "dark Spanish beauty," as the 1906 Medical School yearbook,* The Scope, *called Williams (76). It is an evidence of Williams' own sense of his name's meaning that in several prose pieces, as well as in the first draft of* A Voyage to Pagany, *he refers to this alter ego as "Evans Dio-*

nysus Evans." His Spanish heritage seemed to represent to him that
streak of wildness, of Dionysian abandon, which his poetry so much
needed, and which Williams so much feared.

(Townley 65)

According to Townley, Williams identified with the peasants he saw in
Spain and sometimes spoke in the voice of Carlos, an old Spanish peasant.
This assertion makes no sense at all, as Williams consistently looked back
at an aristocratic Spanish background, but otherwise reaffirms that Townley understood that Williams did value his Hispanic lineage. Inexplicably,
however, even though Townley continues to identify Carlos as an occasional literary device, he contradicts the force of his own previous observations by subsequently claiming that the significance of Williams' Spanish heritage was "impossible to ever understand," and this declaration is
the only justification he gives for simply dropping the subject:

It may be impossible to ever understand what Williams' Spanish heri-
tage really signified to him. His statements on the subject (such as
"Spanish still seems to me synonymous with romantic"—IWWP, 17)
are tantalizing without being informative. Certainly, his feelings about
things Spanish are closely related to his feelings about his Spanish-
speaking mother and, by extension, all women.

(Townley 66)

Up to this point, Townley had been on the right path, but was forced to
return to his original road because his book was intended to explicate the
early poetry of a preconceived Williams that Townley had not planned to
redesign. Nevertheless, Townley himself had already suggested that Williams' "streak of wildness, of Dionysian abandon" was at least one of the
sources of his insistence on defining the American idiom, his invocation
of an American spirit, his opening of English's imagination to new meters.
Townley, in fact, had hit upon the secret behind Williams' counterattack
against the "catalogue" and all the other deadening elements of American society: to defy the social pressure to suppress Carlos. But Townley's
pursuing that discourse to its logical consequences would have indeed
changed in midstream the purpose of his book.

This book was conceived with the express purpose of changing the
face of Williams the poet by establishing that, through Williams' stages of
self-realization over the years, it was the vindication of Carlos that ulti-

mately motivated his work. Behind the politic person of Bill, it was the balancing counterweight Carlos who embodied newness itself, whose foreign heart beats in his most important works; Carlos, not Bill, was fired by the need to prove the "catalogue" wrong and the imagination superior to the mainstream's specious natural laws. Bill was important as the amplifying interpreter, the conduit persona whom Williams encouraged his readers to assume was in sum the poet they were reading. Once Carlos' role is made visible we will begin to read in Williams' work the importance of stasis, the mingled Americanness that he struggled to define.

The "Foreword" to *The Autobiography* opens with the following disclaimer:

> *Nine-tenths of our lives is well forgotten in the living. Of the part that is remembered, the most had better not be told: it would be of interest to no one, or at least would not contribute to the story of what we ourselves have been. A thin thread of narrative remains—a few hundred pages . . . They constitute our particular treasure. That is all, justly, that we should offer.*

(A n.p.)

On the surface, this caveat simply appears to be a general principle of autobiography; writing a life story presupposes a curtailment and selection of details, as well as a necessary demarcation between the literary person "we ourselves have been" and the mundane person whose particulars are of less interest. But the "Foreword" proceeds to give a different nuance to that opening caveat. What we have before us, we are told, is the pertinent "thin thread of narrative," but behind that story remains a "secret," implicitly the proverbial "secret of our lives," which should remain untold:

> *We always try to hide the secret of our lives from the general stare. What I believe to be the hidden core of my life will not easily be deciphered, even when I tell, as here, the outer circumstances.*

(A n.p.)

That part of his remembered life "that had better not be told"—"the secret" of his life—was also his "hidden core," which "will not easily be deciphered." Williams, then, introduces this life story by informing the reader that this book is a depiction only of "the outer circumstances." *The*

Autobiography, in other words, is built on the subdued conceit of Williams' two selves as separated by a wall like the one around the garden in West Philadelphia. In front of the wall stands the poet, the secret-possessing protagonist; behind it stands Carlos, as secretly fecund as the garden. *The Autobiography* is the story of the life of Bill.

But to inform us of that "hidden core," to mention it at all, and declare that it "will not easily be deciphered" only extends an invitation to decipher it. This need to acknowledge that he possesses a secret was, in fact, the core of his untold life story; that revelation itself completes his story, invoking the composite William Carlos. In "The Cure," for example, published in 1944, Williams wrote of his need to write because "when I cannot write I'm a sick man / and want to die." But, in what appears like an unrelated transition, he changes the subject from his writings to the "secret" of his "sources":

> But they have no access to my sources.
> Let them write as they may and
> perfect it as they can they will never
> come to the secret of that form
>
> *(CPII* 67)

The generic "They," he was confident, would never "come to the secret of that form . . . ," although by writing the poem Williams made certain they knew there was a secret. His revealing his having a secret without revealing its content except, as the poem continues, "interknit with the unfathomable ground / where we walk daily," was his "Cure," allowing him to write simultaneously as Bill and as his complete self, William Carlos. But "cure" of what? Of his condition of having to write always guarding a secret, composite self—the condition imposed on him by his narrow-minded country.

For Williams to *be* in *The Autobiography,* therefore, that book too had to consist of the tropes and ambiguities through which he always "cured" his *condition;* his autobiography had to be a work of art, artful in its playing with pliable details, and ultimately justified by Williams' conviction in poetic over empirical truth, a customization of his background that had been a stylistic signature since his earliest poems. "The Wanderer" (*CPI* 108), as will be demonstrated in a later chapter, was so signed. By making his English grandmother his muse in that poem, Williams reinforced the characterization of his Bill persona. In the same vein, his prose is also stamped with that signature. In his preface to *Selected Essays,* written after *The Autobiography,* he married his "West Indies" background to a homogenized summary of his American English-language and English paternal backgrounds identified as "Colonial America":

> *There was also the world of my ancestral background the West Indies and Colonial America . . .*

> (*SE* xii)

Williams' vacillations about what is known of his linguistic and cultural heritage, combined with the true haziness of details of his past, have contributed to his being turned into an amorphous icon onto which his critics have projected their own ideas of what Williams should have been, causing a proliferation of wildly different summations of his background. Van Wyck Brooks described both his parents as born in "the West Indies," an English father and a mother whose background is left unspecified: "His English father and his mother were born in the West Indies . . ." (*The Farmer's Daughters* viii). Harry Levin eliminated the Caribbean background altogether:

> *From his mother, . . . he inherited Spanish and French blood. His English father, . . . never gave up British citizenship.*[5]

But while the *content* of Williams' portrayal of his family is never altogether reliable, where he is most revealing is in his method of writing about it. "Pop and Mother," the chapter of *The Autobiography* in which we are formally introduced to his parents, opens with the declaration that his father William George was "an Englishman who lived in America all his adult years and never became a citizen" (*A* 14). This was true and yet broad enough to be misleading. "America" here signifies, of course, the New World. Although English by birth, at age five William George was taken to the Caribbean where he grew up, as Williams himself tells us— not insignificantly in Spanish—in the poem "Adam":

> But being an Englishman
> though he had not lived in England
> *desde que tenia cinco años*[6]

William George proposed to Elena Hoheb in the Dominican Republic. After they moved to Rutherford, the year before William Carlos was born, the senior Williams worked for a company that sold a cologne called Florida Water. His job kept him traveling to South and Central America. According to Williams he preferred to keep his English passport only because "he said it was more convenient for him to carry British than American papers on his frequent and prolonged trips to South America" (*A* 14). But while that reason may be true, it is also misleading, obstructing the reader's keeping in focus that William George himself grew up culturally mixed. His bilingualism was not a measure of linguistic skill; rather, it was a measure of who he was and where he grew up. This detail is encoded by the otherwise meaningless use of Spanish in the line "*desde que tenia cinco años*" in "Adam," in which the paternal English-lineage symbol diffusely depicted in *The Autobiography* had earlier been drawn more sharply.

"Adam" paints the senior Williams as a cold northern man lost in a hot, amorphous paradise that imagistically encompasses a homogenization of islands and countries, making no distinctions between the places where he grew up and through which he traveled as an adult. The summary image of the man is one of a sad Anglo foil ever facing the telluric Latin forces. Paul Mariani describes the cultural contrast between William George and his setting, also confusing the Caribbean where he grew up with the Latin world through which he traveled on business as an adult:

> . . . *a silent northern figure who found himself growing up in the buzzing tropics of the Caribbean and who tried to distance himself from that world by the ordered harmonies of piano and flute until he managed to exile himself even from that earthly paradise to follow the insistent cicada's cry of duty. Roped in all his life by the idea of duty, surrounded by the carnival lushness of the tropics and the beautiful black and Latin women inviting him to dally a while with them, he went about his appointed round of tasks each day. . . .*
>
> (*William Carlos Williams: A New World Naked* 13)

As silence, culture, and civility embodied, "Adam" walked about stifled in the buzzing tropics, an image that plays up to the readers' stereotypes of the Caribbean and Latins, but that contradicts Williams' description of that *other* world in several other writings: "All The Fancy Things" portrays Elena's past as one of refinement; in the chapter "Dr. Henna" in *The Autobiography*, we learn of William George's close friend from Puerto Rico, a highly cultured man (although Williams does not stress this), who got Williams his internship; in *Yes, Mrs. Williams,* we learn that Uncle Carlos Hoheb was an accomplished musician who described William George as being "no musician."

Similarly questionable is the picture of his father as a bland innocent dragged through the lush tropics by the hook of duty:

> Naked on a raft
> he could see the barracudas
> waiting to castrate him—
>
> . . . .
> . . . .
>
> God's handyman
> going quietly into hell's mouth
> for a paper of reference—
>
> . . . .
> muleback over Costa Rica
> eating patés of black ants.
>
> *(CPI* 409–410)

Although in "Adam" Williams admits that William George's life "was not for one homebound," his tone suggests that Adam would have preferred to have remained home, away from those adventures. This dutiful Adam, who forsook the allures of sinfully aggressive black and Latin women to carry out his tasks, proffers the intended Anglo reader (who presumably harbors a Puritan morality) a symbol with which to identify, but as biography, that image simply doesn't hold up. Duty or not, William George's job was an adventure, and behind the household silence an adventurer's spirit stockpiled many stories:

> *My father was a great storyteller. His accounts of his travels muleback over Costa Rica, the eating of the* patés *of black ants when caught short for a meal far out in the mountains held me rapt.*
>
> *(YM* 7)

This description in *Yes* makes no reference to his father's sense of duty, and instead is part of a detailed rendering of his being "a liberal and something of a socialist," who read the poetry of Paul Laurence Dunbar, forbidden novels, and current Latin American writers. The spirit of that description in the much later *Yes* contradicts the tone of the "God's handy-

man" image in the early "Adam," from which Williams had borrowed the
same memories of his father's adventures.

Also contrary to Williams' portrayal of the man, William George gave
no appearance of being sexually restrained. The barracudas may have
threatened to castrate him, but Latin women surely appealed to him, or
he would not have married Elena, whom Williams himself characterized
as salty and flirtatious. On his frequent and long travels throughout Latin
America, once lasting up to a year, "Adam" was probably not as over-
whelmed by the lush sensuality as Bill wanted to believe and so portrayed.
His picture of his father's sexual squeamishness was probably more an
expression of Williams' embarrassed denial that the contrary was true.
In Williams' autobiographical and psychodramatic "lost" *Endymion*-style
poem "Philip and Oradie," for example, the protagonist's father is depicted as one who "Through forty years of heydey wasting war / Had
grated up his front," an image left unclear. Here the squeamish one is the
narrator who rather than describe the father's conquests expresses his
concern that such revelations would ignite "the throngs" into "sudden
flame and hell of passion." Those conquests, whatever their symbolic
value, were given as the cause for his paying no attention to his wife
Beatrix, who "bitterly . . . wept the seasons through." Consequently, her
child hated his father for making his mother so unhappy.[7] The elder Williams seems to have adopted a Latin double standard and, as did Williams
himself, managed two sexual lives (one hot, the other cool), a pattern that
probably contributed greatly to his wife's unhappiness in this country. His
trips appear to have been prolongations of his distancing himself from
home, where he hid himself in domestic silence, as Mariani writes:

> *What Williams remembered most was the silence. Even when they were*
> *together, there were long stretches when only a few perfunctory words*
> *passed between them, and those dealing with practical matters. . . .*
> *Neither in his letters nor in his* Autobiography *has Williams recorded*
> *more than a few short conversations he had with his father. And even*
> *the poems written about his father are, in one sense, meditations on the*
> *tragic silences between the two.*

> (*NW* 13)

A man absorbed in another, more exciting life, and therefore a taciturn
exterior with a hot inner secret is what one gathers William George was
in fact, so much like the African chief in *Paterson*. The chief is sitting

before his nine wives, the first one worn out and the latest one fresh. He spends his life adventuring but now must be home, where his soul is somewhere else as he floats, unattached:

> Not that the lightnings
> do not stab at the mystery of a man
> from both ends—and the middle, no matter
> how much a chief he may be, rather the more
> because of it, to destroy him at home
>
> . . . Womanlike, a vague smile,
> unattached, floating like a pigeon
> after a long flight to his cote.

(*P* 14)

Like the chief at home, the "Adam" that Bill described was his father's mask, which Williams preferred because it made William George look the most English, the only side with which Williams had any real contact. The other side, his Caribbean side, which like the prince's father in "Philip and Oradie" was "not fit a tongue's report" for being "impious," did not belong to Bill's life.

In sum, the English versus Spanish symbolism implicit in the image of "Adam" repeated in *The Autobiography* grates against common sense and available facts. Throughout his working years in the United States, William George elected to work in offices where Spanish was spoken and in jobs that required that he return to the surroundings from which he supposedly sought to be exiled. His months away from Rutherford on business trips may have been the fulfillment of a sense of duty, but they were also a return to the Spanish-speaking lands in which he grew up. He kept abreast of Latin American writing, collaborating with his son on the translation of the Guatemalan Rafael Arévalo Martínez's popular story "The Man Who Resembled a Horse," as well as translating works by José Santos Chocano, Juan Julian Lastra, Leopoldo Díaz, and José Asunción Silva. Arévalo Martínez's writings, unsurprisingly, were for a while steeped in the spiritualism that William George and Elena practiced for years. Spanish, which the critics customarily associate with Elena, was also his father's preferred language, according to Williams (see Chapter 4). The Arévalo Martínez epigraph with which Williams opened his *Al Que Quiere* was likely a tribute to William George. It was William George, not Elena, who became "furious" because *Al Que Quiere* contained typographical errors in Spanish, mostly in the epigraph (*NW* 13).

The point to underscore is that the critics' routine assumption that Elena was Williams' connection to Spanish relies too heavily on the "English" symbol that Williams consciously made of his father in order to establish Bill's credibility. Williams' joint translations of Latin American stories was a way of bringing him closer to the always distant William George. The same motivation, one has to argue, was likely behind Williams' immersing himself in Spanish literature, his subsequent translations from it and his use of Spanish in his earliest works. After his father's death in 1918, which admittedly coincided with (or possibly helped bring on) his stylistic maturity, the presence of Spanish and Spanish literature in his work virtually ceased (although it re-emerged with his support of the Loyalists in the Spanish Civil War). It can also be argued that his father's absence liberated Williams from having to write in a style closer to the kind of formal poetry that his father preferred, thus opening the way to improvisations and indefinable genres. In contrast, Elena lived on until Williams' old age, and if she alone had inspired him to gravitate to Spanish we would probably not be able to distinguish the phases in Williams' writings in which he was in "hell," Williams' imagistic reference to Spanish. Elena was, of course, an obvious symbol of Spanish in Williams' eyes, but she did not exclusively affect his proximity to Spanish or its literature. Williams' eventually dropping the Spanish touches in his writing was an act of independence and maturity away from Elena's strong influence, as the conventional literary scenario portrays, but as well an independence from his having to emulate William George's loyalty to Spanish.

Equally unreliable is Williams' description of his grandmother, Emily Dickinson Wellcome, who, to be fair to Williams, intentionally kept her history from her grandson. From what Williams was able to gather, she became pregnant with William George in London, gave birth to him in Birmingham, and five years later came to the United States "in a sailing vessel loaded with car rails." In a Brooklyn boarding house she met Mr. Wellcome.

> . . . *up from Saint Thomas to buy photographic supplies. He saw the young woman, married her and took her, with her son, back to the West Indies. There, the boy who was to be my father grew up.*

> (*A* 168)

Grandma Wellcome's story has several versions. Paul Mariani describes her as finally settling in the Dominican Republic (colloquially called in Spanish by its original name, Santo Domingo):

> *Wellcome married Emily and then took his new wife and his stepson*
> *back down to St. Thomas, before finally settling in Puerto Plata, Santo*
> *Domingo.*

(NW 5)

From this version, it would appear that Emily bore her children in the Dominican Republic. The youngest was Rosita, whom Elena "knew in Puerto Rico" (*NW* 7), an acquaintance explained by the version of Grandmother Wellcome's life as Williams tells it in "Dedication for a Plot of Ground":

> met her second husband
> in a Brooklyn boarding house,
> went with him to Puerto Rico
> bore three more children, lost
> her second husband, lived hard
> for eight years in St. Thomas,
> Puerto Rico, San Domingo, followed
> the oldest son to New York,
> lost her daughter, lost her "baby,"
> seized the two boys of
> the oldest son by the second marriage
> mothered them—they being
> motherless—fought for them
> against the other grandmother
> and the aunts, brought them here
> summer after summer

(CPI 105–106)

Grandmother Wellcome apparently had a history of striving to wrest her children and grandchildren away from their Spanish-speaking relations, a pattern that obviously nurtured Williams' developing a dual personality and provoked continual domestic warfare in the Williams household. Furthermore, his grandmother's confrontations with his Latin half also contributed to Williams perceiving her, as well as everybody else with whom he came in contact, as cultural symbols. One of the most dra-

matic moments of his life described in *The Autobiography* is his description of the day when Grandmother and Elena came head to head:

> *Grandmother took me over or tried to. But once Mother lost her temper*
> *and laid the old gal out with a smack across the puss that my mother*
> *joyfully remembered until her death. Her Latin blood got the best of*
> *her that day.*

(A 5)

The reference to Latin blood both characterizes the writing persona
as non-Latin and sets up the symbolism, Mother symbolizing Spanish and
Grandmother symbolizing English, the latter bolstered by the literary
mystique evoked by her personal background and her name. Emily Wellcome's having been adopted by a wealthy family of Godwins prompted
Williams to fantasize about being related to Shelley and Mary [*nee* God-
win] Wollstonecraft Shelley. But, as Reed Whittemore points out, that exaggerated story overlooked that Wollstonecraft had been dead for two
generations.[8] Lastly, one can assume that he conjured over her name,
Emily Dickinson Wellcome. Nevertheless, owing to her fervent defense of
her Anglo self against Latins and the preponderance of literary allusions
in her family names, Williams was apparently prompted to see in her the
embodiment of his Anglo *line,* both sanguine and literary, and the symbol
with whom his readers would most sympathize when she intervened to
save him from being raised as a Latin foreigner. Thus, in the anecdote of
the battle between Mother and Grandma, his misleading syntax keeps
"Grandmother took me over" prominent even though he was actually
telling us that, in fact, she hadn't.

Complementing the importance given to his English-language lineage,
the characterization of Bill also involved customizing his perception of
Latins. Except for his father and great Spanish writers and artists, in *The*
Autobiography Williams paints Spanish-speakers mockingly, subtly invoking social preconceptions and stereotypes. In the course of explaining
his Puerto Rican cousin's "uncertain upbringing," for example, he veers
off into his Uncle Carlos' life. After completing his medical studies in
Paris, Carlos married a French woman. He returned with her to Puerto
Rico where "the gal took one look, abandoned the whole outfit on the
islands and fled back to Paris, where she disappeared" (*A* 37). In his
mocking tone Bill assumes he has the reader's solidarity. The French-

woman didn't just take a look at what awaited her on the island; she reacted to the entire regional culture, the "whole outfit on the islands." Appealing to a stereotype, he posits the defects of the geographical region as moral justification for the woman's leaving Carlos and returning to the higher culture of Paris.

The chapter "White Mule" recalls Williams' claims dealings with the critic and translator Angel Flores, who then ran a small press:

In 1932 Angel Flores broke a different ice by publishing a book of short stories of mine which he had solicited for his Dragon Press.

(*A* 298)

After the publication of *The Knife of the Times,* Williams claims "few books were sold" and he never "heard of Angel Flores again." Actually here Williams was both trying to keep his successes in the foreground and deprive Flores of a moral victory. Along with *Knife,* Williams had sent Flores a book of poems, which Flores took a long time to return.[9] In a letter to the novelist Julian Shapiro, another Dragon Press author, he bluntly asked if Shapiro had poisoned Flores toward him.[10] Williams raised the issue in several letters to Shapiro, "I simply cannot understand what in hell has come over Flores."[11] Flores eventually returned the manuscript, making it clear that he didn't care for Williams' attitude (*NW* 335), a patently reciprocated antipathy if one is to judge from the subtle irony of imagery in "White Mule."

Angel Flores, who was also Puerto Rican, exemplified the obverse side of Williams' identity issue. Flores was a professor who specialized in Iberian literature, and his translations introduced much of Spanish-language literature to the United States. Being of the mindset of his time, save for notable exceptions he usually discounted Latin America. Few but the most renowned Latin Americans were translated by him and none from his own country. Flores' cultural temperament had to figure in the clash between them. Doubtless Williams anticipated better treatment from a (warm, Latin, Caribbean) Flores, who in a way was a critic double of himself. Instead, he encountered a cool and arrogant Europhile. Opening the Flores episode in a chapter titled "White Mule," which only devotes a brief buried anecdote to the publication of his novel *White Mule* (based on his wife Flossie's family), was Williams being vindictive. Flores' complexion was extremely fair and thus white. The white in the title *White Mule,* Williams explained to Edith Heal, came to him because his wife Flossie "is white." Washington, the other character discussed in this chapter, was also white and white-haired (and figuratively a "white mule") but the conceptual wordplay was between Flores and, implicitly, Florence, two contrary kinds of flowers in Williams' life. The kicker, of course, is the "Mule." "Floss, I knew, was a mule," he told Heal. Apparently, so he also thought of Flores.

A weightier satirical tone permeates the chapter "Dr. Henna." Julio José Henna[12] was a physician who collaborated in an 1868 rebellion in Puerto Rico, in which a short-lived independence was declared and briefly defended in the town of Lares. Henna was arrested by the Spanish for allegedly recruiting native Puerto Rican sergeants to commit acts of sedition.[13] The "Betanzes" Williams mentions in this chapter was the exiled separatist leader Ramón Emeterio Betances, who lived out his days in Paris, from where he wrote and continued to lead the independence struggle. Near the end of the nineteenth century, with Cuba on the verge of victory over Spain, Betances counted on Henna in New York, with whom he kept a steady correspondence through letters, to organize a liberating assault on Puerto Rico with the help of Cuban forces.

Like Elena, Henna was representative of the small but largely skilled population of nineteenth-century Latin Americans in and around New York. Among other notables of that period figured the Cuban poet and revolutionary José Martí, a New Yorker for twenty years, who was a major innovator in Latin American poetry and a leader of Cuban independence from Spain. Also part of that generation was the Afro-Puerto Rican Arturo Alfonso Shomberg, who devoted his life to accumulating books on Africana, a collection that grew to become New York's Shomberg Library. At the turn of the century, to that heterogeneous community was added the Puerto Rican Bernardo Vega, a socialist cigar roller whose *Memorias* are a historical landfill in the lacuna of nineteenth- and early twentieth-century New York Latin life. (Cigar rollers, who customarily pooled money to pay the salary of a fellow worker to read for them as they rolled tobacco, became a highly literate class of workers.)

Like Williams, Vega too remembered Henna, but as a considerably more influential figure in both the Latin and non-Latin world than Williams' account would lead us to think. Vega's summary of Henna speaks for itself:

Aside from his revolutionary activities Henna was a renowned physician and man of science. He was loved as a doctor throughout the Latin American, French, and Chinese immigrant communities. He was a highly cultured man who, in addition to his native Spanish, spoke perfect English and French. He could also get along in Italian, German, Portuguese, and even spoke a smattering of Chinese. He was versed in painting, sculpture, and music.

Henna was dean of the Spanish-speaking doctors in New York. He was on the medical staff of Bellevue Hospital, was a founder of the French Hospital, and a member of the board of the Metropolitan Museum of Art. The funeral services for that famous Puerto Rican were an occasion of deep mourning. Thousands of his countrymen filed past his coffin, as did countless South Americans, Frenchmen, North Americans, and Chinese. . . .[14]

Indicative of Henna's influence was his being allowed an audience with Theodore Roosevelt to lobby in favor of the United States' extending citizenship to Puerto Ricans, Henna acting on the prognosis that citizenship would end the epidemic of bigotry that afflicted his compatriots.

Henna, as Williams wrote in *The Autobiography*, had been William George's friend dating back to the "West Indian days," and in New York remained close to the Williams family. Williams himself "helped bring in 1907 at the Spanish-American Club in New York as the guest of Dr. Henna" (*NW* 57). Although Williams portrays him with a measure of irony, Henna loyally watched out for the interests of the son of William George. He was not only the head of residence at the French Hospital, as *The Autobiography* tells us, he was the hospital's cofounder. So he was in the position to give Williams more than a good recommendation: he had been "directly responsible for getting Williams into the hospital in the first place" (*NW* 52). One has to wonder if this influential doctor also had something to do with Williams' entering the special medical program at the University of Pennsylvania. That Williams subtly renders tribute by titling a chapter after him is a better measure of Henna's contribution to Williams' life.

Nevertheless, Bill apparently felt compelled to treat Henna shabbily. His attempt to introduce Williams to a millionaire "Spanish American" widow (it is doubtful Henna would have labeled her so generically) is laughed off by Williams as an illustration of Henna's well-intentioned ridiculousness. The tone of the telling characterizes Henna as crassly materialistic, thus characterizing by contrast the more high-minded Anglo Bill. Allowing Henna to damn himself, he cites Henna's comment to William George: "That's a funny boy you have, Williams. I offered him a million dollars and he merely laughed at me" (*A* 72). Henna, of course, was being materialistic, but Williams besmirched Henna's intention to do good by him, as if Williams had included Henna in this story of Bill's life out of conscience but only grudgingly.

A second episode, this one troublingly dishonest, confirming how he had exaggerated in the telling of the first, opens with that parodic tone sustained: "A little later Henna came up with another one." So his intern could make some extra money, Henna covered for him while Williams accompanied a dying wealthy Mexican, Señor Gonzales, on a railroad trip to Mexico, where the man wished to be at the time of his death. Here the autobiographer postures considerably:

> *In the party was his son, his son's wife—in their thirties, dark-skinned and bitter at all Gringos—and another woman. I've forgotten who. My job was to keep the old boy alive till we made his home town. It didn't look as though I'd do it. More than once I had visions of being lynched if I arrived at the border in a couple of days with a corpse.*
>
> (*A* 73)

According to Bill's account, he never ingratiated himself with the Gonzaleses by revealing his Carlos half. Instead, before the reader at least, Bill plays up being a "Gringo," informing the reader that because his Spanish "wasn't so hot" they "all had a few words in French."

When they arrived at the border where, on the Mexican side, a Mexican doctor was supposed to take over from Williams, "the old boy himself," who had accorded Williams the respect of a true doctor, insisted that the intern be the one to "go all the way with him to San Luis Potosí." Williams' adventure ended in the man's spacious home, among his servants:

> *Downstairs the son counted out ten twenty-dollar gold pieces which he put into my hand, one on top of the other saying, bitterly, as he always did, and motioning about him that I might observe the well-paneled*

room, "You see, we live a little better—un poco mejor quo los ne-
gros,"[15] *and I realized something of what he had been through.*

(*A* 74)

This anecdote misleads the reader on two counts: on how the Gonzaleses might have perceived Williams and on his ability to converse in
Spanish. The French Hospital was founded to care for the French- and
Spanish-speaking immigrant community. Henna's interest in Williams'
applying had not only been to do William George a favor; William Carlos
fit the job description. Whatever the deficiencies of his Spanish or the
limitations of his French, Williams was familiar enough with both languages to handle the job and to bring a comforting familiarity to foreigners. Mariani concurs that Williams "felt he could work up a serviceable
Spanish, at least enough to take care of the patients he would be getting"
(*NW* 43) at the French Hospital.

On his being perceived as a "Gringo," the standoff between him and
the younger Gonzales couple probably resulted from their assessing that
Williams was playing at being the gringo. It is apparent from the logic of
the narrative that Williams did not behave calloused and businesslike
with the old man. At the border, the proud Mexican Gonzales was not
going to insist on keeping the young "Gringo" intern by his bedside if
Williams performed as coolly as he portrays. And on whether the Gonzales family took him physically for a gringo, this contradicts what Williams
himself reveals in the "French Hospital" chapter, in which the autobiographer steps out of his Bill character to let us know he could have been
taken for a Carlos. After he was hired as resident, presumably under his
non-literary name Bill Williams, a competing fellow intern named Gas-
kins took one look at Williams' mug and instantly knew why Williams had
gotten the job:

> *Gaskins would always look for the graft angle in any setup. When he*
> *saw me for the first time, having from my name expected a rough,*
> *sandy-haired Welshman, he let out a wild howl.*
>
> *"There it is, there it is. Didn't I tell you?" He blamed Henna and*
> *family connections and whatnot for my success in getting on the staff.*

(*A* 84)

Bill's posturing that he first realized in San Luis Potosí what the angry
dark Gonzaleses "had been through" in New York also contradicts his

firsthand knowledge of the social prejudices experienced by his mother and undoubtedly even himself. Mariani cites in a 1909 letter to Elena, in which Williams mentions "what his mother had already confided to him: that all her married life she had to struggle in a new world 'among an unsympathetic people who were often hostile and perhaps never understood' her, . . . " (*NW* 61)

Bernardo Vega records that the daily newspapers attacked the Latin newcomers. In 1902, he tells, *The Morning Sun* wrote the following specifically of Puerto Ricans: "These people are no more than savages who have replaced their bows and arrows with guns and knives" (Vega 93). Henna's efforts to spare his compatriots the ravages of bigotry by lobbying to make them citizens further underscores how critical things were. The claim that it took the Mexican experience for Bill to "realize something" of the bigotry around him, especially with what he considered a "foreigner" for a mother, is simply not believable. Those with a "foreign heart" in the United States are defined by their awareness of this imperfection from their incipience, and that awareness becomes a defining motive. What is plausible is that demonstrating that he was cognizant of this social problem since childhood would have been out of character for Bill.

Except for his relatives in France, about whom we have to piece together for ourselves that they were Puerto Rican, what Latins were credited for contributing to the person "we ourselves have been," then, are portrayed chiefly as foils, to cast a brighter light on Bill's being their opposite. Again, this Bill-characterizing device using Latins was not peculiar to *The Autobiography*. In a letter written to Winfield Townley Scott on his return to Puerto Rico in 1956, for example, Williams sarcastically observed that as he prepared to give his reading on the evening of the fourth, a tree frog had begun to pipe, so that he'd felt an urge "'to stop and listen to him with his *coquoc quille* rather than talk to a world of humans'" (*NW* 729). The tree frog, as islanders are fast to inform, was the tiny arboreal frog that uniquely in Puerto Rico makes the sound that became its local onomatopoetic name, "coquí." Here by Frenchifying the frog's call, Bill symbolically assumes toward the local Latins the same distant air that he had taken on in *The Autobiography*.

Consistent with this distant air before Latins, Williams wrote of his two trips to Puerto Rico, in 1941 and 1956, in a way that discourages our reading any literary significance in them. *The Autobiography*, of course, only covers the first trip, but its glancing treatment of it provides a tonal model of how we should evaluate his second trip. Mariani, for example, defers to that tone, suggesting that the 1956 trip was a kind of "gig" that Williams took advantage of for strictly personal reasons. He tells us that it lasted ten days and that Williams read in San Juan at the University of Puerto Rico before proceeding to Mayagüez with a personal agenda:

> *He spent three days in San Juan and then flew to the other end of the island to Mayagüez to see if he could not finally locate the house where his mother had been born and to learn finally just when she had been born. He barely escaped an official welcome by the mayor of the city, read there for a small group, and managed to find in the city hall records the license his mother had received so many years before which allowed her at fifteen to drive a carriage.*[16]

The trip in fact took longer than ten days and Williams traveled to Mayagüez to do more than find out his mother's birth date. Williams flew to the island at the invitation of the president of the University of Puerto Rico, Jaime Benítez, departing on the third of April. The piece in the newspaper *El Mundo* on April 6, the day of his reading, makes it plain that one reason why he was invited, aside from the obvious one that he was an important poet, was that his mother was Puerto Rican and Benítez was therefore inviting a half-Puerto Rican poet. As originally scheduled, on April 17 Williams read at the University of Puerto Rico's Mayagüez campus, an event reported in *El Mundo* on April 18.[17]

Far from the trip's being merely a gig, Williams accepted the invitation for the same reason he jumped at the opportunity to travel to Puerto Rico to the Inter-American Writers Conference in 1941: to refresh his commitment to his intended book on Elena. Even back in 1941, as he told an interviewer for the weekly *Alma Latina,* that trip had been the fulfillment of "un viaje proyectado desde hace mucho tiempo" ("a trip he had been planning for a long time").[18] That first trip, also not without literary significance, came on the heels of his years as a passionate supporter for the Republican cause in the Spanish Civil War, an event that prompted Williams to reflect on his identity. In solidarity with the Republican cause he translated their songs and either expanded on or reviewed his self-given education in Spanish literature for his 1939 essays "Against the Weather" and "Federico García Lorca." The highly productive period between the

1941 and 1956 trips can be interpreted as a byproduct of the prolonged gestation of the biography of his mother, which he had been putting off. While both trips serendipitously fell into Williams' lap, they instantly became part of that gestation, so that the 1956 trip was really a second chapter to that soul-searching 1941 trip. But both trips, as will be discussed in Chapter 2 at greater length, contributed to his finally writing *Yes, Mrs. Williams,* and some of his most important poems (most notably *Paterson*) were poetic sublimations of identity concerns aggravated by his first trip.

It is worth noting that Williams' silence on truly significant literary details of his second trip is probably a measure of how much Williams was self-conscious about them. In 1956 the Spanish poet Juan Ramón Jiménez, after a decade-long hiatus in New York, was living in Puerto Rico. It was unlikely that President Jaime Benítez, or the professors of literature, would have overlooked at least informing Williams of the presence of the prestigious exiled poet Jiménez, whose disciples abounded at the university. Williams, who consulted the Spanish poet Pedro Salinas on Quevedo's language in *The Dog and the Fever,* cited Unamuno, and had written about Lorca, was familiar enough with Spain's "Generation of '98" to be aware of Jiménez's existence. On the other hand, Jiménez, whose politics and aesthetics would have clashed with Williams', understandably remains unmentioned. That Jiménez, while a resident of Puerto Rico, was awarded the Nobel Prize in December of 1956 also would not have passed unnoticed. On the island as well was the Puerto Rican poet Luis Palés Matos, whom Williams had met during the 1941 writers' conference. Williams imitated Palés Matos in a couple of his own poems and translated Palés' poem "Preludio en Boricua." While Jiménez did not contribute to the making of the person "we ourselves have been," in a modest respect (to be shown later) Palés Matos did. Williams' reticence on him and Jiménez both affirmed Bill and has further encouraged his critics to not see literary importance in his trips to Puerto Rico.

Williams' first awareness of his destiny to struggle with another self in his writing is revealed in *The Autobiography* in the chapter titled "Ezra Pound," which covers Williams' days at Penn. Bill's confrontation with his other self in writing came in the form of his first long poem, which he compared to Keats' *Endymion,* "a narrative in that vague area of thought that associated itself with a romantic past" (*A* 59), and whose title he claimed he couldn't remember. It tells the story of a prince who, "from some one of the romantic (and real) motives that were always the agents in such cases," was poisoned at his wedding celebration, along with the entire royal family. Fortunately, he was saved by his "ancient" nurse, who gave him the antidote and laid him on a bed still breathing:

> *The poem itself began at that point, the young prince had been ab-*
> *ducted in his dream state and taken to a "foreign country" at some*
> *distance from the kingdom which was now his.*

(A 59)

In this "'foreign country'" the people spoke a language he could not understand:

> *No one was there to inform him of his whereabouts and when he did*
> *begin to encounter passers-by, they didn't even understand, let alone*
> *speak his language. He could recall nothing of the past.*

(A 59)

Given *The Autobiography*'s murky-past motif, Williams' detailed discussion of this poem is important because it reinforces that very theme. Like the prince's past, Bill's past vanished: his mother's family disappeared with the eruption of Mt. Pelée on Martinique; his father's lineage was erased by Grandma Wellcome's secrecy. That Bill's grandmother took over his upbringing while the inexperienced young Elena cared for her second baby corresponds to the "ancient" nurse's saving the prince with her "antidote," one *doting* against another. The prince is saved only to be "abducted in his dream state and taken to a 'foreign country.'" The words *foreign country* are in quotation marks, noting that the country was not foreign to the speaker but foreign to the prince. This too parallels Bill's biography: if his parents had not traveled to the United States, he would have grown up in their Caribbean kingdom.

Bill's summation of the prince's story amounts to a recapitulation of Carlos' story:

> *This was no more or no less than the aimless wandering, for the*
> *most part, of the young prince in his effort to get home again as well*
> *as to discover what had happened to him—he had not been able to re-*

> *call the details, merely "sensed" them: that there had been a beautiful*
> *bride, a father, a mother; that a disastrous event of some sort had oc-*
> *curred of which he was the victim. So he went on, homeward or seek-*
> *ing a home that was his own, all through a "foreign" country whose*
> *language was barbarous.*
>
> (*A* 60)

Note that Williams again affixes quotation marks around *foreign*, confirming that the modifier meant foreign from the prince's point of reference. Also noteworthy is Williams' use of "barbarous," Spanish's conventional condemnation of Protestant English, what Romans labeled the Germanic tribes. (In *The Great American Novel*, Williams writing as Carlos refers sarcastically to General Washington as "that German George.") Lastly, the themes of chanced birth and wandering are not unique here, reappearing as transformations in numerous images of birth, flowers, spring, sexuality. In a later chapter of *The Autobiography*, Williams reiterates his sense of being born here by accident:

> *I had begun to think of writing* In the American Grain, *a study to*
> *try to find out for myself what the land of my more or less accidental*
> *birth might signify.*
>
> (*A* 178)

Mariani quotes from Williams' epic, which is documented as being at Yale. That version of the poem, for reasons unexplained, was not found. There was, however, an apparently earlier, handwritten manuscript titled "Introduction," along with a cover letter to "Viola" (Baxter) from "Billie." This one, catalogued as "Philip and Oradie," begins differently from the one Mariani cites,[19] although it proceeds to tell the same narrative. From that handwritten manuscript we learn that Bill failed to mention that the setting of his epic was Spain and the prince's father was Don Pedro. This version doesn't begin at the point of the prince's receiving the antidote or his being abducted, as Williams recalled, but with a description of Don Pedro, Prince of Navarre, "an Altamont":

> . . . who loved an eager toil,
> Defiant, still to bruise those heraldries,
> Though forty years of heyday wasting war
> Had grated up his front. Oh I could sing

Of his brave deeds until the harking throng
Clayed with flat peace would fly like midnight birds
Into the sudden flame and hell of passion
Heedless of torment toppling kingdoms down—
But to what end? For they were impious all
Nor fit a tongue's report.

The images that characterize Don Pedro crackle with autobiographical allusions: "Pedro" from the Latin for rock, "Navarre," suggesting sail, "Altamont" the sexuality of high peak and power, the three painful points that distanced Williams from William George. The "eager toil" parallels his father's constant working. His "brave deeds" is an image of William George's adventures in foreign lands, but which if reported would cause the throng to fly into "the sudden flame and hell of passion / Heedless of torment toppling kingdoms down." From this early stage Bill sublimated his father's sexuality away from home. The editorial "But to what end?" is ambiguous: why did he do those things or why bother to tell? Pedro's exploits were "impious" and not "fit" to report; odd for an epic to circumvent battles, if indeed they were conquests of a military nature.

Don Pedro had poisoned the household metaphorically before he poisoned it literally. He had poisoned even his own life, as he eventually does at the wedding. Because of the "rock" Pedro, the prince's mother Beatrix lived constantly miserable:

. . . Could flowers gleam pure as she
How spring would beam with loveliness. But then
Rush meddler fortune here unconsonant,
Wide, natural-severing ways in bond to knit,
Why didst thou so; to wed her to that man;
To grief and loneliness, she who was made
For unrestrained clear mirth, for all the world
To gaze upon and turn refreshed away
As they had drunken of a crystal spring,
And here decree she'll die of languishment?

Consistent with Williams' preference to suppress his father's sexuality, his fictive prince was born as if from the rib of Beatrix's loneliness, and he grew up exclusively hers:

> For bitterly she wept the seasons through,
> Wept spring to summer, summer into snows
> And snows to melting—then her child! He came!
> He came, he came! Ye faint ribbed mid-May skies
> Whence, whence this flooding o'er mild ecstasy,
> That we may sip, we too of that deep well?
> But no, for now imagination flings
> With puzzling Beatrix through that infancy
> When here, in short, there grew an upright boy,
> A slender serious featured boy who knew
> By truth's sheer grace his father not at all
> And loved his mother like the breathing [unintelligible] . . .

Beatrix filled the boy's mind with stories of "foreign kingdoms[20] o'er the sea," which transparently correspond to Elena's infusing in her little Carlos' soul her own romantic nostalgia for Puerto Rico:

> Of sands that shone like sheeted gold—of waves
> And calm, of auzure [sic] skies so pure and deep
> No clown so low but sang it witless praise
> At magic morn's uncloaking. All of which
> Young Philip breathless for delight drank in
> And wove among this warp of history
> A woof of faery dreams, exalting all
> Till there grew up a wide and tenting world
> Of fabrics o'er him, who soon saw the cool,
> The actual round all golden through its mesh
> And thus came on his more eventful life.

Don Pedro was impatient with his son, who cared not for such manly and practical things as war and spent his time at his mother's side. This corresponds to Williams' father's dislike of his son's wasting time with writing. In reaction, because his mother Beatrix was "vilely used," the young prince detested the name of Altamont and requested permission to take his mother and his Oradie to Italy. After surviving the poisoning, the prince wanders in dreams and in reality, in an adventure that the manuscript leaves unfinished.

Mariani reasons that Williams destroyed the poem only after it had served its psychological purpose:

What probably happened, though, is that he had worked out the
problems that were troubling him sufficiently to realize that what
was left . . . could now be discarded like an old skin.

(*NW* 55)

According to Mariani, aside from venting differences with his father, the
poem also points to a need to start fresh by being away from his parents,
whose high expectations of him made them difficult to relate to:

> *. . . what Williams was working at here was his own psychodrama,*
> *and part of the problem he was trying to work through was his own*
> *reading of how his businesslike father must have been looking at his*
> *oldest son with his penchant for dreamy poetry. . . . The poem . . .*
> *points to Williams' deeply felt need to erase as effectively as he could*
> *his dependence on his parents and to strike out on his own into a brave*
> *new world, as terrifying as that experience might initially be. . . . If he*
> *found himself constantly bested in his talks and letters to his parents,*
> *at least here in his long poem he could work out his relationships by a*
> *radical beginning again under the aegis of the one relative he could*
> *relate to: his renegade Grandma Wellcome.*

(*NW* 54–55)

Mariani is right in general about how Williams responded to his family,
but like Williams, he fails to mention that "Philip and Oradie" is set in
Spain and that the entire family is Spanish-speaking, a context that clearly
underscores other things that Williams was trying to resolve in that poem.

For in addition to "Philip and Oradie"'s working through Williams'
own reading of his father, it also worked through Williams' identity crisis.
Philip no longer wanted to be an Altamont but did want to belong to his
mother and her dreamlike past. He wanted them to live in Italy, just as
Williams' "Spanish" cousins had escaped Puerto Rico to become Parisians. The poem loses its way because in his new land Philip really has
no role to play, suddenly becoming a "foreigner" and possessing no identity or noble title. Like the prince, the poem becomes open-ended and
wandering. At this point too, Williams probably first realized that he had
written this epic in the spirit of Carlos, a frightening discovery consider-
ing the implications. In throwing (or saying he threw) the poem in a "furnace," he was putting his Latin consciousness among the flames with
which he associated it: a purgation with fire, a cleansing away of Carlos.

It would take five decades, after which Carlos came around to writing *Yes, Mrs. Williams,* before the wandering Philip would finally find his way back to Beatrix and the remnants of his lost past.

While Carlos does not explicitly figure in her investigation, Ann W. Fisher-Wirth affirms that to become an American poet ("American" in the conventional Anglo sense that Bill used the word), Williams had to destroy "Philip and Oradie," because he realized that his Spanish prince was really himself at that point in his life:

> *Had he not done so [burned the poem], had he held on to "Philip and Oradie," there would never have been what we know as William Carlos Williams. For "Philip and Oradie" is not just a poem with autobiographical elements, a poem in which one can recognize certain real people and events in the poet's life. It is Williams' first attempt at autobiography, to come by means of art to a sense of his inner standing. Philip is Williams, as Williams perceived himself to be during this early state of his life.* [21]

Once "Philip and Oradie" was incinerated, Williams tells us, "The Wanderer" "took its place." This poem was now Williams' *first* long poem, in which he is reborn in two senses: as the poet-wanderer baptized in the waters of the Passaic, seeking to mirror the modernity around him, and as Grandma Wellcome's Anglo boy, the lost prince reborn as Bill and only another of numerous rebirths Williams underwent in his writings. In the Stecher Trilogy, he will be reborn as Flossie, with an acceptable mainstream background. He will be reborn as Kore. He will be reborn as Evans. He will be reborn again as Carlos in *Yes, Mrs. Williams.* But so that Bill may thrive, Carlos' poem had to cease to exist. The prince had landed on the beach of a "foreign" country where he had no place and so he simply evaporated, as happens in and to "Philip and Oradie."

Apparently believing that all copies of that first epic no longer existed or would not be read, Williams told Edith Heal that the new long poem was "a reconstruction from memory" of the first poem. Even more important in his explanation is how he correctly aligned each poem with the corresponding cultural symbols in his life:

> *It's actually a reconstruction from memory of my early Keatsian Endymion imitation that I destroyed, burned in a furnace! . . . The old woman in it is my grandmother, raised to heroic proportions. I en-*

dowed her with magical qualities. She had seized me from my mother
as her special possession, adopted me, and her purpose in life was to
make me her own. But my mother ended all that with a terrific slap in
the puss.

(*I Wanted to Write a Poem* 25–26)

Williams' anecdote on the struggle between his grandmother and mother
gives us further psychological insight into how he perceived the two
poems as representative of that very struggle inside him. "Philip and Oradie" celebrated his mother as the defining genius of his identity as Carlos; "The Wanderer" elevates his grandmother, and in it he is Bill.

But in *The Autobiography,* which predates the interview with Heal, he
had translated the significance of these two poems into strictly telling us
that "The Wanderer" was its restructuring, Bill steers the discussion to
what he claimed was the dominant concern in the writing of both poems,
his central interest in the "'line'":

> The Wanderer, *featuring my grandmother, the river, the Passaic River,*
> *took its place—my first "long" poem, which in turn led to* Paterson. *It*
> *was the "line" that was the key—a study in the line itself, which chal-*
> *lenged me.*

(*A* 61)

Note his quotation marks around *line.* They ostensibly give emphasis but
in fact signal Williams' playing encoding games: the "'line'" refers to both
the bloodline as well as the poetic line (see Chapter 5). This ambiguity,
like the autobiographical omissions that help to characterize Bill, is an
important cipher that illustrates how Williams "interknit" his personal
wanderings into the language of his poetry, continuously translating his
struggle into the structure of his work.

This includes the structure of *The Autobiography,* the life story of the poet
Bill, which Williams restructured from details selected from the life of the
man William Carlos. Factually unreliable, the autobiography is, by Williams' admission, an account of "feelings": "I decided if I was going to
give an account of my feelings I wasn't going to let people tell me what I
feel" (*IWW* 85). But this flippant summary, diverting us from the idea of
scheme, bestows on his book the appearance of an improvisation. However fast and inaccurately written, as Williams tells Heal, *The Autobiog-*

raphy must be read for its artful language and poetic devices. Names of people, places, and episodes have imagistic or symbolic value. Contradictions are blatantly left to stand at the expense of mundane truth, to be justified in the totality of the work, a contradictory style that reconciles otherwise irreconcilable particulars at an aesthetic level, a focusing of a cubist's eyes on himself.

In its defense, this contradictory style also expressed Williams' spirit of independence. Behind the pressures from his parents and the social pressures—including pressures coming from the "catalogue" that governed the literary world—that would attempt to mold him into some logically expected model, existed his determination to become whom he willed himself to be, certain that he would convince all doubters. To succeed as a poet against the challenges of his "weather" called for extraordinary measures, and his exemplary determination was expressed in *The Autobiography* when he recalled having spent a bad night at a party at Arensberg's, when he complimented Marcel Duchamp, and felt condescended to:

> *I realized then and there that there wasn't a possibility of my ever saying anything to anyone in that gang from that moment to eternity— but that one of them, by God, would come to me and give me the same chance one day and that I should not fail then to lay him cold—if I could. Watch and wait. Meanwhile, work.*

> (*A* 137)

The prince, finding himself in a "foreign" place, had vowed to himself to work as hard as it took in order to one day reign. He harbored no doubts that he could lay claim to a new kingdom in this land that spoke English and admired French. In its own oblique way, then, *The Autobiography* also celebrates Bill's triumph against an array of obstacles—his biculturalism, his parents' doubts, and "that gang," be they the academics, the entrenched literary Europhiles, or the "catalogue"'s guardians—before whom he politically assumed amorphous transformations.

Marsden Hartley reflected on this shifting feature of Williams' personality. In a 1903 letter to Alfred Stieglitz, he described Williams as multifaceted, "a small town of serious citizens in himself":

> *Williams you know is a very lovely fellow for himself and he certainly has made a splendid struggle to plasticize all his various selves and*

he is perhaps more people at once than anyone I've ever known—not
vague persons but he's a small town of serious citizens in himself. I
never saw so many defined human beings in one being.[22]

Hartley's ability to detect this multiplicity in Williams parallels Demuth's
perception of a fragmented identity. For besides the evocative possibilities
of Williams' poem "The Great Figure" (*CPI* 174), Williams' multifarious
appearance and dichotomous inner structure surely figured in Demuth's
making a cubist portrait of his friend.

That duplicitous deep structure can also be decoded from *The Autobiography,* which on the surface purports to be colloquial, although Fisher-
Wirth believes that Williams' duplicity results out of a genuine innocence:

> *One thing is certain, though: the water flows much more deeply than*
> *Williams permits us to see in his* Autobiography. *The* Autobiography *is*
> *not a deliberate falsification; Williams' other writings show that inno-*
> *cence, as he portrays it here, was a quality he did possess. But* The
> Autobiography *is a one-sided self-portrait in which certain facets of*
> *Williams' experience are cleverly highlighted and others firmly sup-*
> *pressed. Both the highlightings and the suppressions serve to*
> *strengthen the theme of innocence, as becomes clear once one perceives*
> *that the things suppressed are* eros *and* thanatos—*those great desires*
> *that drive the psyche and consternate Americans—while the things*
> *highlighted are the public virtues derived from sublimation.*
>
>   (Fisher-Wirth 39)

Fisher-Wirth here has described Bill in the clearest of terms, pointing
to his suppressed treatment of Carlos, who doesn't figure at all in her
exegesis of *The Autobiography.* With Carlos suppressed, so too was *eros.*
Thanatos, however, was not completely suppressed, as it briefly entered
into his account of his family's involvement in spiritualism, a discussion
centered on Elena. Carlos symbolized *eros* and Elena *thanatos* (the dead
yet living past). Nevertheless, Fisher-Wirth's conclusion that "the high-
lightings and the suppressions serve to strengthen the theme of innocence" is true, if incomplete. Bill suppressed Carlos' eroticism and emphasized Elena's spiritualism in order to highlight the trait that would win
him the public's acceptability: moral virtue, the antithesis of what Anglos
stereotypically associate with Latins. Here, to differ with Fisher-Wirth,
Williams is being consistent. The genuine innocence that Fisher-Wirth

perceives in his other writings was really artistically rendered innocence, a lack of innocence demonstrated by his politic and protean portrayals of William George, Grandma Wellcome, Angel Flores, and Dr. Henna.

Bill's innocence being a performance, *The Autobiography* can't even stand as the poeticized life of Williams. The Bill in that book did not live haunted by an inner foreign voice, without which Williams would never have produced "Asphodel," or *Paterson,* or "The Desert Music." Williams created those poems out of a compulsion to both claim a new kingdom and recover his old one, to fuse and balance his divergent parts into a composite whole, like the name he chose: William Carlos Williams. His inner conflict between divergent personae and postures, his inconsistent interpretations and subsequent contradictory rectifications require a portrait in which the Bill of *The Autobiography* is simply a flat publicity photograph affixed to a broader canvas. The true, fuller autobiography should be a collage, a combination of *The Autobiography* and the many expunged or customized particulars: the range of elements that automatically emerge once we restore to the composition the person who was foremost in the making of the poet, the most mistreated in Bill's story, his mother Elena.

Chapter 2

The Female Totem

Very seldom does a man get a chance to speak intimately of what has concerned him most in the past. This is about an old woman who had been young and to a degree beautiful a short number of years ago—this is as good a way as any to pay her my respects and to reassure her that she has not been forgotten.

(*Yes, Mrs. Williams* 38)

We are the spawn of the Caribbean, crouched here on another arm of the same great ocean; the same salt water as on the shores of Puerto Rico, Santo Domingo, Martinique combs the eelgrass and winnows the sand on this shore. And above us in the shadows sits and listens—the central thread, the tough core, this female totem.

(William Eric Williams [1])

Throughout *The Autobiography*, Williams condescends to his mother:

Poor, darling mother, she had her way, little as it got her. I could only chuckle at it and applaud her. I guess I was a strange son in her eyes.

(*A* 161)

He also characterizes her as an outsider with a language problem: "Mother was still a good deal of an outsider because of the language difficulty." The portrayal projects her as marginal to the person "we ourselves have been," and so expresses Bill's solidarity with his readers' world by playing to its prejudices; Elena was not just a foreigner, she was also "unquestionably, a foreigner to me." Albeit true in diverse ways, if left bare and out of context, that statement suggests a separateness between them and an unimportance about her that contradicted the facts. Williams wrote *The Autobiography* during a time when he was gathering the material and the fortitude to write a book exclusively about her. The reason for this contradiction should by now be clear. Being the mother of Carlos, Elena really did not figure in the life of Bill. Nevertheless, in their respective contexts, both depictions of Elena were tenable to him; Williams was concomitantly the son of the marginal mother in *The Autobiography* and of the central figure in *Yes, Mrs. Williams.* That binary secret told Williams' whole story. To understand the sense of this contradiction, however, we must return to "beginnings," to the lost prince's undying devotion to his Beatrix and her contribution to the making of the poet.

Raquel Helene Rose Hoheb (1847–1950) was born in Mayagüez, Puerto Rico to a mother originally from Martinique and a Puerto Rican father of Dutch ancestry, both of whom had died by the time she was fourteen. Elena's marriage to Williams' father, William George, was a link in a chain of unfortunate coincidences. While studying art in Paris, she received word from her physician brother Carlos that, owing to his personal financial losses, she would have to discontinue her studies and return to live with him and his family in Puerto Plata, Dominican Republic. Anglo American literary history might have been different if shortly before her departure she had not discovered that, out of love for her, her Spanish lover had jilted another woman. Incapable of accepting a love so tainted by deliberation, she broke with the Spaniard—a decision that, judging from Williams' tone, the entire family lived to regret:

> *From Paris she returned to those meager islands. She married at the home of one of those same Monsantos and pretty soon had two boys on her hands. I call it her vicarious atonement.*
>
> (*YM* 5)

In 1882, at her brother Carlos' home, Elena met William George. Still bitter with herself for having left her Spaniard and with little to look forward to in Puerto Plata, she followed William George to Rutherford. They married at the home of her cousins the Monsantos, and in 1883, she gave birth to William Carlos Williams.

Of the two parents, Elena was destined to leave a deeper impression on Williams. First, she was the mainstay of the home, ever present while William George traveled throughout Latin America for weeks, months and, once, for an entire year. Second, there was the necessary deference paid to her culture and language. Elena spoke no English and her husband, who was at home in her culture to begin with, spoke fluent Spanish.

In an interview with John W. Gerber and Emily M. Wallace, Williams describes the household into which he was born as Spanish-speaking, suggesting that he and his brother started out as bilingual or monolingual speakers of Spanish before, at some unspecified time, they "dropped" it:

> *We've dropped it in our day, curiously enough, but my parents spoke Spanish, preferable to English, and my brother and I heard it and understood it because they said things in Spanish that they didn't want us to understand.*[2]

This version of Williams' linguistic formation contradicts the emphasis in *The Autobiography,* in which his childhood as a Spanish-speaker is never mentioned. The truth of the matter was that Grandma Wellcome became a symbol of English because she stood out in the household as the sole person that he couldn't associate with Spanish.

Bill's circumventing Spanish in his autobiography's account of his linguistic formation has contributed to our not associating Williams with biculturalism; a cool, anglicized Bill persona prevails, giving little reason to pursue any Spanish language influence in his writing. As Bill, Williams only admitted to a *background* that spoke Spanish:

> *I feel close to Spanish-speaking people . . . simply because I have heard so much of the language at home and knew so many Spaniards among my parents' friends.*[3]

Williams here defers to popular prejudices by "upgrading" his background: his parents' friends were "Spanish" in the loose sense that means they were Spanish-speaking, from *hispanos.* "Spaniards" too was employed in that loose way. None of his parents' friends appear to have been from Spain.

Bill's separating himself from Spanish symbolically separated him from Elena, a symbol system that his critics adopted. Mariani, for instance, muddies the linguistic context of the Williams household by portraying the confluence of Spanish and English in the Williams home as a "strange, heady, unorthodox linguistic minestrone":

> *And though many of her friends were English, for most of them Spanish came as naturally to them as English. We must recall, they were friends from Puerto Rico or other islands and Elena didn't speak English. What Williams heard as a young man, then, was Spanish from*

the lips of the Hazels, the Lambs, the Dodds, and the Forbeses. And English from the Monsantos and Enriquezes of Brooklyn. It was a strange, heady, unorthodox linguistic minestrone Williams tasted growing up.

(*NW* 17)

The Hazels' or Dodds' speaking Spanish perfectly wasn't any more "unorthodox" than William George's fluency in Spanish or Elena's in French. Children who hear two or three languages spoken routinely at home do not find the bilingualism of others confusing. Williams' problem was not that he grew up hearing different languages; rather, what confused him was his society's ranking of them, which taught him that they were incompatible.

Regarding Williams' supposed linguistic confusion, Mariani adds that Elena had taught her son the "language distinctions" between "French and Spanish patois." The former literally exists, but except for words here and there Elena herself may have picked up from her mother, it's unlikely that Williams would have heard French patois spoken because the French his mother learned was from her very proper French school in Mayagüez, where many Europeans had settled. Mariani's invented "Spanish patois," on the other hand, celebrates the common misconception of an impure and corrupted Caribbean Spanish. In fact, as is true of the Spanish throughout Latin America, Caribbean Spanish is simply regionally enriched, with no significant syntactic changes. A Puerto Rican or Cuban or Dominican patois is nonexistent; what does exist is a variety of American Spanish, a variant of Iberian Spanish as Huck Finn's English is a variant of that of Sherlock Holmes.

Mariani's diffuse image of Elena causes him to stumble over several contradictory descriptions of her. On page 2 of *New World Naked,* for instance, Elena is described as a "mother who spoke French first and then Spanish and—when necessary—a very broken English. . . . On page 6, he distances her from her own native tongue: "It was French *she* wanted, French and a serviceable Spanish." On page 17 we are told that "Spanish was the language she used as home" and that she "practiced her beloved French whenever she could find someone who could speak that 'civilized' tongue." And on page 447 she is "that marvelous hybrid creature of French, Jewish, and Spanish descent, whose whole life had been shaped by this island where she had been born. . . ."

Despite those inconsistencies, Mariani bends toward the French version of Elena, and owing to his over-Frenchifying Elena in his mind, he feels free to Frenchify Williams:

> . . . *Williams reacted by joining the Carlstadt Turnverein there. That was nothing more dangerous than a gymnastics club, but his own mother was furious that her son, who was half English and half French (to oversimplify), had elected to side with the Germans in spite of what those "barbarians" were doing to her beloved France.*
>
> (*NW* 170)

Although the subject of war motivated her use of the epithet "barbarians" just then, even if the Germans hadn't invaded France, Elena would have still considered them barbarians. As noted earlier, when referring to Teutonic culture "barbarian" is as common in Spanish as in French. Mariani's reference to Elena's reaction was taken from Williams' autobiographical novel *The Build-Up*, which Mariani cites as literal truth. In that scene the mother of Joe's "son-in-law, the doctor" is said to be "half-French" and does react furiously at her son for joining the German gymnasium: "'You are half-English and half-French, . . .'"[4] But here one can argue that Bill was merely projecting ingratiating symbols of himself. Characterizing Williams as "half-French" in Elena's eyes, even in the most figurative of terms, may be blandly supported by Bill's posturing but is absolutely unsupported by the dominant Spanish vein that runs through the better part and the best of his writings. His Frenchification is even unsupported by Williams' own better conscience as the narrator, who immediately corrects his fictive mother's remark by adding "though that was not quite true."

Misinterpretations of Elena, one needs quickly to interject, are also understandable, being as much the fault of Williams' own shifting cultural emphasis. When speaking as Bill and having to highlight his foreign roots, Williams placed greater emphasis on French. In the opening to *Yes, Mrs. Williams,* for instance, Williams stresses his maternal grandfather's mixed breeding and circumvents the mixture of his maternal grandmother. Elena is described as "half French, out of Martinique," even though in the next breath he tells us that her mother "was of Basque stock." In "From Notes about My Mother," which was incorporated into *Yes, Mrs. Williams,* Bill's rationale for his way of "telling things" includes another Frenchification of Elena:

Perhaps my way of telling you this isn't exactly what you might prefer or expect, but in this family you are expected to understand what is said and interpret, as essential to the telling, the way in which it is told—for some reason which you will know is of the matter itself. That is to picture it. "Figure to yourself," as my mother would often say— obviously translated from the French."[5]

Elena's "Figure to yourself," which according to Williams came "obviously from the French," is not necessarily and unlikely from the French but from the Spanish, in which "Figúrate" is a common idiomatic exclamation, meaning "Imagine that!" or "Who would have thought!"

French also figures, but more subtly, in Williams' intentionally contradictory style in *Spring and All*. Just before embarking on an extensive exposition of the new aesthetics exemplified by his favorite artist, the Spaniard Juan Gris, Bill praises Cézanne and dismisses "the Spanish" for clinging to their favorites:

I don't know what the Spanish see in their Velázquez and Goya . . .

(I 111)

His fascination with cubism and the new art coming out of France also bolstered the impression that he was drawn to remote French roots, but his two major idols of that French scene were really the Spaniards, Picasso and Gris, with whom he identified because they were Spaniards.

In fact, Williams finally rectified in *Yes, Mrs. Williams*, he heard little French while he was growing up:

French we did not hear very much though we were conscious of it from the letters Mother occasionally received from Paris, . . .

(YM 4)

One motivation for mixing around Elena's history was loyalty. Elena's French side, the "Hurrard or Hurrand" line, disappeared with the eruption of Mt. Pelée, while her Hoheb side descended from an unclear line. More important, its haziness covered over a racial secret. This combination gave Williams' maternal side a foggy past to parallel the cloud on his paternal side. If William George had sworn to Grandma Wellcome that he would not reveal a secret about her past and dutifully kept that promise, then Williams was probably emulating his father in keeping Elena's past blurry; his changing story about her identity was part of his filial defense.

In a 1950 interview, for instance, he gave Elena's background with a minimum of embellishments, identifying Elena's mother as French and her father as Puerto Rican:

> *And well, switch to Mother, she was born in Mayagüez, Puerto Rico, of mixed parentage she was, her mother coming originally from Martinique, a French woman, and her father being a Puerto Rican.*

> (Wagner 5)

In the "Introduction" to *Yes*, Elena's paternal side is simply described as "a mixed breed, the Hohebs, Monsantos, . . ." Later in that book he elaborates, telling us that no one recalled how many generations earlier the Hohebs had arrived on Puerto Rico:

> *Apparently the Hohebs came from Holland—Amsterdam most likely. Carlos tried for years to locate some connection, or even to trace the name, but without success of any sort. She remembers oil portraits in Dutch costume. But Cousin Sissy hated old things and all were lost or destroyed finally. Hoheb, the father, was of a first marriage and the half brothers Enriquez were often in his hair. How many generations there had been of them in Puerto Rico and how they had mixed with the Spanish there is completely lost.*

> *(YM* 53)

While the Dutch were rare as immigrants to Puerto Rico, Holland was always present in the Caribbean, whose larger islands the Dutch constantly sought to wrest from Spain. In the seventeenth century the island was attacked frequently and briefly occupied by Holland. In a 1644 letter, the Bishop of Puerto Rico Damián López de Haro complained of the constant fear of the Dutch. Puerto Ricans felt so besieged by them that they didn't "dare take out boats to fish for fear of being captured by the Dutch."[6] Holland, of course, ended up with Curaçao and one of the Guyanas. That in the crosscurrents of the centuries, a Dutch-Caribbean Hoheb could have landed on Puerto Rico and remained was quite within the realm of possibility. Williams' assumption that the Hohebs had to have arrived directly from Amsterdam is unfounded. The point being stressed is that given the maelstrom of Caribbean history, the murkiness of Elena's past and Williams' sense of being historically lost is a not uncommon Puerto Rican legacy.

That Puerto Rican legacy prompted him to praise what took place in

the nineteenth century Caribbean, when Sol Hoheb found himself admired by a "girl" from Martinique, a union that Williams interpreted as
the races mingling:

> *Yet the races mingled with man and woman sensing the new in superb*
> *disregard for a tradition which, indeed, they had left behind, simply*
> *didn't know anymore. The girl admired Sol Hoheb—and I suppose*
> *they learned each others languages fast enough.*

(YM 136)

This racial question in Elena's lineage surfaces in other writings and is
treated in code. Elena's father's half-brothers were surnamed "Enriquez,"
a name her father himself bore for a time while he grew up (*YM* 30). More
commonly spelled "Henríquez," in Puerto Rico this surname is legendar-
ily associated with African blood. In her unusually long life Elena undoubtedly dropped this tidbit of Puerto Rican lore. In the segment "12/18"
of *The Descent of Winter* Elena speaks of her father's half-brother: "But
his half-brother Henríquez, there's plenty of that in my family, . . ." (*I* 264).
The "of that" is ambiguous. To the reader, the half-brother may imply the
proliferation of illegitimate children. But to a Puerto Rican mind, because
"Henríquez" hints at black blood, the "of that" also encodes racial mixing.

In another subtle racial allusion in *Yes, Mrs. Williams,* Williams tells
us that Elena's father complained that the Enriquez half-brothers "were
often in his hair." Among Puerto Ricans blackness is measured by quality
of hair as much as by darkness of skin. Hence the litmus test of whether
someone has *pelo bueno* or *pelo malo* ("good" or "bad hair"). This popular convention was also something that Williams would have inevitably
picked up from Elena. Williams' encoded suggestion is that beside being
meddling half-brothers they were "in his hair" genetically. Had only the
half-brothers been partly black, then Williams' racial doubts about the
family would have been localized, but Williams doesn't make this point.
At the end of *Yes, Mrs. Williams,* he discusses his racial doubts bluntly:

> *Nothing is known of our family beyond the last three generations and*
> *not all of that—other than vague rumors, enticing, irritating, scandal-*
> *ous—racially doubtful in certain cases.*

(YM 132)

In another encoding in *Yes, Mrs. Williams,* Elena's mother is said to
have married Enriquez after the death of her first husband. That was

Hoheb, whose name Williams cites as "Job," spelling it in Spanish as Elena probably pronounced it (with the "J" sounding like an English "H") for the sake of a biblical allusion that results when read in English: his grandfather was reputedly very patient (*YM* 30). It was this "Job" who was raised by "Enriquez," bearing his surname until "he assumed his own name in later life," probably when he realized the racial connotations of his adopted name. The two paragraphs that follow the one that tells of Enriquez, if left undecoded, are a cryptic leap of logic:

> *Old Mrs. Wingate, Mother said, was the one who told me about my father. She said he was a great dancer in St. Thomas. That is where she knew him. All the girls wanted to dance with him.*

> (*YM* 30)

Although we know nothing of Hoheb, except that he had an "Enriquez" for a stepfather, by immediately inserting that Elena's father was a good dancer, Williams appears also to belabor a racial stereotype. One comes to that conclusion because in the subsequent, otherwise non sequitur paragraph, Williams celebrates how throughout the Caribbean islands "the races of the world mingled," proclaiming that mixture as being "in the best spirit of the New World":

> *In the West Indies, in Martinique, St. Thomas, Puerto Rico, Santo Domingo, in those days, the races of the world mingled and intermarried—imparting their traits one to another and forgetting the orthodoxy of their ancient and medieval views. It was a good thing. It is in the best spirit of the New World.*

> (*YM* 30)

So while the specifics of the racial doubts in Elena's family are left murky, Williams' conviction of racial mixture in him is clear. His certainty of having been conceived in "the best spirit of the New World" gave him the confidence to see himself as a "pure product of America." This realization turned a background that he, seeing the world as Bill, formerly thought "meager" into a source of power.

A nuance of that racially mixed legacy, which Williams himself doesn't relate to the question of his background, was his attraction for dark women. They were always present, if invisible, in his life. William George had worked among Latin women and traveled to regions where black, Indian, and Latin women drew him away from his family. Black women appeared to predominate among Williams' patients, and several of his poems are about them. From *Yes, Mrs. Williams* one infers that Williams traced at least one source of that attraction to Elena's bloodline. He recorded, for example, her fascination with the distinctiveness of the African-Puerto Ricans. After quoting an anecdote about black dancers on New Year's Day on the island, he cites and translates one of Elena's refrains:

> Con la sal que derrama una morena
> Se mantiene una rubia semana y media
> (With the salt you'd take for a brunette
> You'd keep a red head a week and a half)

> (*YM* 109)

Although Williams translated the gist, the refrain literally says

> With the salt a dark woman spills
> A blond can keep going for a week.

In Spanish, *sal* (literally "salt") also figuratively signifies both sexual secretion and expressiveness or wit.

Williams' attraction to dark beauty as expressed in his writings, to be discussed in greater detail in Chapter 6, was emblematic of his idealization of his Caribbean inheritance. The dark woman symbolized nonconformity and fusion. Like the Caribbean, she embodied the New World spirit, a breaking down of the concept of racial "purity," a mingling spirit that Williams wrote of as his inheritance by way of Elena:

> *It is precisely the racial solidarity, the traditional aloofness of the nomadic tribe, the ancient, the classic "purity of race" which forms the basis for Nazi action. It is precisely this that the West Indian tradition abhorred also and tended to break down. It would have been unlikely that there would have existed there, in St. Thomas, the incentive to such spurious integrity of race—such spurious "purity" that it would have been held laudable for individuals to be governed by its tenets.*

> (*YM* 137)

After the arrival of the Europeans, the Caribbean produced a gold greater than the kind the conquerors came to find, a resistance to "the devil of conformity," a model for the "good":

Great gold came from these things, greater than the metal they killed the natives for and drove them to death by group suicide to circumvent. The devil of conformity which peopled them under Torquemada wasn't allowed to sleep entirely in New Spain. Evil opposed good. The line is sharply drawn as it is in the character of my mother.

(*YM* 136)

In abhorring the divisiveness epitomized by the Puritan, the "catalogue," and the poor visibility of Ezra Pound, the Caribbean at its best was the model for Williams' ideal America.

Elena Hoheb was, with apologies to today's pseudo-racial connotations of "Puerto Rican," simply and typically a cultured woman from nineteenth-century Puerto Rico. Her cultural identity was the same as that of Julio Henna, her brother Carlos, Angel Flores, Betances, and Madame Trufly, who all inhabit *The Autobiography.* But to have a factual picture of Elena, we must separate the historical person from the literary symbol Williams made of her. We also have to dismiss efforts to turn her into something other than Puerto Rican, a false image put there by biographers and critics for whom the idea of Elena as Williams' mother did not elegantly coincide with American English's stereotypes of "Puerto Rican." Over the years, her French, Dutch, and even Sephardic lineages have taken precedence over and often covered completely her Spanish Caribbean origins. Those other multiple heritages may sound exotic and may therefore even have piqued Williams' imagination, but Elena's cultural mixture was not extraordinary in the Caribbean. French, especially French Catalan, and remote Spanish Sephardic lineages are common in Puerto Rico, and her words in *Yes, Mrs. Williams* leave no doubts about her sense of what she was not. To her, the French, German, and English people she knew in Mayagüez were "all foreigners" (*YM* 44).

But because she herself lacked a clearly-defined cultural character, "bridging two cultures," Williams described her as a "grotesque":

Neither one thing or the other, grotesques were drawn on the walls of grottos, half human, half leaves—whatever the fancy made obligatory to fate. So in her life, neither one or the other, she stands bridging two cultures, three regions of the world, almost without speech—

(*YM* 94)

The bridge between two cultures was an image that Williams surely heard often in the years leading up to 1952, the year of the "Commonwealth" plebiscite in Puerto Rico, and numerous times during his 1956 trip there. After World War II, to placate a United Nations mandate to dismantle the world's colonies, Washington and the colonial government of Puerto Rico launched a media campaign to sell (to Puerto Ricans, Americans, and the UN) the virtues of a newly-conceived "Commonwealth" status.[7] The propaganda hook was that the island was to become a "A Bridge between Two Cultures," a catch phrase that after the 1952 plebiscite continued to figure in the Commonwealth's public relations campaigns to invite industrial investors. These often took the form of full color supplements in the *New York Times,* spreads in *Life* magazine, and press coverage in other national publications. The island's miraculous economic transformation was constantly being pushed by publicists (good news that competed with less pleasant reports on the lives of poor island immigrants in New York who, as part of that economic miracle, had been encouraged to abandon the island). Williams' reading in 1956, at the invitation of the University of Puerto Rico's president Jaime Benítez, one of the leading ideologues of the new "permanent union," was a perfect "bridge" example of the "Commonwealth"'s cultural policy. Unwittingly, Williams' trip contributed to its propaganda. In short, it was unlikely that Williams would have arrived in heavily industrializing Puerto Rico without having already heard or read the "Bridge between Two Cultures" phrase several times. In fact, in "The Desert Music" (written in 1951), Williams had already used the "Bridge between Two Cultures" image. On that bridge he placed another "grotesque," this time a reflection of himself. In both the 1951 poem and the 1959 book, Williams' "bridge" image could not have been conceived in a vacuum unrelated to the highly suggestive, personally relevant, and ubiquitous original bridge in the Commonwealth propaganda.

Williams' negative use of the "bridge" image implies a condemnation of the Commonwealth bicultural model as a perpetuation of "grotesques" like Elena, thus touching upon the important detail that Elena lacked a sharply defined sense of identity because Puerto Rico lacked one. While the island gained a better sense of itself in the second half of the twentieth century, the island's undefined cultural identity has been its historical burden. Early on after its conquest, because the gold ran out quickly, Spain abandoned Puerto Rico, treating it as a military outpost. In the nine-

teenth century, when liberal ideas threatened the dissolution of its empire, Spain kept a tighter grip on its remaining American colonies, Puerto
Rico and Cuba, its two military "keys" to the Caribbean shipping gateway
to a dreamed reconquest of its lost continents. For those islands this
meant that any commerce of ideas was severely censored, education was
restricted, and intellectuals, especially revolutionary types like Henna
and Betances, were banished.

These oppressive policies made Puerto Rico even more pathetic than
it had already been. For unlike Cuba, Puerto Rico didn't even have a university, and would not until the U.S. Department of Defense founded the
University of Puerto Rico in 1903.[8] Throughout the nineteenth century, as
Latin American countries became independent, nascent nationalistic impulses were constantly watered down by the demographic pattern of arriving conservative exiles, who supported oppression and censorship, including the crown's policy against education. Those who could afford it
looked to and traveled to France. By the mid-nineteenth century, as illustrated by the brief-lived *Grito de Lares* that catapulted Dr. Henna to New
York, the island had lost its Spanish consciousness—but without having
actually forged a national one, a confused identity reflected in Elena's
mood swings between her nostalgia for her lost Paradise and her nostalgia for France because there was "nothing" in Puerto Rico.

Elena's Francophilia was also perfectly reasonable and contemporaneous with her Latin American generation. Among educated nineteenth-
century Latin Americans, French was *de rigueur*. Many political and
intellectual leaders received a French education. France, the temple of
Liberalism, had inspired Latin American independence, including the
Puerto Rican *Grito,* as well as provided a countermodel for Spanish
culture. From 1864 to 1867, Mexico was ruled by Napoleon's brother
Maximilian. Romantic French writers became the literary standard. The
Cuban-born, half-French José María Heredia became a major French
poet as did Jules LaForgue, who was born in Montevideo. As was also true
with U.S. writers, this literary adulation of France by Latin Americans
lasted into the twentieth century, notably in the example of the influential
avant garde Chilean Víctor Huidobro, half of whose poetic production
was in French.

In Williams' immediate background, the Puerto Rican painter Francisco Oller worked among the Impressionists in Paris before returning
to Puerto Rico to paint island scenes. His "El Estudiante" hangs in the

Louvre. The aspiring artist Elena received a French education on the island and later studied painting in Paris. Her brother Carlos and Julio José Henna studied medicine in Paris, as did many others of their social class. Henna's political and medical colleague Betances, who had also studied in France, continued to lead the movement for Puerto Rican independence from his exile in France, where he was eventually awarded the Legion of Honor. Before he died there, Betances authored in French a political romance about Puerto Rico, *La Vierge Borinquén* (1859). The identity of educated nineteenth-century Puerto Ricans, therefore, was an admixture of a love of France, a rejection of Spain, and a romantic, undefined national consciousness.

All this adds up to Elena's being representative of the Puerto Rican gentry of her time. Having received a private French education, and being a conventional woman of her social class, she pursued her French roots, which also happened to be in vogue. But she was not French. When she came to New Jersey, she found herself having to surrender to a life in a country that she disliked and that expressed hostility to foreigners in general and assumed its supremacy over, among others, Spanish-speakers—her cultural predicament differing not at all from that of later Puerto Rican and other Latin American immigrants. The Spanish-American War in 1898 had to have left Elena even more amorphous about her identity. While she might have welcomed the triumph of liberal democracy over Spain, the outcome probably branded in her heart the metaphor of her trapped condition: Puerto Rico was lost to the United States. The island was now in the hands of barbarians, gone forever with the wind, a reality that she sternly rejected. She was left with her memories and her imagination. (That about the Spanish-American War, or the Jones Act of 1917, which thrust U.S. citizenship upon Elena, Williams remains reticent raises the suspicion that anything there was to report would have affected Bill adversely.)

In sum, Elena's being a pure product of nineteenth-century Puerto Rico explains her cultural amorphousness and her appearing a "grotesque" when reflected in the mirror of Anglo American ignorance, including Williams'. For her amorphousness, contradictory as it might sound, has been a characterizing trait of Puerto Ricans as Puerto Ricans. Luis Palés Matos made that very point in his poem "Canción Festiva para Ser Llorada" ("Festive Song to be Wept"), whose refrain pairs the three larger Caribbean islands with images popularly associated with them:

Cuba—*ñáñigo* and good times—
Haití—voodoo and gourds—
Puerto Rico—*burundanga*—

(*Poesía Completa y Prosa Selecta* 158)

Čuba was at that time identified with good times and *ñáñigos,* members of a secret society of Afro-Cubans. Haiti evoked voodoo and (probably folk art made from) gourds. But Puerto Rico failed the poet's imagination: *burundanga,* an African-derived onomatopoetic word that signifies an undefined mixup, what Williams labeled a "grotesque."

But Elena's appearing to lack a cultural identity didn't preclude her having certain cultural traits, and her passing them on to him. Williams exhibited, for example, a perspicuously Puerto Rican characteristic discernible from what Mariani cites as "the key to Williams' character":

> *a single-minded ability to see a thing through his way, a refusal to be hassled into following the lead of others, including, finally, even his rabbit-swift friend, Pound himself.*

(*NW* 33)

The emblem of a turtle on Williams' college stationery, "slowly stepping over the word *"j'arrivai:* I will get there," universalizes this character trait; but his manner and strategy display what Puerto Ricans call *Jaiba* (prounded *high-ba*), a term derived from the name of a river shrimp that hides under the stones, which denotes a quiet, unswayed shrewdness that attains its objective obliquely. Such *jaiba* is evident in statements such as: "I knew French which impressed Pound and he thought I knew more Spanish than I did. I never let on" (*IWW* 7). Similarly, Williams' letting the literary world turn on its axis without his physical involvement while he attacked it instead from the fringes, convinced that his writings would "get there" before they did, also exhibits this *jaiba.*

This trait was poetically defined in a popular 1944 poem by Luis Lloréns Torres, in which a *jíbaro* ("peasant" or "hick") is accosted by *pitiyanquis* ("statehood advocates," from *petite yanqui*), who try to recruit him into the statehood movement:

Llegó un jíbaro a San Juan
y unos cuantos pitiyanquis

lo atajaron en el parque
queriéndolo conquistar.
Le hablaron del Tío Sam,
de Wilson, de Mr. Root,
de New York, de Sandy Hook,
de la libertad, del voto,
del dólar, del Habeas corpus . . .
y el jíbaro dijo: Njú.

A *jíbaro* came to San Juan
and a band of wannabe Yankees
cut him off at the park,
to woo him to their camp.
They talked of Uncle Sam,
Wilson and Mr. Root,
New York and Sandy Hook,
freedom and the vote,
habeas corpus and the dollar . . .
and the hick replied: Uhuh.[9]

The *jíbaro,* exercising *jaiba,* feigns stupidity, resisting passively.

The *jíbaro*'s *jaiba* is not exclusive, of course, to Puerto Rican culture and only a local expression of the universal shrewd country bumpkin. But Williams didn't grow up in the country. More to the point, Elena probably made him aware of this "country bumpkin" character trait in him. In Book Four of *Paterson* (1951), in a poem about the funeral of an unnamed elderly woman who from the details and the poem's being published in 1951, two years after his mother's death, we must conclude was Elena, he informs us that "country bumpkin" was her affectionate way of address-ing him: "She used to call me her / country bumpkin" (*P* 189). But that term was inconsistent with her thickly-accented English usage; Williams was clearly translating. Elena more likely expressed affection in Spanish, and the term she apparently used was the common Puerto Rican form of affectionate address to a child, the diminutive of *jíbaro, jibarito.* Hence it should not surprise us that Williams frequently identified with this *jíbaro* role in his writing. He plays it, for example, before Valéry Larbaud in *In the American Grain.* Bryce Conrad describes that encounter as one in which Williams wears a bumpkin mask:

Williams, however, adopts his own symbolic mask. His pretended fear that Larbaud has "presumed too much" and will ask him questions he cannot answer—whatever its apparent basis in the "facts" of the diary and letters—certainly speaks such a mask, for Williams indeed answers more questions than Larbaud can put to him. Williams gives us a playful twist on the American folk motif of the country bumpkin who outsmarts the cultivated city dweller.[10]

Williams' story "A Visit to the Fair" also explores this subtle manner that bides its time. The widower Fred approaches the married Bess with an invitation to the fair. He had always taken his wife to the fair and tells this to Bess, who out of sympathy agrees to accompany the poor man. Bess gets her husband's consent and spends the day with Fred. It is an innocent outing, with subtle tinges of wrongdoing: her car is kept in his barn, so as not to have the neighbors misconstrue; her friend sees them together, surprised to find Bess escorted by a man not her husband. But Fred behaves impeccably and even extends a very generous offer that Bess move her entire family, which happens to be in financial trouble, to live and work on his land. At the end of the day, Bess doesn't know how to repay Fred for taking her to the fair, and Fred's response is exemplary of *jaiba*:

> *You've been wonderful to me and I've had a really great day.*
> *Well, he said, Mrs. Rand, I'm glad you did, I'm very glad you did. I wanted to treat you right because, well, he said, I wanted you to have a good time because I thought if you did, maybe sometime you'd go out with me again.*
>
> (FD 13)

Indeed, this country *jaibería* whose astuteness takes the soul underground, making it impervious to tests others may put it through, may be interpreted as universal; but Williams eventually realized that in this he imaged his mother. His poem "Eve" confesses to his discovering late in life this secret, survival side to her. His ability to keep a hidden core to himself is the very trait that in time he began to see as Elena's own strength:

> When Adam died
> it came out clearly—

Not what commonly
might have been supposed but
a demon, fighting for the fire
it needed to breathe
to live again.

(*CPI* 411)

The question of Williams' receiving anything from Elena's Puerto Rican culture had also been overshadowed by his turning her into a symbol
of a Spanish literary legacy. In the absence of a clear notion of her immediate cultural legacy, which he only knew to be "meager," Williams
clung to the pedigree afforded by the older roots of her spoken Spanish
and its literature. Puerto Rico and Spain became interchangeable, as they
would have been for Elena, who was born in a Spanish colony; her actual
geographic origins played no role in this symbolic system. According to
this system too, Williams' English implicitly became a form of patriotism,
the language of the industrial United States, and a standard against which
to define "Spanish," which signified Elena's romanticism and ideation,
which he as Bill also projected on all speakers of her language.

Privately, however, Williams understood that this system was a distort-
ing oversimplification. His 1939 essay "Against the Weather," written in
the persona of Carlos, praises Spanish thought's courage to face the real:

> *Read carefully, the icy chastity of Spanish thought comes through the*
> *reality of the event from which the man does not flinch—nor does he*
> *flinch before the consequence.*

(*SE* 228)

And Spanish literary realism did eventually affect his perception of Elena,
as will be discussed ahead; but this remained a secret, so as not to affect
Bill's symbols, which continued to rely on his youthful impression of her
as a romantic, a contradiction that, despite his respect for Spanish literature, he was able to keep with a straight face because Williams really
associated that literature with his father. William George was the knowl-
edgeable reader of Spanish-language letters in the household. Except
for writing two translations with Elena, projects to keep her busy in old
age, and referring to her Quevedo anecdotes (popularly known even by
non-literary Hispanics), Williams does not portray Elena in any signifi-

cant literary context. To him she symbolized Art, a latticework of questions about art and the aesthetics of language, all of which ultimately also affected his writing, as will be demonstrated subsequently. But, even though Elena continued to symbolize "Spanish," his regard of Spanish literature as a role model remained divorced from his perception of her as the foreignizing romantic element in his grittier American life. Day to day, Elena's "Spanish" idealism and nostalgia appeared dishonest or ridiculously anachronistic when measured against the starkness of industrial Rutherford. That at least was the Anglo Bill's stock summary of her, not knowing that despite her ostensibly anachronistic manner she was actually concordant with her true background and time: Latin America's belated romantic century.

Romanticism came to Latin America in the nineteenth century and overlapped with *fin de siècle* isms (realism, naturalism, positivism), often creating impure stylistic and ideological alloys, not unlike Williams' own mingled romantic/anti-romantic style. We are, of course, dealing with an *age* whose features spanned the hemisphere, and continued to persist even in the more advanced North America, which in Williams' youth was still putting its romantic phase behind it. Williams' depicting his Bill persona as the triumph of his more concrete English over his mother's "romantic" Spanish was in the spirit of that casting off of romanticism in Anglo America. But that figurative declaration of independence further distorted Elena's cultural influence: his obsession with concreteness and things over abstractions, with an unfailing language unafraid to address reality, coincided exactly with how contemporaneous Puerto Rican writers rejected the romanticism that characterized Elena's generation.

The doctor-novelist Manuel Zeno Gandía (1855–1930) broke with romanticism in his series *Chronicles of a Sick World,* begun at the end of the nineteenth century. His *El Negocio (The Deal,* 1922) was a realistic portrayal of city lives. His earlier *La Charca (The Stagnant Pool,* 1896), although set in the country, is naturalistic. In it, the socially conscious landowner Juan del Salto reflects on the pathetic lives of the rural poor, as well as on the future of his homeland as symbolized by his son Jacobo, studying in Europe, who evokes the Jacob who dreamed the ladder. After reading Jacobo's letters that gush with patriotic nostalgia for his remembered island, Juan's reflection on his son perfectly serves to describe Elena:

Apart from that he kept his homeland engraved on his spirit: he
dreamed it more than he experienced it. He gazed at it through the
prism of his romantic soul.[11]

Juan del Salto's reaction to his son's romantic distortion of the island's
reality also voiced for the first time a theme that would prove to recur in
post-romantic Puerto Rican writings, the islander's proclivity for denial:
"Reality, that's the anchor!"

The book-long essay *Insularismo* (1934) by Antonio S. Pedreira (1898–
1939) expressed the same concern for the Puerto Rican's evasion of
reality. An intellectual whose writing was otherwise representative of
Westernist and racist assumptions of his day, Pedreira contributed impor-
tantly in castigating his society for its *retoricismo* or penchant for euphemism and circumlocution. Seeing this trait encouraged by nineteenth-
century aesthetics, he lauded the death of romanticism in Puerto Rico,
which in a literary context he dismissed as a long "poetic pneumonia."
Pedreira specifically criticized the poet José Gautier Benítez (1848–1880),
whose work was the epitome of the island's romantic poetry, in words that
aptly parallel Williams' criticism of Elena:

He turned his lyricism into a nostalgia and perceived Puerto Rico as a
reflection in a mirror of water, on the verge of a departure or a return,
"like the memory of a deep love," with that lover's emotion that im-
pedes a man's arriving with incisive penetration into the marrow of
things.[12]

Pedreira called for a language that is direct and concrete, pruned of
facile emotions. This he felt was key if Puerto Rico was going to develop
a national consciousness, the self-awareness that can only come with an
efficient language that doesn't euphemize harsh reality. Thus he opened
his preface with these stern words:

These words will lack that flattering tone that our complacency has de-
vised to measure reality in Puerto Rico.

(Pedreira i)

Pedreira was essentially calling for a language that does not fail its
speakers, and speakers with the courage to use their language efficiently.
This call predates Williams' declaration in *Paterson:*

> The language, the language
>   fails them,
> they do not know the words
>   or have not
> the courage to use them .

(P 11)

Needless to say, in their anti-romanticism Puerto Rican writers were also not unique and responded in concert with their generation throughout Latin America. For underlying the aforementioned parallels was the hemisphere's ongoing objective to define a mixed-up America composed of both European and non-European legacies. *Insularismo* is one of a number of important Latin American essays of the twenties and thirties in which writers attempted to summarize the collective psychology of their respective societies. Williams' *In the American Grain* was a northern expression of that hemispheric American urgency. That it should spring from a writer whose soul was half-Latin American should not surprise. English-language Americans had yet to contemplate their Americanness, which up and down the continents, centuries after Columbus, was still an exotic and unprestigious concept. In brief, Williams' apparent Anglo response to Elena's "Spanish" romanticism was, in fact, as much an expression of his own Americanness as a Latin.

The major obstacle to our seeing Elena's importance to Williams' writing has been his rebellious and censoring persona as Bill. This posture toward Elena camouflages Williams' genuine sense of being betrayed by those traits in her that he most admired when he was Beatrix's young prince Carlos. Her romantic idealism, her ostensibly higher standards, and her dream-like memories of refinement in Puerto Rico had once been things upon which Williams had also counted and which, when he tried to harmonize them with his New Jersey surroundings, failed him:

> *She died with a tranquil smile on her face, just went to sleep from pneumonia. What dream she was following at the moment of course we will never know. The truth and its pursuit was always at the front of my mother's mind. It was a long time before I came to realize how her romantic ideas had deceived her and me in the modern world which we in our turn had to push behind us to come up fighting or*

smiling, if we could make it, or just to find some sunny spot where we
could stretch our bones, . . .

(*YM* 20)

His reference to having to struggle, to push the modern world "behind us
to come up fighting or smiling" is left vague, but one can deduce what
was intended. A society, as described by Williams' son William Eric, "in-
fested with WASP entrepreneurs who cared not a *centimo* for her religious, social, or cultural background" (*YM* ix), had to have brought on
complications to Elena's children as they grew up.

Williams' targeting Elena's being "Spanish" as the origin of his sense
of betrayal must be understood as the ruminations of his Bill persona, the
one that evolved from his first gut impressions as the child of immigrants.
When he felt like an outsider and wished to be at one with his readers,
Bill blamed Elena. Because of her, he was deprived of a mainstream lineage in his own country:

> *It was all in a great yard with a painted wooden fence of boards, cut*
> *out into a scroll design and painted green and red—that stood above*
> *his head—but he could peek through and see the people passing.*
>
> *Behind him his smaller brother, six years old or less, came follow-*
> *ing while the mother leaned upon the balustrade of the balcony that*
> *encircled the house and watched them play.*
>
> *There above them, as they played, leaned nothing of America, but*
> *Puerto Rico, a foreign island in a tropical sea of earlier years—and*
> *Paris of the later Seventies.*

(*YM* 116)

As the vignette shows, this was Williams' childhood impression, a fear of
his society's retaliation, which he was able to turn into a literary device.

An example of Bill's turning his child-of-immigrant's fear into a literary conceit is the poem "All the Fancy Things." In it, Bill portrays Elena's
response to her harsh social reality in the United States, by reflecting on
the refinement of her remembered past in Puerto Rico, as immoral:

> music and painting and all that
> That's all they thought of
> in Puerto Rico in the old Spanish
> days when she was a girl. . . .
>
> . . . .

> *ma chere*
> must withstand rebuffs
> from that which returns
> to the beginnings—

> (*CPI* 268–269)

Invoking spiritual values and, by extension, refinement, in the face of Yankee utilitarianism was a common defense mechanism among Latin Americans of Elena's day. In 1900 the Uruguayan José Enrique Rodó's essay *Ariel* called on the younger generation of Latin America to counter the encroaching materialism of the United States, symbolized by Caliban, by drinking from their built-in fountain of humanism and spiritual values, whose symbol was Ariel. Actually Rodó was reiterating a convention among Latin Americans, especially of the educated class, based on the Latin versus "barbarian" idea, so Elena didn't need Rodó's advice on how to defend herself in the harsh north. But his essay illustrates that Elena was simply reacting in keeping with her culture and generation.

For his part, Williams, who through his Anglo socialization had turned her into a symbol of foreignness and "Spanish," at the time that he wrote "All the Fancy Things" was not yet prepared to contemplate Elena for herself. This inability to see her as a person is, in so many words, what he confesses to later in "Eve." But in "All the Fancy Things," lacing his angle with that moral tone that often accompanies a rationale for bigotry, Bill postures with a moralistic air about Elena's nostalgia for the old and her rejection of modernity. The "rebuffs" that return Elena to dreams of her "beginnings" are kept abstract, lacking particulars—typical of Bill, on this subject. The only thing clear is his portrayal of her haughtiness, her denial, her pride: sins of her foreignness. Juxtaposed to his down-to-earth reality, Elena's world is pathetic.

Beneath the surface of this poem, however, awaits another poem, about an Elena who spits her own codes back into the mainstream's eye and challenges her son by preserving an image of herself that was more culturally refined than the society telling him to reject her. This made her difficult and debilitating to Bill, who years later would come to realize how much he had emulated that very independence. In the surface poem, fully empowered by his language and his readers, Bill stands up to her strength. By his rejecting her "older things" (Spanish), siding with modernity (English), and loftily admonishing Elena for her preferring to be, according to the stereotype, prototypically Latin, he claimed his Anglo America, whose collaboration in this drama is implicit. On the other hand, had Bill detailed what was meant by "rebuffs," he would have invoked Carlos, Elena's prince and defender, whose presence would have changed the poem: as it stands, the poem is the frustrated Bill's monologue disguised as a critical portrait of his mother.

Another of Bill's overshadowing characterizations of Elena is of her as spiritualist medium. Even though William George was a believer and Grandma Wellcome was herself a medium (*NW* 6), Elena is the focus of all discussions about spiritualism. This was because she was the person in whom Williams saw himself, and as medium of a foreignizing practice she also foreignized him from "normal" American culture. His reaction therefore had to be normal, making him one with his reader, whose popular reflex was to ascribe to such activities "from the islands" some stigmatizing, racially dark seed. Ironically, spiritualism in Puerto Rico descended from France as a by-product of romanticism, and was based on the writings of Allan Kardec.[13] It was introduced and practiced widely among the white gentry. This background, irrelevant in retrospect, would have removed some of the exotic tinge that helped Bill characterize himself as independent of his mother and her culture.

Williams' fear of Elena's spiritualist trances is quite understandable, as they were both an unusual phenomenon and a powerful symbol of so much that he needed to reject. For, in Williams' defense, his Bill persona was an expression of a deeply rooted tradition in U.S. history, the American persona of every child of an immigrant or marginal culture, on whom the culture imposes the challenge of having to earn acceptance. To consummate this identity always involves a figurative rebirth, as an acceptable, unforeign Anglo American, and the invention of an alter ego, usually reflected in a rechristening to an Anglo name. As that persona, the new ego becomes a spokesperson of mainstream values and, of course, its prejudices. In the case of Bill, who was therefore also under the influence of Anglo American xenophobia, Williams felt ashamed of his mother's public display of embarrassing foreignness. Her Spanish accent was one kind of display, of course, but the most dramatic was her spiritualism. In "Eve," Williams admits that seeing Elena in one of her spiritualist trances—as well as seeing her being seen by others—shamed him:

I realize why you wish
to communicate with the dead—
And it is again I
who try to hush you
that you shall not
make a fool of yourself
and have them stare at you
with natural faces— . . .

It not so much frightens
as shames me.

(*CPI* 412)

But because Bill is never pure and always somehow, whether in code
or contradiction, culturally balanced, in "Eve" he also admits that in reality Elena was not as he had just painted her, an exotic contrast to his
Anglo self. He obliquely confesses to realizing that all along she had been
defending herself by disdaining his Anglo half, the very thing that he held
as superior to her. While he saw her through a hostile society's eyes, she
had been looking back at him with the same shame at his surrender to its
hostility, ashamed that her son should elect to see her through the eyes of
that barbarian society:

Pardon my injuries
now that you are old—
Forgive me my awkwardnesses
my impatience
and short replies—
I sometimes detect in your face
a puzzled pity for me
your son—
I have never been close to you
—mostly your own fault;
in that I am like you.
It is as though
you looked down from above
at me—not
with what they would describe
as pride but the same

> that is in me: a sort
> of shame that the world
> should see you as I see you, . . .

(*CPI* 410–411)

Bill admits that he had "been a fool" who, until "Adam" died, failed to understand or appreciate her inner passion that had been stifled by— and here Bill characteristically omits particulars—her trapped situation and William George's exterior cold. In "Eve," then, William Carlos marks when he finally understood that what he had previously dismissed as his mother's escapism was Elena's using her imagination to survive.

But even after "Eve," Bill continued to paint Elena as lost in the past and among spirits. Nowhere in *The Autobiography* do we get a sense of the lost prince's young mother to whom he was so attached, or of the aging woman celebrated in "Eve." The only discussion of "poor Mother" as a young woman is limited to her strong temper (her "Latin blood"), some examples of her nostalgia and, foremost, her spiritualism, all tributaries to his original shame. This was how Bill rendered Elena in *The Autobiography,* while in his conscience hovered Carlos' unkept promise "to write a book" about his Beatrix.

Thirty years passed between Williams' first promising to write *Yes, Mrs. Williams* and its publication. His chief obstacle was his having to confront a flesh-and-blood person who for the better part of his life had been a symbol. The notes, receipts, letters, and scribblings that he gathered for the project only reaffirmed the historicity of his subject. He also had difficulty writing in his naked personal voice, which is what a biography would have demanded of him. This problem of self-confrontation is reflected in the point of view of its originally intended title: *Your Grandmother, My Son.*

He first planned to write a straightforward biography, but with Elena as symbol of a Spanish literary lineage. On 8 March 1941, a month before the Inter-American Writers Conference in Puerto Rico, he wrote an outline that was obviously affected by the words he planned to say at the conference on the value of Spanish literature "to us":

Writing plan for the Biography:
1. *The Introduction said as it is—possibly with a cut or two here and there.*

2. *Section I—in Mother's own words with 3 or 4 rather long interpola-*
   tions by "the author," independently and freely written (in the style
   of the Introduction) of comment and explanation of the child's gen-
   eral circumstances—parents etc.

3. *Her student life in Paris. Again—comments and a word or two of*
   explanation. The account must move smoothly, not jerkily but
   more freely than in the first section, the text and the comments
   more blended (?)

4. *Married life: these headings to be definitely stated—bringing the fo-*
   cus to a sharp point on what is being spoken of. Now autobiographi-
   cal interpollations [sic] of "the author" (her son) are permitted.

5. *A word or two and then the translation, perhaps cut a little where it*
   drags—the cuts to be indicated by . . . A note on Quevedo might not
   be out of place, Q. and his times, Cervantes, Lope and Góngora—
   their significance for us.

6. *Her letters: Note—their imagery and their language. Not English*
   but a new start from a base. Old age.[14]

As if the book was to be written by someone else, Williams refers to himself as "'the author.'" This sense of a narrating persona apart from himself is also evident in point 4, in which he parenthetically adds "(her son)"
beside "'the author.'" This effort in the outline to separate son, author,
and subject parallels the trinity of Bill, Carlos, and Elena.

Another outline, undated but closer to the final book, introduces translation as a leitmotif and framework, but loses the emphasis on objectifying and distancing Williams from his subject. The plan designed the book
as a portrait of Elena's body, mind, and soul:

1. *Introduction (present day) The translation (mention the earlier*
   one?) and preliminary remarks—her mood relative to stories: Que-
   vedo—how during it remarks were picked up and jotted down.
   Laughter. A bit here and there quoted—representing the scope of life.
   Order. Vitality. Anger.—

2. *—entirely quote. No remarks. No translation.*

3. *France. Marriage. U.S. Spiritualism. Seances. Music. Painting. Uni-*
   tarianism. (Quoted) but with remarks. Transl.

4. *Deafness and blindness. Age. The Translation carried through. Fi-*
   nis. Last quotations.

5. *Selected letters.*[15]

A reflection of his own dichotomy, the outline isolates as "mind" her past activity, beliefs, memories, and reflections, while labeling as "soul" her physical erosion with age, suggesting a spiritual distillation. The "body" section was redundant, as it would have consisted entirely of her words, which could have been put under either mind or soul. Despite the three categories, Williams was in fact highlighting a mind/soul duality, one that paralleled his own "author"/son dichotomy; the author related to her intellectually and the son spiritually. The bridge between mind and soul, and thus author and son, was the translation of Quevedo's novella.

Different from the first outline, here the struggle over point of view is absent. His design had evolved from an intended copy of her in a realistic portrait to a re-creation of her disjointed essential components, mind, body, and soul. Her body resided in the United States ("no remarks, no translation"), her mind dwelled with the dead and her more triumphant moments in the past, and her soul only became visible to him once her body eroded. Telling about her in a representative narrative was giving ground to painting her component images: the book was on its way to becoming another work of poetry. For in the final analysis, Williams was no more capable of writing about his mother journalistically than he was capable of writing about anything without his personae. Only the work of art fused, balanced, or reconciled his contradictory views of her as author and son, and so only after turning Elena into an object of art was he going to compose himself so he could write this book.

This interpretation is further supported by the circumstances surrounding the delay in its writing. By 1924, the date that he tells us in *Yes* he started thinking about writing it, Elena was becoming an old woman. Her late blossoming upon her husband's death in 1918 and her will to live endowed her with universal qualities that, in his now mature eyes, transcended his younger concerns over her being foreign. Seeing her with new eyes, he also realized that the very same thing that he, as Bill, had formerly denounced as escapist and immoral and endemic to her being Latin was actually inseparable from that other valuable gift that she had also imparted: her imagination. This revision did not itself make his "agony of self-realization" any easier, but through his new insight into Elena he appreciated the power of the imagination to transform his troubling situation into a resource, to survive through the imagination as Elena had. Unsurprisingly, after the disappointing response to his flaunting his Spanish in his first books and after his father's death, his reflection of that positive legacy from Elena produced the radical series of writings that showcased the uniqueness and native Americanness, as opposed to the foreignness, of his "strange courage": *Kora in Hell* (1920), *Spring and All* (1923), *The Great American Novel* (1923), and *In the American Grain* (1925).

Williams was apparently unaware of how complicated his dichotomous identity would make the task of writing *Yes;* at first, the idea of his writing a book on Elena prompted high aspirations. "I hope to make [my mother's] biography one of my major works—if not *the* major one."[16] Between 1924 and the book's publication year, however, he kept renewing his commitment to it while he also kept postponing its writing. In "Eve," published in 1936 in *Adam & Eve in the City,* and as if to make a public contract with himself, he expressed his intention to immortalize Elena in a book:

> If you are not already too blind
> too deaf, too lost in the past
> to know or to care—
> I will write a book about you—
> making you live (in a book!)
> as you still desperately
> want to live—
> to live always—unforgiving

(CPI 412–13)

In 1938 he and Elena had already completed their translation of Quevedo, a project begun in 1935 and that Williams used as a means of extracting more from Elena's mind and soul. Afterwards, Williams wrote "Raquel Helene Rose," an introduction to the translation, which he later incorporated into the introduction of *Yes, Mrs. Williams.* But one must conclude that even though he had gotten closer to her, he really needed a better sense of her background, which really meant he still lacked a necessary sense of himself. Thus he jumped at the opportunity to travel to Puerto Rico in 1941, where he was reported in the San Juan weekly *Alma Latina* as having elected to participate in the Inter-American Writers Conference because the trip was " . . . the fulfillment of a trip he had been planning for a long time" so he could work on that biography:

Para el Dr. Williams, quien nunca ha visitado la Isla pero cuya madre,
Helene Hoheb de Williams es puertorriqueña, la Conferencia Inter-
americana de Escritores en Puerto Rico será la realización de un viaje
proyectado desde hace mucho tiempo. Williams está escribiendo una
biografía de su señora madre (siendo joven ella estudió pintura en
París bajo la dirección de Carolus Duran) y la visita a Puerto Rico le
suplicará material de primera mano para la obra.

(22 March 1941: 51)

[For Dr. Williams, who has never visited the island but whose mother,
Helene Hoheb Williams, is Puerto Rican, the Inter-American Confer-
ence of Writers in Puerto Rico will be the fulfillment of a trip he had
been planning for a long time. Williams is writing a biography of his
mother (as a young woman she studied painting in Paris under the di-
rection of Carolus Duran), and the visit to Puerto Rico will give him
firsthand material for the book.]

But even though intellectually committed to investigating his Puerto
Rican half, Williams was not ready to confront it head on. Much to our
benefit, he channeled his self-confrontation into poetry. He continued to
write poems on a broad range of subjects (*The Pink Church, Journey to
Love* [both in *CPII*]), also fiction (*The Build-Up, Make Light of It* [in *The
Farmer's Daughters*]), among other writings, but throughout and concomitantly he also worked in earnest on *Paterson,* a poetic autobiography
that logically results from the long-simmering commitment to write his
book on Elena. This claim makes more sense if we set the poem in the
circumstances of Williams' life. To begin with, the subject of his beginnings was obviously aroused during his 1941 trip to Puerto Rico. There,
in addition to his expressed objective of gathering background for the
book on his mother, he was given Luis Palés Matos' book of poems *Tuntún
de Pasa y Grifería,* which reaffirmed for him his American vision expressed in *In the American Grain.* Palés Matos' book also appears to have
given Williams the scheme for how to approach his planned but as yet
undesigned epic (for more discussion on this, see Chapter 6).

Before this island experience *Paterson* had first been imagined as a
summing up, based on a sense of his immediate place:

The first idea centering upon the poem, Paterson, *came alive early:*
to find an image large enough to embody the whole knowable world

about me. The longer I lived in my place, among the details of my life, I
realized that these isolated observations and experiences needed pull-
ing together to gain "profundity." New York City was far out of my per-
spective; I wanted, . . . to write about the people close about me; to
know in detail, minutely what I was talking about—to the whites of
their eyes, to their very smell.

(*A* 391)

Not surprisingly, as occurred with *Yes, Mrs. Williams,* between knowing
what he wanted to do and actually attaining it Williams encountered considerable inner obstacles; *Paterson* came out "constipated" and grudgingly over several years. As he discovered with his book on Elena, Bill's
effort to summarize his poet's life was made difficult by his inability to
handle a summing up that included his hidden core. This ultimately
translated into another "agony of self-realization," the rich identity theme
that also gave him "The Desert Music."

That *Paterson* burdened Williams with his problem of self-realization
is confirmed in the opening sentence of the final chapter of *The Autobiography,* "The Poem Paterson." The sentence pronounces that a poet is
blessed with a "secret and sacred presence." That secret presence parallels the secret and hidden core in the "Foreword" of his autobiography.
The earlier secret, we recall, started out sounding like the proverbial "secret of our lives," but actually referred to an intentionally enciphered
"core." Just as illogically, this "secret and sacred presence," which at first
is celebrated as a boon, suggesting the poet's genius, is immediately
transformed into a malignant attachment:

Even though the greatest boon a poet grants the world is to reveal
that secret and sacred presence, they will not know what he is talking
about. Surgery cannot assist him, nor cures. The surgeon must himself
know that his surgery is idle.

(*A* 390)

The inability to surgically remove this "secret . . . presence" evokes the
inability to vomit up the agony of self-realization in "The Desert Music";
the world's inability to "know what he is talking about" parallels the reader's inability to decipher Bill's "hidden core" or "the secret of my form."

In both the "Foreword" and "The Poem Paterson," then, Williams rhetorically shuffles around the mystery of poetry and his Carlos self, sophis-

tically equating the intrinsic indecipherability of the former with his encoding of the latter. In this way his personal secret is organically fused
with the poet's secret presence. Thus his declaration simultaneously ap-
plies to both: "Even though the greatest boon a poet grants the world is
to reveal that secret and sacred presence, they will not know what he is
talking about." The only thing that made possible the revelation of his
ambiguous truth was the poem, which in this case was *Paterson:* a composite of his two cultural spirits, multifaceted present, and dual personae
into a contemporary English that in the reader's imagination continues to
regenerate semantic layers beyond its autobiographical foundation.

Paterson, then, burgeoned from the autobiographical curiosity sown
when Carlos promised to write a book on his mother, an idea that Bill
translated into a poem about his life story—Bill again offering "The Wanderer" as his answer to "Philip and Oradie," *The Autobiography* as a
counterweight to the inevitable *Yes, Mrs. Williams. Paterson* thus became
the story of the poet's life imaged on the surface of the Passaic. But beneath those reflections lurked the same obstacles that stared back at him
when he attempted to write *Yes;* gestated and written at the same time as
both *Yes* and *The Autobiography, Paterson* joins them to form a single
semantic piece. So while *Paterson* has nothing explicitly to do with Elena,
it is Williams' self-portrait in a cosmology in which she is the spiritual
core. As the Passaic was the bloodline of Paterson the city, she is the river
running through the heart of the personified Paterson, embodying the
mystery of how deep Williams' life's river ran. The river itself, therefore,
is a transformation of Williams' female principle and, building on the conceit, the confluence of many streams, like his mother's many blood-
streams, with her currents converging into a currency, a tongue, a mother
tongue, "the language":

> Haven't you forgot your virgin purpose,
> the language?
>
> What language? "The past is for those who
> lived in the past" is all she told me.

(P 187)

Language was his umbilical cord to spirits of the past. Through language
he became a poet, which Williams understood as a form of being woman.
That is why he has a "virgin" purpose, and inquires

—and did you ever know of a sixty year
woman with child . ?

(*P* 187)

But he needed to ask himself "What language?," only to hear in his
own ears his Grandma Wellcome's response, "The past is for those who /
lived in the past." We know his English grandmother is the speaker because that same line is repeated in Book Five, and there we are informed
that the words are uttered in "Cockney." She was telling him to stop poking into her past, which is what *Paterson* is all about. But the second time
that Williams quotes her she tells him to stop in (misspelled) Spanish:
"The past is for those who lived in the past. *Cessa!*" Although missing
from the first time he quotes her, the idiom mixing, mixed tributaries,
represented by "*Cessa!*" was really what prompted him to ask here "What
language?" For, as this study will subsequently show, the river in *Paterson*, which had also passed through "The Wanderer," has tributaries that
may well have originated in the river in the *Coplas* by Jorge Manrique
and in Luis de Góngora's *Polifemo y Galatea.* These spirits also flow into
the river of his mixed "language," no longer English, which springs from
the womb of his female principle, which is ultimately Elena, the secret
and "deepest level" of his Passaic. Appropriately, the chapter "The Poem
Paterson" ends *The Autobiography* with an anecdote that evokes the
"agony of self-realization" during which *Paterson* was written. Williams
relates the day that he took his grandson Paul to the river: "'How deep is
the water?' asked Paul. 'I mean at the deepest level?'" The autobiography
ends there, with an unanswered question ending a chapter on an unfinished poem about an unresolved obsession. The closest thing to an answer to that final question was *Yes, Mrs. Williams.*

Of course, this chain of imagistic associations makes sense once
one interprets Elena as the Kore in Williams' life. Mariani, for example,
had made Williams' grandmother central and focused instead on Marcia
Nardi as the immediate impetus that in 1942 "actually got [Williams]
started again on *Paterson*" (*NW* 466), overlooking Nardi's patent similarity to Elena. Nardi was the kind of woman who insisted "on art school
rather than college—and came to grief because of it." She was a survivor,
"who refused to give in following her first defeat and came to the city with
determination" and who "taught herself French." Coming on the heels of
Williams' impassioned identification with the Spanish Republican cause,

a year after his trip to Puerto Rico, and during a time of his renewed thoughts of a biography of Elena, this encounter with a version of the younger Elena surely triggered in Williams a series of associations that also figured in the writing of *Paterson.*

Kerry Driscoll also affirms the similarity between Nardi and Elena:

> Like Cress, Elena is *"a woman dying of loneliness" (P 87), isolated, un-*
> *happy, oppressed by circumstances, and thwarted in her artistic aspi-*
> *rations. Alienated from the mainstream of patriarchal society, the two*
> *women turn to the poet for companionship and emotional support.*
> *Their appeals to him are characterized by an underlying urgency and*
> *despair, since both have difficulty in communicating with others, and*
> *believe that he alone can help them.*
>
> (*William Carlos Williams and the Maternal Muse* 82)

The point here is not that *Paterson* is about Elena, but that she figures conceptually, as a symbol of the stasis operative behind the poem's spiritual summation of Bill. Without that statis, Williams wouldn't have been able to write the poem. Driscoll's discussion of the similarity and differences between Nardi and Elena helps illustrate this stasis model. The question of stasis first comes up in Driscoll's response to Jerome Mazzaro, who in *William Carlos Williams: The Later Poems* compares Williams' making Nardi's letters a part of *Paterson* to his making use of Elena's recorded remarks in *Yes.* Mazzaro proposed that Williams included the letters in *Paterson* to produce a "'stasis'":

> If any "marriage" of Paterson with "C." is to evolve from this stasis, he
> may want it to occur not on the page but in the minds of the readers. A
> similar feature of balance occurs in his biography of his mother.[17]

Driscoll agrees that Elena in *Yes, Mrs. Williams* and Nardi in *Paterson* establish a balance of male and female voices, but questions Mazzaro's analogy as being a "purely stylistic" one, based on the general incorporation of female texts into male writing. Driscoll argues that the balance found in each work is different, "protean"; the relationship with Cress is antagonistic, while in *Yes* Williams' voice blends with Elena's, a type of stasis "only obliquely hinted at in *Paterson*" (*MM* 85–86).

That Williams' relationship with Cress is antagonistic is irrelevant. Taking from cubism and from examples he came across when he researched Luis de Góngora (see Chapter 5), Williams used the technique of simultaneism: including in a portrait of himself the contrary perspective of a criticism made of him. Nardi's passion for writing was his voice in her body; it was genuine and only happened to be directed at him. She spoke for him. Furthermore, Nardi's passion, her womanness, her heat made her a symbolic version of Elena, and however different the women might have been, in both of them Williams saw that hot, procreative side of himself: Carlos. What Mazzaro and Driscoll identify as the female voice, then, is actually an extension of Williams' lengthy catalog of heat imagery, the vital sensuality that ultimately made his writing survive, a sometimes conscious and sometimes subdued variant of Carlos' spirit. Thus, more than hinted at, Williams attains stasis through becoming Nardi, who represents Elena.

In sum, his coming to see something redeeming in Elena after his father's death in 1918 began a new phase, in which Williams sublimated his obsession with his identity until the Spanish Civil War, during and after which commenced yet another, final phase, one of reconciliation. "The Desert Music" and *The Autobiography* were products of that final phase. In a balancing way, the Stecher Trilogy, in which Bill is reborn as Flossie, was also part of that self-exploration. One can consider these writings all fortuitous detours from a book he had been putting off, the most important of these detours being the one that began with *Paterson*, Book One, but that eventually forks, with one road ultimately bringing him to write his final book, *Yes, Mrs. Williams*. And maybe Williams planned things to be that way, knowing that the longer he postponed that promised book, the longer he could turn obsessions and self-interrogations into poetry.

In this trajectory of the soul should we understand the prolonged gestation of *Yes*. During the forties and early fifties, Williams completed the first four books of *Paterson*. In 1949, the year in which he published Book Three, Elena died. "Two Pendants: for the Ears" resulted from his watching her die. That poem was part of the summing up taking place in his life as he wrote *Paterson*. In 1956 Williams returned to Puerto Rico, during which trip he devoted more time to learning of his and Elena's background. On his return he wrote "Puerto Rico Song," which really had nothing specifically to do with Puerto Rico and so later had its title changed to "Calypsos" (*CPII* 426–427), evoking the English-speaking islands as well as the Greek sea-nymph, and which according to Mariani, "caught in their short circular rhythms" (*NW* 725) the calypso music he had heard in the islands. Well, calypso was never a music of Puerto Rico, so he wouldn't have heard it there. The change of titles, however, is significant. The former title suggested a poem by Carlos; its new title turned it into a poem by Bill, the wanderer sidetracked by Calypso.

Meanwhile, a different mood was spreading throughout the country. In 1956 Martin Luther King, Jr., triumphed in desegregating the buses of Montgomery. The Puerto Rican immigration, now a decade old, had become a journalistic staple. In 1957 *West Side Story* opened on Broadway, a play that humanized the Puerto Rican María, who had to suffer the rebuffs of a cold land and endure being ostracized from the "catalogue" of the Jets. Williams' once obscure and exotic background had become newsworthy. The time seemed to be right for a self-confrontation. Was Williams taking advantage of the situation or, now an old man, did he simply feel free to write of "what has concerned [me] most in the past"? Whatever the motive, after a three-decade gestation, *Yes, Mrs. Williams* was published in 1959, and despite the appearances of its being about Elena, it should also really be read as a prefiguration of the confessional literature that proliferated in the sixties and seventies.

Yes, Mrs. Williams begins with a strangely-organized "Introduction," which opens with a brief paragraph on "determined women" against whom Williams had to contend. In the second paragraph, three sentences are on his mother, followed by a discussion on his father which continues for a page and a half until, after briefly discussing Spanish, "the language spoken among the staff" in his father's office, two more paragraphs on his mother appear; this is followed by another lengthy section on his father until Williams himself, aware of the digression, notes: "Though this book is mainly about my mother, and should be so, it must dwell somewhat for its character on the man she lived with most of her life, my father." Twelve pages later we return to his mother, who is described in a spiritualist trance. Two paragraphs on her death follow, and thus ends the first half of the "Introduction."

Williams' explanation for the background to this preface accounts for the impression one gets that he was padding with what he could find:

> *Norman Pearson came to me in 1954, telling me about a group of men at Yale who had more or less sponsored a small offset printing firm. There was an opening for a book. Did I have anything? I fished out the Quevedo thing. It wasn't quite long enough. "Can't you add an Intro-*

duction?" Pearson said. I looked through papers written twenty years
ago and found an Introduction I'd started, stopped in the middle of a
sentence. It needed more, so I wrote it. And the book, to be a book, still
needed more. I had also found a piece about my mother, her childhood,
so I made it into the true story of our work together on the translation.

(*IWW* 91)

What is important here is the content used to pad. The subject of his book,
the symbolic Elena (Carlos), needed the balance of William George (Bill),
who symbolized English to the reader even though privately symbolizing
a balance of English and Spanish to Williams. As a young man he had
perceived his involvement with Spanish literature as a form of emulating
his father, and translating Quevedo was something that even in his mature years Williams naturally associated with William George.

In the introduction's second half, which incorporates the 1938 essay "Raquel Helene Rose," Williams describes how he arrived at the
"scheme" for this book, an account of his interaction with his mother
as they translated Francisco Quevedo's *El Perro y la Calentura*. That
seventeenth-century work was their second translation together: from
1928 to 1929, with the same purpose of keeping Elena entertained, they
had collaborated on a translation from the French, Phillipe Soupault's
Last Nights of Paris, whose title explains why Williams chose that work
for Elena to translate. This project would have also brought him closer
to her, but being from the French it offered no imagistic value to the
"scheme" at hand, which is why he skips over that translation as a stage
in the evolution of *Yes:*

Once we translated a French novel together. Then, finally, I hit on
the scheme I wanted. Casting about for something to translate, the fit
object offered itself in the form of an old book.

(*YM* 25)

By referring to the translation as a "scheme," Williams suggests that
something more than a project to occupy Elena was involved, which certainly was the case. Translating that "old book" became his metaphor for
understanding the old woman, about whom, outside of the "outer circumstances" of her being foreign, her once-frightening spiritualist ways, and
her being a social liability, he knew little. But she and Quevedo were fused
in his imagination:

She has frequently in her life referred to Quevedo, telling one or an-
other of the salty stories connected with his name, showing that she
enjoyed them exceedingly well. Were it not for these stories she has
told me, the old book would not have attracted me and nothing more
would have come of it—even the idea of the biography would not have
taken form beyond the vague idea I had of it.

(YM 36)

He makes the metaphorical comparison explicit: "Like her it is old,
though far older than she" (*YM* 36). And like Elena, the novella dwelled
with him, and had often been in his hands, but remained unread. As a
workable conceit, Elena was now material that his personae could write
about:

It . . . had been lying about the house unread for many years. I had
held it in my hands many times without ever having had the courage
to dip into it, . . .

(YM 36)

The word "courage," as seen in "El Hombre," was also Williams' cipher for Spanish and its consciousness. On the surface, of course, Williams is confessing he would have had trouble with the language. But
"courage" additionally encodes that he felt deficient in the inspiriting
Spanish substance. The reference to "lying" about the house is an intentional pun, reminding us that Bill saw Spanish as romantic and therefore
"lying," as in the Latin "lying music" in "The Desert Music." The book
could also have been "lying about" the Williams "house unread," some
private meaning that Williams understood about the household itself.
Certainly the book was "lying" throughout the house in appearing to be
unread, as it is impossible to believe that Williams, who since his Spanish
(hell) phase had read or translated from numerous authors, would have
allowed this Quevedo novella to escape his curiosity.

Another point of comparison between Elena and this book was their
mutually clouded history. This particular edition of *El Perro y la Calen-*
tura was an original seventeenth-century edition that had passed through
many hands:

The various owners of the book since 1700 have scribbled their names
and a few faded notes among the fly leaves at the front and back. A
young librarian, a friend of mine, on taking up the book discovered at

once—a thing I hadn't noticed—that two of the front (flyleaf) pages
had been gummed together. He held them up to the light and there was
a name between them—perhaps that of the original owner.

(*YM* 36–37)

A final point of comparison was the book's and Elena's having been
rejected by Ezra Pound, who disdained Spanish and its literature and had
always given Elena the cold shoulder, a psychological association that
Williams patently harbored, as revealed in his explanation of how he
came to possess the book:

I got the book from Ezra Pound, . . . He was not interested in Spanish
literature so much as in Italian and the literature of Provence. I don't
think he spoke Spanish; certainly I never heard him speak it to my
mother, though she knew him well.

(*YM* 25–26)

Besides evoking his mother, however, the book's author also dwelled
warmly in Williams' imagination for several other reasons. To begin with,
owing to Quevedo's having clubbed feet and wearing thick glasses, he
was, like Elena and Williams, an outsider. Also, as a writer in the great
realistic tradition of Spanish literature, he is legendary for his scatalogical
and linguistic wit, one of the first great antipoets, whom one latter-day
critic called a "contemporary in the past." Thus, Quevedo was one of Williams' ancestral alter images. Through lessons picked up from Quevedo,
as well as from Luis de Góngora, Williams developed his own duplicitous,
encoded style (see Chapter 5):

To tell that story, to have it accepted by a Spanish-Catholic audience,
Quevedo had to write cryptically—you can imagine the problem this
was to the translator.

(*IWW* 91)

Lastly, Quevedo's very name, the basis of numerous jokes, plays with an
oxymoron that parallels Williams' encoded counterpoint in his given
names:

So much for Quevedo. I might have gone on writing a scholarly thesis
upon his name. . . .

(*YM* 23)

"Quevedo" morphologically breaks down into the sound of the relative pronoun *que*, "that," which is homonymic with the interrogative pronoun *¿qué?*, "what?" The two remaining syllables form the word *vedo*, which has two semantic possibilities. One is the first-person singular of the verb *vedar*, whose meanings can be "to cover over" or "to hide from view." *Vedo* also suggests the past participle form *-do*, from which popular Andalusian and Caribbean speech drops the intervocalic *d*. An *-edo* ending is nonexistent but *vedo* suggests an invented overcorrection of a past participle back formation from *veo*, which happens to be the legitimate first person singular of the verb *ver*, "to see." This hint of linguistic confusion is best illustrated with an anecdote. In one of the Quevedo stories the poet is supposed to have been caught defecating in a garden. A proper lady came upon him and sighed *"Dios mío, ¿Qué Veo?"* ("My God, what do I see?"). Don Francisco is said to have corrected: *"No, señora, Quevedo,"* which arrogantly identifies him and suggests a grammatical correction often made when the intervocalic *d* of a real past participle is dropped, even though he was saying his true name, which also happens to denote "What do I cover up?"

In sum, the "scheme," that at first appeared to refer to the idea of using a translation as a way of keeping Elena occupied, really signified the scheme for the style and structure of the book in the reader's hands: the scheme was to write *Yes, Mrs. Williams* as Quevedo wrote, scheming. In *The Autobiography*, to illustrate, Williams also identified Quevedo's stylistic design as a "scheme":

> The scheme of it is a putting down of the facts about the corrupt court, but not openly, which Quevedo couldn't afford. Instead we have a story told in terms of proverbs of the people, among the scenes and sounds of the farm where he then was staying. It is all by implication, nothing is directly stated—very much as might be done today.

(*A* 350)

In other words, by himself playing with the idea of *veo* and *vedo*, both revealing and covering up, Williams the narrator unfolds the story in fragments, by implication and indirectly, the same way in which he came to learn about his mother over the years.

The *concepto* or "conceit" in this book begins with the very title, which at once affirms Mrs. Williams' desires ("Yes, Mrs. Williams, whatever you say") and emphasizes a fact despite expectations to the contrary ("Yes, it was Mrs. Williams after all"). Equally duplicitous is its "Introduction," which is really, as is true of other introductions by Williams, integral to the work. But the most important example of Quevedo-esque wit is the central conceit of the book's being a translation of Elena. The pieces that comprise the main text are essentially about translating a foreign spirit into English:

> *How would you say in English? How would you translate it?*
> Y esta es aquélla? *(And this is she?)*
> Y esto [sic] es aquél? *(And that is he?)*
> *It was two who used to be lovers. They were going each with a*
> *friend and they passed the one they had been in love with years before.*
> *And he said to his friend:* Y esta es aquélla? *He couldn't believe it. And*
> *she said too:* Y esto [sic] es aquél? *You couldn't translate that into En-*
> *glish without a long sentence explaining what it was.*
>
> (*YM* 72)

In *Yes, Mrs. Williams*, then, as he had done intermittently throughout Williams' career, Carlos materializes in poetry. Through Elena's fracturing English, she became Carlos performing novel language tricks: "It was two who used to be lovers. They were going each with a friend and they passed the one they had been in love with years before." This book is a compendium of such found prose poems, another collage of improvisations inspired by Williams' "Kore" and "core" submerged in the hell of Spanish. Consistent with that design, like *Kora*, this book on his mother was actually written to characterize its author. The reader is forewarned that the "real story" of this book is Williams himself:

> *I'll speak of all these things as if she told them to me while we were*
> *translating—only the pretext: the real story is how all the complexities*
> *finally came to play one tune, today—to me—*
>
> (*YM* 26)

This mention of a "real story" parallels the secretly encoded layer in *The Autobiography*, only here the secret is revealed. Whereas from *The Autobiography* we are led to infer that the story told constitutes the essence of a poet's life, the *Yes* introduction borrows the "music" metaphor from Williams' opera on George Washington, referring to that essence as a "tune." Thus, the varied prose pieces in *Yes*, in collectively invoking Elena's spirit, evoke the true William Carlos; her story is of interest to us only because it is really a fulfilled portrait of Williams himself. However we may wish to interpret several themes in this book, or whatever Williams' description of them, this book is foremost the completion of Bill's earlier autobiography, an incomplete book that had awaited its balance, the spirit of Carlos, and therefore the necessary stasis to complete Williams' "grinning mug."

Elena's centrality throughout Williams' career cannot be overstated, but except for the amends he made in *Yes, Mrs. Williams* at the end of his career, Williams more often distorted the true nature of her influence, encouraging the reader to believe that his poetic maturity resulted from his sprouting Anglo wings and flying out of her Latin cocoon:

> *I was conscious of my mother's influence all through this time of writing, her ordeal as a woman and as a foreigner in this country. . . . I was personifying her, her detachment from the world of Rutherford. She seemed an heroic figure, a poetic ideal. I didn't especially admire her; I was attached to her. I had not yet established any sort of independent identity.*
>
> *(IWW 16)*

And over the years critics have taken Williams at his word when, speaking as Bill, he claimed that at some point he matured away from her. Representative of critics who pursued that line, in his *William Carlos Williams: An American Artist* James E. Breslin observed that from his mother Williams received an artistic sensibility and a sense of refinement, but that her influence was essentially romantic and uncreative:

> *But the direction of her influence was not immediately creative, since it inspired a sense of beauty that was dreamily nostalgic: it was she who led him to Keats. Behind all of Williams' later attraction to the elegant, his frequent squeamish distaste for the common, lies the refined and remote figure of his mother.*[18]

Contradicting Breslin on the extent of Elena's influence, Kerry Driscoll investigated her importance to Williams in *William Carlos Williams and the Maternal Muse:*

> *Beyond their obvious blood ties, mother and son shared an aesthetic kinship. Williams believed his creativity was an extension of Elena's artistic impulse, and looked to her as both a muse and poetic ideal.*[19]

As Driscoll affirms, Williams never did break away to establish his own identity, even his personal identity, and actually matured emulating Elena as both man and poet:

> *The source of Williams' abiding fascination with Elena, which served as a crucial factor in his surmounting of the perceptual barriers typically imposed by gender difference, was his intuitive recognition of the extensive physical, spiritual, and psychic similarities that existed between them. Because the poet believed that he and his mother were, in many respects, fundamentally alike, he came to regard her as a living text in which he could read and discover the secrets of his own identity.*
>
> (*MM* 8)

Williams' lifelong preoccupation with Elena resulted from his obsession with his own reproductive impulse, which Williams called "the woman in us":

> It is the woman in us
> That makes us write—
> Let us acknowledge it—
> Men would be silent.
>
> ("Transitional," *CPI* 40)

This sense of being female as a poet explains why Williams saw himself imaged in woman symbols such as Kore, Cress, Grandma Wellcome, Flossie. They all had "Helen" in them because they each reflected the woman in him, who was Elena. As Driscoll notes, because his identification with her proceeded from his understanding of his own capacity to create, in his writings mother and son symbolically converge, becoming fused into a single identity:

> *The concept of female "otherness" thus yielded in the case of Elena to a perception not only of resemblance, but symbolic convergence. Within the fictive universe of Williams' writing, the figures of mother and son complement one another, conjoining male and female elements to form a single, unified whole. . . .*
>
> (*MM* 8)

In brief, whereas earlier critics gave Elena no role at all in Williams' lasting contribution to American letters, Driscoll makes her "crucial," so that *Yes, Mrs. Williams,* which was seen as an insignificant addendum to his career, suddenly becomes central to our appreciation of Williams:

> *. . . Elena—or more precisely, Williams' conception of her—is crucial to the development of his poetics. His complex fictive representations of Elena chronicle the evolution of his identity as a writer; she is the poet's grotesque double, the other through and against whom he defines himself. In this regard,* Yes, Mrs.Williams, *which has long been considered a weak addendum to his extensive canon, assumes a new centrality and significance.*
>
> (*MM* 25)

In her elevation of Elena, Driscoll indeed takes the criticism on Williams through a little-explored area, but her analysis fails by her imposing on it, whether consciously or unconsciously, parameters that cause her to leave unresolved important implications that proceed from her own thesis. While her book shows that in Williams' struggle with his two cultural selves he, both as man and poet, ultimately succumbed to Carlos, nowhere does Driscoll literally mention his identifying *culturally* with Elena. Tellingly, Driscoll discusses the "extensive physical, spiritual, and psychic similarities" between mother and son only in Williams' own Bill-consciousness metaphors of Elena's Otherness—images of warmth, the "South," the aristocratic impulse. Like her predecessors, then, Driscoll subsumes the subject of his cultural identity in a discussion of Williams being confused about his identity, an identity crisis also consistently spoken of figuratively, such as in the following account of an inner North-South Civil War (with only glancing mention of that metaphor's semantic referents):

> *The pattern of oppositions proposed in this passage—north/south, Maine/Puerto Rico, coldness/warmth—clarifies the antagonism between aristocratic and democratic impulses mentioned in the letter to Marianne Moore by identifying the divergent connotations Williams associated with each of his parents. His father represented cool detachment, his mother warmth, passion and sensuality. And while these associations convey an implicit preference for the latter, both this passage and the letter itself indicate that the primary legacy of the poet's mixed blood was divisiveness and confusion—an internalized "civil war," north versus south, by which he himself was enslaved. Williams'*

determination to establish an American identity was strongly moti-
vated by a desire to reconcile these antagonistic aspects of his ancestry;
however, as time passed, he realized that the synthesis he had hoped
to achieve between them was all but impossible. A choice between the
two strains was inevitable, and he ultimately allied himself with the
"south" represented by Elena.

(*MM* 125–126)

While Driscoll is right to conclude that Williams ultimately allied himself with the "south," and the danger does exist that one might belabor
the obvious by redundantly specifying what that "south" represented, she
doesn't discuss those meanings at all, except in other symbols, thereby
obviating having to venture into her thesis' most radical implications: that
Williams was destined to identify with his Latin half, an image of Williams
not sharply evoked by this book. Driscoll develops her thesis on Elena's
importance, but she manages to do so without allowing the implications
of her thesis to alter the reader's preconceptions of Williams. In this, her
ground-breaking book is also unfortunately a paradigm of the ethnocen-
tricism typical of the criticism on Williams. This tacit restriction on her
scope can be seen in her earlier analysis of the following pieces from
Kora, which she discussed as evidence that the earlier work is "an essential precedent for" *Yes, Mrs. Williams:*

This that I have struggled against is the very thing I should have cho-
sen—but all's right now. They said I could not put the flower back into
the stem nor win roses upon dead briars and I like a fool believed
them. But all's right now. Weave away, dead fingers, the darkies are
dancing in Mayaguez—all but the one with the sore heel and sugar
cane will soon be high enough to romp through. Haia![20] *leading over*
ditches, with your skirts flying and the devil in the wind back of you—
no one else. Weave away and the bitter tongue of an old woman is eat-
ing, eating, eating venomous words with thirty years' mould on them
and all shall be eaten back to honeymoon's end. Weave and pangs of
agony and pangs of loneliness are beaten backward into the love kiss,
weave and kiss recedes into kiss and kisses into looks and looks into
the heart's dark—and over again and over again and time's pushed
ahead in spite of all that. The petals that fell bearing me under are
lifted one by one. That which kissed my flesh for priest's lace so that I
could not touch it—weave and you have lifted it and I am glimpsing

light chinks among the notes! Backward, and my hair is crisp with
purple sap and the last crust's broken.

A woman on the verge of growing old kindles in the mind of her son a
certain curiosity which spinning upon itself catches the woman herself in its wheel, stripping from her the accumulations of many harsh
years and shows her at last full of an old time suppleness hardly to
have been guessed by the stiffened exterior which had held her fast
till that time.

(I 62–63)

According to Driscoll the first piece is an expression of triumph of Williams' liberation from Elena's influence:

He is suddenly liberated from a delicate, but stiflingly oppressive bur-
den: "The petals which fell bearing me under are lifted one by one."
This image of a dying flower dropping its petals signifies, on one level,
Elena's loss of beauty, youth, and vitality, yet it can also be read as
a metaphor for the religious and ethical values she passed on to her
children.

(MM 97)

Williams' most obvious intention, of course, was to recreate in reverse
his own birth, reiterating the rebirth motif throughout his work: back before the prohibition by "They" (his social "weather") to see her for what
she was, to know her at all, back before her bitter life (bitter for having
been brought to a reluctantly-accepted new life), now "eaten back" to
Mayagüez, where he vicariously relives her past as he imagines her
memory of romping through the cane field, then further back to before
the first kiss that led to other kisses. The pivotal sentence is masterfully
ambiguous: "The petals which fell bearing me under are lifted one by
one." Each petal that was the oppression he was "bearing" under her
harsh life was being lifted; the overbearing fallen petals, once lifted, were
giving him birth, thus "bearing" him under them. Either way, as they rise
back to the stem they resurrect the rose, Raquel Helene Rose.

The liberation and rebirth being extolled was his having found the
aesthetics that liberated him to "interknit" Elena into his writing. This
liberation also resulted from his father William George's death, a rebirth
for both Williams and Elena: her true heat rose to the surface and Wil-

liams himself was free from his father's formal poetic tastes and the Spanish poetry in which the son had immersed himself both to possess his mother and emulate his father. Once free to find himself, Bill discovered in Elena's *Kora-zón,* his core/Kore: Carlos. Looking back, on an imaginary plane, different from how he would write of her even years later, Bill saw Carlos' young mother not as the shame-inducing spiritualist from a "meager" island in the "West Indies," but a strong, essential woman into whose stormy and frightening "heart's dark" he peers, a ceremony he had performed "over again and over again."

But his true triumph was his having come through, Bill the poet in America, without losing Carlos, even though "They said I could not put the flower back into the stem nor win roses upon dead briars." Beside the obvious meanings of rose as his mother and stem as her past, Williams here also identifies the poet with the flower, which "they" said he couldn't reconnect with its foreign "stem," or regain the lost heritage of his mother, "roses," from a dead past, "dead briars," a plant with origins in Southern Europe, her symbolic cultural origin. But on those very dead briars Williams did win the prize roses, and so he renders tribute to the thing he had struggled against, which should have been "the very thing I should have chosen": the free, *jaiba,* underground spirit of Elena. Like her, his Kore in *Kora* proceeds to explore whatever it discovers, defying expectations, preconceptions, and propriety, including the rigid rules of his mainstream cultural "weather." Finally allowing his inner self to burst out free, in *Kora* Williams celebrates his own private language (one of the categories that the "catalogue" excluded), a non-English free flow that was also a sublimated, personae-balanced, prefiguration of *Yes, Mrs. Williams.* Understandably *Kora* was Williams' own favorite book.[21]

What Bill discovered in the secret recesses of Elena's heart was Carlos being born, "my hair is crisp with purple sap and the last crust's broken." Driscol interprets the hair image as one of Williams "transformed into a Dionysian figure, . . . a satyr," an interpretation that is valid but incomplete. Of course, Williams did see himself as Dionysian. Rod Townley observes that in a first draft of *A Voyage to Pagany* Evans was to be named Evans Dionysus Evans (*Townley* 65). But, as is also obvious in his putting Dionysus in Carlos' place, Williams associated Carlos with sexual energy. Carlos is Williams as Dionysus; the satyr and rebirth images are one and the same.

Driscoll's incomplete interpretation of the satyr image is consistent with her pattern of stopping short of applying her own evidence that would change our perception of Williams. As if Williams' cultural dualism, to which she had devoted a book, were not real in his life, she finds this passage in *Kora* "infuriating and problematic" because it supposedly doesn't explain what he saw in Elena's heart:

> *Despite the fascinating glimpse this passage provides into the mother/ son relationship, it is at once infuriating and problematic since it does not adequately explain what Williams discovers in the secret recesses of Elena's heart that could engender such a profound change in his character.*

> *(MM 98)*

If Williams was the product of a bicultural background, then the most reasonable explanation of what he found in her foreign heart's secret recesses was the spiritual source of his own: in Elena's core Bill had a vision of his "hidden core."

But the answer seems inconceivable to Driscoll who, having discounted the genuineness of Williams' ethnic inner drama, is therefore equally baffled by Williams' second paragraph, which also appears to offer no answer:

> *The reader is instead presented with a baffling tale of conflated identity wherein the poet's investigation of his mother's past somehow becomes a vehicle for introspective analysis.*

> *(MM 98)*

The second paragraph tempers the first's Dionysus-Carlos spirit by rewriting its essence in the cooler, abstracting, observing, third-person narrative voice of Bill, who tells us that the subdued metaphorical loom that had been "weaving" before was his curiosity about Elena as the source of Carlos. In this paragraph, Carlos is symbolized by a physical quality: suppleness. By catching the woman in the spinning of his curiosity (*"spinning upon itself,"* implying that he was reflecting on his very curiosity), Bill strips away *"the accumulations of many harsh years,"* revealing her stuff. Thus having stripped her, Bill reaches her core, and he is surprised, having judged from the *"stiffened exterior,"* that its suppleness blends harmoniously into his own material, by implication his Anglo persona. Despite appearances that the second paragraph reiterates the first, the pieces complement from different points of view. The second reinvents the first. The counterpoint (Dionysian/cool; Carlos/Bill) in each one's way of telling is an image of the stasis that epitomizes Williams' whole self.

Unable to imagine what Williams saw in Elena's heart, however, Driscoll moves on to a broader question radiating from the previous one:

> *His opening remarks in the prologue to* Kora in Hell *offer some poten-*
> *tial, albeit vague, clues as to what this mysterious discovery might be;*
> *however, it is not until the appearance of* Yes, Mrs. Williams *nearly*
> *four decades later that the matter is fully examined and resolved.* Kora
> *and the memoir, which are respectively his first and last published*
> *pieces of prose, thus form distant, interlocking halves of the same*
> *puzzle—namely, what does Elena ultimately signify for Williams?*
>
> (*MM* 98)

Driscoll proceeds as if her first question on what Williams saw in Elena's heart had simply been another phrasing of the second one that inquires what Elena signified to him. That second question, she finds, is answered in the opening to the prologue to *Kora:* "in the ultimate connection Williams perceived between his mother and his writing." Williams explains his understanding of that connection with an anecdote about his mother's tendency to get lost and her inability to learn from previous experience. Driscoll sees these traits as metaphors for the "genuine reasons she occupies this lofty position in the poet's mind; . . . a more intangible quality he observes in her language" (*MM* 99). What follows is fine, except that we have moved quite a distance from the original question of what Williams saw in Elena's heart. A considerable difference separated how "Williams perceived" as Bill, and how he perceived as Carlos, the ultimate connection between himself and Elena. For Bill, the connection to Elena was language; for Carlos the connection was spirit.

Driscoll's disregard of Williams' biculturalism as a working premise also results in her missing a substantial portion of Williams' duplicity. For example, she mentions that in *Kora* Williams offers Longinus' *On the Sublime* as a remote precedent to the style of the prologue. She then goes into some detail on stylistic and structural features that both texts share, her analysis culminating in the allusion's connection to Elena:

> *But the most important link between the prologue and Longinus' work is Williams' tacit—and perhaps even an unconscious—association of Elena with the notion of the sublime.*

(*MM* 100)

This was certainly true, but again there is more. Longinus is the accepted name given to an unknown author, a duality that parallels Williams' personae. The allusion to Longinus, then, was also intended to point to Williams himself. Moreover, it encodes that he was *sublimating*, i.e., modifying a private, instinctual impulse to a socially acceptable manner, which in this case was his translating visceral concerns into the language of poetics.

Proceeding in her argument, Driscoll demonstrates that although Williams identified Elena with the sublime, owing to the naive forthrightness of her language (which could often be graphic and crude), she also represented a totality of the world's experience. Williams therefore imitated her way of shocking through language by juxtaposing those two extremes of beauty and grossness. Based on this observation, Driscoll concludes that Elena's "critical significance to Williams thus lay in 'open[ing]' up the world" to him:

> *. . . not by means of religious and ethical instruction, but rather by the unconscious example of her language, raucous humor, and habits of mind. The legacy he uncovers in her "heart's dark" involves the reconciliation and synthesis of moral polarities, the knowledge that sublimity and snot are products of the same "gutter, where everything comes / from, the manure heap." In this way, Elena incarnates the essence of his own aesthetic philosophy.*

(*MM* 108)

Elena is finally revealed for what she truly signified to Williams, a far cry from the romantic foil that Bill promoted.

But to the end Driscoll evades the initial question, about the "legacy" Williams "uncovers" in his mother's "heart's dark": we are told instead what ideas it "involves." As Driscoll demurs in realistically factoring in Williams' sense of his "Spanish" lineage, she fails to see that Elena's aesthetic sublime/crudeness actually paralleled the romanticism/sexuality dichotomy with which he associated "Spanish," a shocking contrapuntal style that he directly inherited from his readings of Góngora, Quevedo, Juan Ruiz, Lope de Vega, and Cervantes. This Spanish literary style is what he finally recognized was epitomized in Elena. So what he saw in Elena's "Heart's dark" was the full measure of his being Carlos, and only because that became clear to him did he as Bill understand all the things that Driscoll tells us that legacy involved, "The reconciliation and synthesis of moral polarities."

Nowhere, however, does Driscoll flatly state that in the end Elena's legacy was *cultural*. What Driscoll essentially and implicitly argues throughout is that Williams was bicultural, and despite his efforts to claim an Anglo American identity, he knew that in his heart he would always be Carlos first. This statement, as demonstrated earlier, is buried in a language that facilitates the reader's retrofitting her proof of Elena as maternal muse onto the standard image of Williams. Had Driscoll allowed Bill his Carlos heart, which she patently proves he had, then she would have shown that in his weaving his mother's voice with his own he was consciously creating a writing that was structurally and spiritually bicultural, and whose ultimate objective was to change the "catalogue"'s idea of "America" to a land that he could recognize as his own. For Williams' need to prove to Elena that snot and the sublime come from the same gutter was only the obverse side of his need to prove to the social "They" that they were no better than she.

Finally, Williams' coming to grips with his Carlos self contradicts Driscoll's assertion that Williams was *confused* by his dual identity, an idea based on Williams' having a mixed legacy, which is really a euphemism for his mother's being Puerto Rican. His background, as he has indeed written, offered unreliable data, leaving much to the imagination, but nowhere does Williams say that he was *confused* by it; critics have been, by his biculturalism, and project that confusion on to him. Williams was *burdened* ("The petals that fell bearing me under . . .") and ultimately absorbed by his legacy: "This that I have struggled against is the very thing I should have chosen—but all's right now." But the breadth of his work only shows that he evolved to become quite clear of what he was in a society that, lacking an understanding of its own Americanness, failed to appreciate his essentially American mix.

Thus, his mission to show his readers that the Puritan-descended

American was a "grotesque" imposed on the continent was simply an affirmation of his own cultural identity. In this conviction, writing as Carlos, Williams enjoyed a great confidence in his Americanness:

> *Of mixed ancestry I felt from earliest childhood that America was the only home I could possibly call my own. I felt it was expressly founded for me, personally, and that it must be my first business in life to possess it; that only by making it my own from the beginning to my own day, in detail, should I have a basis for knowing where I stood.*[22]

Here Williams was discussing *In the American Grain* and, as in that book, the "America" in question is not narrowly the United States, but the hemispheric America that Columbus stumbled onto. Elena's being from Puerto Rico, one of the sites where Columbus is believed to have actually set foot, and from a Spanish-speaking line that mingled its blood with the continent, made that "America" Williams' legacy. He was American and a "pure product of America" *because* his mother was Puerto Rican.

Of course, this clarity became less clear when muddied by Bill's Anglo-ethnocentricity, but the result was not confusion; rather, this contradiction nurtured a creative search for stasis and reconciliation. In Bill's social milieu, his two minds were irreconcilable. As Driscoll concludes, Williams "realized that the synthesis he had hoped to achieve" between his two cultural minds was impossible. Williams' expression of this impossibility, Driscoll offers, is the frustrated love of the characters Dev Evans and his sister Bess in *A Voyage to Pagany*. Each represents one half of Williams' duality:

> *She was her father's daughter while Dev was of the southern side of his family which was so mixed that no one ever had been quite certain what they were, except that there was a strong Basque strain there associated with the somewhat mythical name of Hurrard.*
>
> *(VP 27)*

Their symbolic incestuous union being impossible, they separate, Bess going north and Dev "going south, south" (*VP* 256). Of course, Bess and Dev do symbolize Williams' impossible union of Bill and Carlos. But Driscoll overlooks the importance she had earlier given to art. For "the synthesis he had hoped to achieve" between his two selves was simply another way of expressing the incestuous fusion he sought between himself and Elena, and of that convergence, Driscoll herself had noted that

Within the fictive universe of Williams' writing, the figures of mother and son complement one another, conjoining male and female elements to form a single, unified whole; . . .

(*MM* 8)

As he resolved his desire to be Elena in his fictive universe, so did he consummate the love of Bess and Dev in the narrative; Williams unites them in the act of *writing* their story, in making them exist as symbolic halves juxtaposed on the plane of his creation, the canvas of his self-portrait. This exemplifies Williams' understanding of writing as *being:* his personae were reconciled in his performance because only in the performance was he his composite self, in the same way that in the act of writing he was simultaneously himself and Elena. Elena as trope imaged him, and she was just one of numerous alter images in which Williams saw himself and through which he elaborated on his ever-unfinished collage of himself.

Chapter 3
Alter Images

> *History adds that before or after his death he found himself facing God and said:* I, who have been so many men in vain, want to be one man, myself alone. *From out of a whirlwind the voice of God replied:* I am not either. I dreamed the world the way you dreamed your work, my Shakespeare: one of the forms of my dreams was you, who, like me are many and no one.
>
> (Jorge Luis Borges, *A Personal Anthology* 116–117)

In his essay "Everything and Nothing," Borges describes Shakespeare as a face behind which there was nothing:

> *There was no one in him: behind his face . . . and behind his words . . . there was nothing but a bit of cold, a dream not dreamed by anyone. At first he thought that everyone was like himself. But the dismay shown by a comrade to whom he mentioned this vacuity revealed his error to him and made him realize forever that an individual should not differ from the species. . . . Thus beset, he took to imagining other heroes and other tragic tales. And so, while his body complied with its bodily destiny . . . , the soul inhabiting that body was Caesar, . . . and Juliet . . . Macbeth. . . . No one was ever so many men as that man: . . .*[1]

As poets Williams and Borges would appear to be polar opposites. Williams' aesthetics was rooted in a faith in change, in novelty; Borges celebrated permanence, the repetition of a handful of metaphors. And yet, parallels and shared characteristics emerge. Both, for instance, were obsessed with conflictive legacies. Intellectually steeped in the West, Borges sought to reconcile his European cultural legacy with barbarous Argentine surroundings. Williams, a "pure product of America," worked to reconcile his roots with his nation's nostalgia for when it was a remote province of Europe. Perhaps owing to this inverse parallel their writings intriguingly coincide: both were drawn to write about Shakespeare and Quevedo. But the point is not to elaborate a comparison; Borges only serves here because, among other things, he alerted us to the metaphysical issues underlying the relationship of the writer and the writing. In Borges' cosmos the poet and God created with the same objective, to *be*. Related to that concept, Borges also perceived time as circular, so that when, say, his character Pierre Menard sets out to write, word for word, the *Quixote*, or when Borges creates a Pierre Menard, we witness in the consequent acts the reincarnation of Cervantes. Borges, then, interpreted a writer's interest in past authors metaphysically: out of a desire to resurrect earlier incarnations in those antecedents.

Borges' observation aptly formulates what Shakespeare embodied for Williams, which makes sense because Williams' picture of Shakespeare is identical to Borges',[2] which also reminds us of the picture of Williams that Marsden Hartley rendered in his letter to Stieglitz: "I never saw so many defined human beings in one being":

> *The secret vitality of Shakespearean characters is that the writing does not seem to be about the characters—but it is, in effect, the mouth of the character when in all he says is saying [sic] always the same thing himself. In all the characters this is the same since Shakespeare is no one. He* must *have done this, to do it invariably, man or woman, king or fool, by a tyrannical necessity over which he had no power. He did it to be.*
>
> (*The Embodiment of Knowledge* 100)

Williams' idea of Shakespeare as writing "to be" is really a semantic transformation of the description of himself in the preface to *The Autobiography*, as the person "we ourselves have been," which meant himself as writer. Like Shakespeare, outside of his writing Williams felt that he was "no one," an idea repeated in several works. In "The Desert Music," his "agony of self-realization" is resolved in the poem, which "calls" the music "into being" (*CPII* 275). The opening chapter of *White Mule*, the first novel in his Stecher Trilogy, is titled "To Be." Writing is also synonymous with being in *A Voyage to Pagany*:

> *Evans had practiced medicine all his adult life, so far, up to his present fortieth year, in a continuously surly mood at the overbearing necessity for it—wanting always to do something else: to write! Why? Because*

then only, when he was stealing time for his machine and paper, did
he live.

(*VP* 4)

Every time he wrote, in fact, Williams was reborn in the imagination in the form of "the best of him." The act of writing was his self-realization:

A writer is a person whose best is released in the accomplishment of
writing—perhaps it is a good variant to say—in the act of writing. He
does not necessarily think these things—he does not, that is, think them
out and then write them down: he writes and the best of him, in spite
even of this thought, will appear on the page even to his surprise, unrec-
ognized or even sometimes against his will, by proper use of words.

(*EK* 7)

Is Williams again using "will" punningly here, "even sometimes against his will," meaning in the non-English voice of Carlos? And does "proper" here play on the Spanish sense of *propio,* closer to the Latin that means "one's own"?

But *being*-in-writing was not the sole characteristic that Williams revealed of himself through Shakespeare. Like Williams, the Bard got his material from lived experience and not from books:

There is a unique element in Shakespeare, unique that is, up until his
time, that has baffled scholarship which has been at a loss to place it, a
new element, a "naturalism" which clashed with all earlier and classic
formalizations. And why not? Shakespeare knew nothing of these
things. He wrote outside the scholarly tradition.

(*EK* 138)

Williams thus celebrated his own "naturalism" in the life of Shakespeare, whose daily life was not that different from his own:

. . . for myself concerning Shakespeare: he was a comparatively unin-
formed man, . . . lived from first to last a life of amusing regularity
and simplicity, a house and wife in the suburbs, delightful children, a
girl at court (whom he never really confused with his writing) and a
café life which gave him with the freshness of discovery, the informa-
tion upon which his imagination fed.

(*I* 121)

Williams, of course, saw his English blood mirrored in Shakespeare. Bill substituted the café life with the art scene, and one infers that, behaving as Carlos, he occasionally kept a "girl at court." Like his namesake too, the poet Bill was also a playwright. Adding in their respective need to *be* in writing, and their naturalism, Williams understandably made of Shakespeare "a recital" that converted him to an antecedent of modernism. In that reading, Shakespeare is a modernist despite himself. Shakespeare's aphorism "about holding the mirror up to nature," Williams argues, has done harm because it has led us to misinterpret what Shakespeare thought he was doing: "He holds no mirror up to nature but with his imagination rivals nature's composition with his own" (*I* 121). By virtue of Shakespeare's lacking scientific training, having nothing by himself to say, he reached into the imagination, which detached his creations from reality in the same way that the new painters had liberated art from being representational:

> *His actual power was purely of the imagination. Not permitted to speak as W.S., in fact peculiarly barred from speaking so because of his lack of information, learning, . . . He speaks authoritatively through invention, through characters, through design.*

> (*I* 122)

In other words, contrary to his own English father William, Shakespeare would have seen the merits of Williams' poetry. This explains why Williams figuratively adopted Shakespeare as his "grandfather" in his "An Essay on William Shakespeare: My Grandfather" (*EK* 110).

Ironically, however, what made this wholehearted embrace of Shakespeare possible was that Carlos too found something in Shakespeare with which to identify. This hidden condition of adoption came out in the 1940 essay "A Letter," in which Williams likens Shakespeare to "a great conceptualist," transforming the crafty, encoded style that Williams admired of Shakespeare into an English-language incarnation of Góngora's and Quevedo's literary school:

> *Be the Shakespeare of your own day, write well, skilfully [sic], covertly, deceitfully, with every faculty under a hood or blanket concealed from public view, . . .*
>
> *So what, huh? After all, man being human must believe himself at times a great conceptualist (read your Spanish lit.: . . .), at least for*

> *home consumption, or lie down and die of disgust at the sights he sees*
> *about him.*
>
> (*SE* 239)

Williams translated *conceptista* "conceptualist," playing as well on the conceptualism of Peter Abelard's school that argued that universals are concepts in the mind that reflect the objects similar to them in reality. Hence his punning argument that man must act as a great "conceptualist," whether as a *conceptista* who skillfully guards his core by keeping "every faculty under a hood," or as one who philosophically believes in the fertile connection between the wealth of concepts in his mind and the multitude of objects about him. In so punning, Williams illustrated the point he was making by writing in the *conceptista* style. He was also underscoring that Shakespeare figures as an English-language antecedent of the style that Williams first learned from the Spanish writers.

"A Letter" was written on the heels of Williams' years of identifying with the Spanish Republican cause, and the year after he wrote the essay "Federico García Lorca," in which he devoted nearly half his words to Góngora, the great *conceptista* whom Williams respected immensely, emulating him in a few writings (see ahead and Chapter 5). The other great "conceptualist" whom Williams emulated, almost as second nature, and from whom Williams always seems to want to distract our attention ("covertly, deceitfully, with every faculty . . . concealed from public view") was Quevedo.

Although both *conceptista* poets were like Shakespeare in artfully revealing by using layers of meanings that also covered, Quevedo wrote to *be* through his creations. In his essay "Quevedo" (*Otras Inquisiciones* 55), Borges observed that the Spaniard's range of genius, his mastery of so many tones and forms, made the poet immemorable, owing to the absence of a central image with which to associate him. Quevedo, to interpret from Borges' thesis, surrendered his unhappy social existence (he wore thick glasses and was physically deformed) to *be* someone else in his writings. Williams' fusing his Spanish and English masters in "A Letter" in 1940 (well after his Spanish phase) signifies that when he wrote about Shakespeare in *The Embodiment of Knowledge* (late twenties, just out of "hell," to early thirties), he was mindful that the Bard was really the embodiment of his *conceptista* spirit. By identifying a "conceptualist" Englishman as his grandfather, he was also rendering tribute to the

English-born, Caribbean-reared, bilingual William George who begat William Carlos Williams. In other words, as Bill publicly celebrated the English Shakespeare, Carlos superimposed on that icon his own "conceptualist" grandfather, an imagistic fusion of Góngora and Quevedo. Williams' privately-interpreted bicultural Shakespeare, then, was the antecedent that he claimed as his grandfather. Williams' use of allusion here also exemplifies another stylistic signature that naturally resulted from his "agony of self-realization": Williams alludes to a writer or artist who images some aspect of himself, with a subset of this device being his personifying things that also serve as mirrors. Out of his sense of being a composite, Williams perceived everyone or anything that helped compose his life, as a contributor. These he turned into *alter images* of himself.

Williams' alter images were all children of the primary alter image, William Carlos Williams, who like Evans Dionysus Evans, was Williams' idealization of himself in cultural and psychic balance. This ideal, pregnant Bill, the vessel of Williams' secret and female other, Carlos, was also the embodiment of an America that itself needed to be realized, an America able to accept Williams' biculturalism. For this reason the ideal William Carlos was invoked in any optimal design that fostered *conversation* or *union* because these acts in turn evoked that other alter image, the ideal America. Conversely, any sowing of discord, miscommunication, or disharmony undermined Williams' ability to be whole. Thus, in his own writings Williams worked to devise the proper design that would allow him *to be:*

> *Conversation has come to be impossible save among specialists in a certain pen, between the lists no languages reaches. This is childish. Is there no conversation or communication between farmers and engineers? Strange to say I have found a very general language.*
>
> *A very simple, easily worded abstract design: a clarity as gracefully put as I am capable of putting it with respect to the meaning. Not too short but not too long. A steady development of what I understand . . . as well as I am able to think, and pretend no more. Then another design and so on to others to embody America and myself in it.*
>
> (*EK* 46–47)

Characteristically, Williams left it up to the reader to assume his meaning of "America." *The Great American Novel* and *In the American Grain* had already been published, so this was a conscious language trick

that he was playing on the reader, who took for granted that he was referring to the narrower Anglo "America," unaware that Williams had superimposed on the conversation an America defined by the roots, spirits, and
history of the hemisphere, not the country sown and nurtured by a xenophobic religious community. For what *he* understood by "America" was
what the complete William Carlos Williams physically embodied, and this
was a conviction as strong in him as that of a revolutionary dreamer
whose country waited to be born. He himself was a new George Washington, as in "Della Primavera Trasportata al Morale":

> —she
> opened the door! nearly
> six feet tall, and I . . .
> wanted to found a new country—

> (*CPI* 331)

The metaphorical comparison between procreating by inseminating the
woman's tall geography and populating a new nation is consistent with
Carlos' depiction of the Spanish explorer's penetration of female America in *In the American Grain*. It is also consistent with Bill's discovering
in George Washington an unexpectedly passionate and, therefore, mingling man.

In the preface to *The First President* (1936), an opera libretto based on
Washington, Williams explains that he was drawn to a dichotomous, enig-
matic public man with a deceptive "frigid" exterior:

> *A first difficulty is that people think the man to have been stolid—a*
> *cold rod of no subtlety of interest, certainly no emotional appeal. He*
> *worked, he married and he died. He was indeed a voluminous writer,*
> *one of the world's most prolific writers. But his exterior was frigid.*
> (*Many Loves and Other Plays* 303–304)

Washington's cold mask obviously evoked another externally cold George:
Williams' father. Like the elder Williams, Washington too "spoke, it was
commonly believed, seldom and formally" (*ML* 304). Both possessed a
frigid exterior while seething inside with adventuring, sensual spirit.

Williams asked himself: "What in the world, retaining his obvious vitality, can you do with a character like that?" His answer was a biography
that captured the essence beyond the outer circumstances of the man:
"Music must be the answer. The character creates a music—it must have

created a music for its escape" (*ML* 304). Lives that accomplish things, Williams was insisting, are by their nature artistic performances, and "the externality of events" should conform "to the actuality, the music of conviction" (*ML* 307), a succinctly formulated definition of an existentialist biography—or autobiography: the true Washington was a sum of his acts, however incompatible or contradictory the details might appear. Music and the imagination provided the media in which appearances, true and invented facts, conscious and unconscious causes and effects, coexist compatibly:

> *Yet music and the imagination are the keys. They open to a common*
> *world into which both history and the present can step on an equal*
> *footing of basic agreement. There the figure of Geo. Washington*
> *can join us with advice—a realization of his performance and its*
> *significance.*
>
> (*ML* 303)

As a performance on Washington's performance, this libretto foreshadowed Williams' later compositions (*The Autobiography, Paterson,* "The Desert Music") on the "music of conviction." Washington as protagonist was Williams' mouthpiece, even Williams himself, not in the first president's exterior, but in his "flaming" kindred soul: "inwardly flaming, [giving] his life a fragmentary surface but a tremendous continuity and singleness of purpose" (*ML* 309). This flame, in Williams' lexicon, is also sexual. In *In the American Grain,* Williams describes Washington as a "great wench lover":

> *America has a special destiny for such men, I suppose, great wench*
> *lovers—there is the letter from Jefferson attesting it in the case of Wash-*
> *ington, if that were needed. . . .*
>
> (*AG* 143)

As Washington's exterior was said to be "taciturn," which is here synonymous with the earlier "cool," the inward flame made of Washington an Anglo shell with a Carlos heart, a kindred spirit of Uncle Carlos of the "amorous disposition."

The preface of *The First President,* then, prefigures the foreword of *The Autobiography* in its delineation of a protagonist with a hidden core:

*It was a music which Washington must constantly have felt from the
beginning to the end of his life within the secrecy of his shuttling
thoughts.*

(*ML* 304)

This preface, of course, also completely contradicts Williams' reasoning
for keeping his own core hidden in *The Autobiography*. Here Williams
argues that to understand the first president it is essential to get a glimpse
of his hidden core; the central theme of Washington's life was his "inner
drama."

*To invent a theme, an operatic theme, of whatever sort—revenge,
love, persecution, ambition or lyric fancy—on which to string the
man would be fatal. It would at once falsify the true theme which is the
inner drama of his life.*

(*ML* 307–308)

Obviously, besides seeing William George, Williams saw himself imaged in Washington's conflictive cool public mask and secret sexual inner
spirit, also seeing his own life as an artistic performance whose "externality of events" was secondary to the "music of conviction" that made up
his essence. But while *The Autobiography* purports to narrate the story
about "what we ourselves have been," it gives the reader only the "externality of events." That he felt compelled to reveal that his secret core was
encoded in the externals he offered is the measure of Williams' own sense
of the inadequacy of his autobiography. The earlier preface on Washington confirms that only in his expressing that compulsion in *The Autobiography* did Williams give us a glimpse of his true self.

Williams' idea of being his truest composite self in his performance was
also embodied by the Spanish artist Juan Gris, a key alter image. To begin
with, Juan Gris was the name adopted by José Victoriano González. Although his just having an alter ego would have probably drawn Williams'
imagination, the imagistic value of González's chosen bilingual professional name was not lost on the "conceptualist" Williams. In either Spanish or French, *gris* signifies "grey," a haze, a compromise between black
and white. Thus *Gris* evoked Williams' own personal and artistic temper-
ing of spiritual halves, suggesting as well their ambiguity and fusion. The

name of Williams' protagonist Evans ("even") plays with the ideas evoked by *Gris*, as does the title of the poem "A Portrait in Greys." The name also figures in *A Novelette,* a prose work based on the aesthetics of Gris:

> *As the gates closed and the bridge slowly swung open wasting his time—*
> *enforcing a stand-still, he thought again of "Juan Gris," making a*
> *path through the ice. That was the name of the approaching tug boat*
> *seen through the branches of a bare beech tree. It had a white cabin*
> *and a black stack with a broad yellow band around it.*
>
> (*I* 284)

Bilingually punning on "one grey" (note the absence of an article before the boat's name), Williams "thought again on 'Juan Gris,' making a path through the ice." The verbal phrase "making a path through the ice" ambiguously modifies both "Juan Gris" and the "he." The setting is the Northeast, where the beech tree grows. As the bridge opens, Williams is forced to wait, "wasting his time," so the sighting of the tug boat "Juan Gris" makes the time fruitful. While physically detained, the poet's spirit progresses on the tug, so he and "Juan Gris" together cut through the ice, their respective "weathers." Cutting through the ice, "Juan Gris" forms cubist patterns, as well as makes graphic a favorite Williams imagistic counterpoint between alter images of heat and cold.

Because Gris' painterly techniques contributed to Williams' own, Williams renders tribute by writing *A Novelette* and *Spring and All,* a collage of poetry and prose that collectively illustrate by their performance the book's and Williams' new aesthetics epitomized for him in Gris' art, which says that a painting is a picture of itself, not a picture of reality:

> *The only realism in art is of the imagination. It is only thus that the*
> *work escapes plagiarism after nature and becomes a creation.*
>
> (*I* 111)

In rendering this tribute to Gris, Williams is also aware of receiving through the Spaniard's work his artistic lineage, "the impressionists, the expressionists, and Cezanne—and dealing severe strokes as well to the expressionists as well as to the impressionists groups" in order to get to "what will prove the greatest painting yet produced" (*I* 117).

Williams describes a black and white reproduction of a Gris painting, "The Open Window," noting that it "separates things of the imagination from life" (*I* 107); things that are "familiar, simple" are detached "from ordinary experience to the imagination" (*I* 110):

> *Thus they are still "real" [sic] they are the same things they would be if photographed or painted by Monet, they are recognizable as the things touched by the hands during the day, but in this painting they are seen to be in some peculiar way—detached.*

(*I* 110)

So also, in a poem, Williams' words are detached from the symbolism or meaning of a discourse in nature, although they are still "real" words, making a "jump between fact and the imaginative reality" (*I* 135):

> *What I put down of value will have this value: an escape from crude symbolism, the annihilation of strained associations, complicated ritualistic forms designed to separate the work from "reality"—such as rhyme, meter as meter and not as the essential of the work, one of its words. . . . The word must be put down for itself, not as a symbol of nature but a part, cognizant of the whole—aware-civilized.*

(*I* 102)

Williams' poem as a painting, specifically like Gris', is illustrated by the painterly techniques in "X":

> The universality of things
> draws me toward the candy
> with melon flowers that open
>
> about the edge of refuse
> proclaiming without accent
> the quality of the farmer's
>
> shoulders and his daughter's
> accidental skin, so sweet
> with clover and the small
>
> yellow cinquefoil in the
> parched places. . . .

(*I* 118)

Images are juxtaposed to overlap illogically. Each is its own image, and visually arresting, but they are painted to be seen in relation to each other, within the framing "universality of things."

To take, as Gris did, disparate things and have them fuse into one thing while still allowing them to remain themselves, results in what Williams called a "Fierce Singleness," the title of a vignette in *A Novelette*. That unity of imagery simultaneously juxtaposes disconnected themes, whose composite is itself their discourse, what Williams identified as a "conversation as design," whose only effect is its being:

> To be conversation, it must have only the effect of itself, not on him to whom it has a special meaning but as a dog or a store window . . .
>
> It must have no other purpose than the roundness and the color and the repetition of grapes in a bunch, such grapes as those of Juan Gris which are related more to a ship at sea than to the human tongue. As they are.
>
> (*I* 287)

As Williams did with everything else that touched his life, however, his seeing himself in Gris resulted from his projecting himself onto Gris. "That man was my perfect artist," Williams wrote of Gris to Charles Henri Ford, "He embodied all the personal faults with which I am so familiar myself."[3] This meant that Gris' work was useful in explaining his own life, which he implicitly compared to a work of art evincing the aesthetics of the Spanish painter. In "Conversation as Design," a section of *A Novelette*, Williams carries on a conversation with his "wife" (literally Flossie, but also his female half and Elena), who is told that she is part of a unity that is his fragmented life: "By this SINGLENESS do you, my dear, become actually my wife." (*I* 286) In the subsequent vignette he expands on the conceit, referring to some of his life's scattered components as converging in a "Fierce Singleness" that he is assembling in the piece that he writes:

> You, I, we, cannot you see how in the singleness of these few days marriage and writing have been fused so the seriousness of my life and common objects about me have made up an actuality of which I am assembling the parts?
>
> (*I* 294)

Contradicting his eschewing of metaphor in *Spring and All*, Williams turned Gris' aesthetics into a metaphor:

> As you by becoming pure design have become real. In the singleness of this epidemic which is like the singleness of Juan Gris?
>
> (*I* 287)

Williams' identifying with Gris' aesthetics is complemented by his also identifying with the painter's bloodline. Washington had only been figuratively Carlos-hearted; but Gris was a flesh-and-bones reflection, in whom Williams saw an unromantic self without betraying his warmer Latin side. As a painter who worked in France, Gris was also an Elena ("you") who was not romantic:

> *Because he was not Picasso—nor discouraged by him—but a Spaniard full of admiration for French painting and lived in Paris where he worked: like you.*

> (*I* 283)

Williams' associating Gris with Elena leads to an even richer aesthetic development. Kerry Driscoll observes that Williams found in Elena's speech and writing a reiteration of Gris' concept of art:

> *Elena's disregard for conventions of written English is amply demonstrated by the wrenched syntax, lack of punctuation, and use of nonparallel structures in the passage. . . . these grammatical distortions greatly enhance the vividness and immediacy of her account. In particular, her rapid conjunction of the phrases "he went to my father's room howl and howl went all over, the house was in mourning the master was gone," creates a strong impression of simultaneity; actions and details overlap, but their outlines remain crisp, unblurred. Hence, it is in the way Elena wields words rather than a paintbrush that she most resembles Juan Gris; she achieves with language the same innovative effect he produced with color, line and mass. Through the unusual juxtaposition and emphasis of elements, both artists revivify the thing being represented and "make it new."*

> (*MM* 65)

Driscoll proceeds to demonstrate how in *Yes, Mrs. Williams* the design of vignettes of varying lengths juxtaposed are "like the geometric shapes in Juan Gris' canvas" (*MM* 66), and that the language and structure of that book replicated Elena's haphazard way of speaking and thinking. Although Driscoll limits her demonstration of Elena's linguistic influence to *Yes* and other writings in which Elena is the subject, her argument also proves that Williams' most mature and innovative style actually reflected Elena's speech and thought patterns, which mentally translated her private Spanish to a fractured public English.

But what needs to be underscored is that in its unusual way Elena's fractured language also made her a model of the *unity* that Williams praised in Gris' style in "The Open Window":

Here is a shutter, a bunch of grapes, a sheet of music, a picture of sea and mountains (particularly fine) which the onlooker is not for a moment permitted to witness as an "illusion." One thing laps over on the other, the cloud laps over on the shutter, the bunch of grapes is part of the handle of the guitar, and the mountain and sea are obviously not "the mountain and sea," but a picture of the mountain and the sea. All drawn with admirable simplicity and excellent design—all a unity—

(*I* 110–111)

Elena survived by that internal conversation with herself, a unity despite the appearances of being scattered. In this she also embodied Williams' fusing of the contradictory components in his life, a unique design that, even if it didn't comply with logical expectations of "reality," in an imaginary reality was justified, like Gris' painting, in its unity.

Although the alter image device is most readily identified in allusions, Williams also repeated a number of things or abstract images in whose deep structure he saw himself. Images of temperature are one category. In "The Marriage of Souls," an unhappy union reminiscent of Elena and William George is abstracted into a metaphor of opposite temperatures:

> That heat!
> That terrible heat
> That coldness!
> That terrible coldness

(*CPII* 233)

The couple had remained together, the poet repeats, "Like to like," which resounds with semantic layerings—affinity, preferring to like rather than to love, or two of a kind:

> Like to like
> In terrible isolation

> Like to like
> in terrible intimacy
> Unfused
> And unfusing

> (*CPII* 233)

They are "Like to like" in their isolation and intimacy and yet one is terribly hot and the other terribly cold.

But the couple in question can be of another sort, two selves unhappily married in one self, Williams' signature of imagistic balance between extremes of temperature:

> *Upon a great round hot and cold mass of eighty odd indestructible materials I am thrust in an unconscious state . . .*

> (*EK* 154)

Of course, the couple can also be Williams and Flossie, whose marriage served as a metaphor of Williams' dialogue with himself in *A Novelette:* "By this singleness do you, my dear, become actually my wife" (*I* 286).

Consistent with what should by now be an obvious pattern, Williams' hot images encode the Latin Carlos; the cold images encode the Anglo Bill, Williams' *yin* and *yang,* with Bill the male principle and Carlos the female. But these are not equally distributed in any given work: a single image might be the counterbalance of pages of the opposite temperature—or the balancing element might even be encoded. Cold was Williams' default temperature, his public exterior, as Bill was the understood spokesperson of his enterprise. In Bill's cool voice, Carlos' heat often serves as a means of seeming provocative and Dionysian to the Anglo reader, the object of Bill's moralizing, because Carlos is highly sexual and therefore hot:

> *I have been reasonably frank about my erotics with my wife. I have never or seldom said, my dear I love you, when I would rather say: My dear, I wish you were in Tierra del Fuego.*

> (*I* 22)

This heat/cold motif, implicit in his Bill-English/Carlos-Spanish dualism, was present in Williams' work since his earliest poems. In his *Endymion*-style epic, for example, he refused to sing of Don Pedro's brave deeds lest the throngs "fly like midnight birds / Into the sudden flame and hell of passion." The lost prince escaped on water, as did "The Wanderer," who was reborn on the river that, although muddy and dirty, was also cool:

> Then the river began to enter my heart,
> Eddying back cool and limpid
> Into the crystal beginning of its days.

                                                                                          (*CPI* 116)

Williams' ideal was to find a figurative midpoint between his two temperatures, however subtly. For example, that section of "The Wanderer" from which the quotation is taken is titled "St. James' Grove"; the text refers to it as "Santiago Grove," Santiago being the Spanish, or hot, version of James.

In *The Tempers,* his second book, there is a clear intention to balance temperatures, starting with the Latin-rooted title. "Temper" has several meanings, most referring to states of mind. As a verb it denotes to alter or modify a thing. Two archaic noun denotations are "a compromise between extremes" and "physiological condition," as defined by the mixture of the four humors. In the plural, all the senses apply, evoking compromise and balance between states and extremes, substances and humors. And true to its title, *The Tempers* was designed to be balanced. Although written in English, with its language evincing Williams' Keatsian influence, it was dedicated to Uncle Carlos. It also contained four translations from the Spanish seventeenth-century selection of folk poems known as "El Romancero."[4] As the languages and cultures served as temperature symbols for Williams, these elements also represented a balance of hot/cold imagery.

The poem "The Ordeal" is emblematic of the book's temperature consciousness. In that poem Williams prays to the mythical salamander, a *fusion* of heat and cold. He appeals to the salamander to come to the rescue of "our fellow," to bring him "home again":

> Swim in with watery fang,
> Gnaw out and drown
> The fire roots that circle him
> Until the Hell-flower dies down
> And he comes home again.

                                                                                            (*CPI* 8)

The poem weaves with threads of opposites. The fire is oxymoronically described as a form of burning liquid. A salamander, whose legs are rudimentary, is also phallic: "Salamander" is another name for a poker, and "crimson salamander" paints a red-hot poker. On the other hand, "crimson" evokes the female principle: the color was originally produced from pulverizing the shells of dead female Kermes insects. The image "O crimson salamander," said three times, also echoes the vaginal "O" in "Ordeal," whose etymological roots evoke "trial" (also echoed in the poem's motif of fire). The "Hell-flower" (hot and cool; damnation and regeneration; Kore in Hell) is both attractive and repellent. Both male and female, the cool/hot salamander deity will "Gnaw out and drown / The fire roots" that encircle the phallus-antecedent of "him," "our fellow," a pun on the Spanish *falo*, "phallus."

He (penis, poet) is whom the flames threaten to "disman," an uncommon word in American usage, meaning to remove men or a garrison, but employed here in the sense of "unman," which can signify the same as "disman" as well as to cause to lose courage or, applied more literally as Williams does, can suggest a spiritual castration, a return to the unmanly state of a boy:

> Swim
>> the winding flame
>> Predestined to disman him
>> And bring our fellow home to us again.

(CPI 8)

But "disman" further plays on another, more subtle motif, from the Spanish *desmanar*, an archaic word, one of whose meaning is "to remove something from use, to separate." (Williams' intense interest in seventeenth-century Spanish poetry, as discussed in Chapter 5, doubtless resulted in his picking up etymologies and archaic Spanish forms.) By evoking the unrelated *desmanar*, "disman" thus encodes the poem's collective consciousness. Whether "he" signifies the speaker or his penis, he is "our" fellow coming home "to us," those far from the flames. This collective consciousness makes sense because "The fire roots" image is consistent with Williams' associating being Hispanic with high sexual charge, something dangerous to the English-speaking "us." The mythic salamander, which can survive fire, thus fusing cold and heat, is the only power that can "Gnaw out and drown" (that is, coolly extinguish) the "fire roots" and thus return him to harmony with his puritanically, sexually cool "home."

Once "our fellow" is home and the poet sees that he, our fellow, is "unchanged with burning" (an ambiguity, whose meanings can also include his having *escaped* being burned as well as his having *survived* even though burned), then the salamander (and here Williams repeats Shakespeare's famous pun) can have its "will with him," meaning that the salamander can take him through both fire and ice, because despite the fire Williams will safely remain the cool Bill.

This salamander spirit reappears in "Appeal," a poem that Williams published in *The Collected Earlier Poems* as part of *The Tempers*, but that according to the Litz and MacGowan edition was originally published in *Al Que Quiere*. But this poem was obviously written soon after "The Ordeal," as its counterbalance, even containing a line that addresses the salamander of the previous poem: "crimson salamander, / hear me once more." As in "The Ordeal," fire here is an image of sexual urge. Contrary to its previous function, however, here the flame is positive. The cold opposite of flame is a "fiend":

> The fiend was creeping in.
> I felt the cold tips of fingers—

Williams appeals to the "crimson salamander" to

> Give me one little flame,
> one!
> that I may bind it
> protectingly about the wrist
> of him that flung me here,
> here upon the very center!
>
> (*CPI* 68)

The "flung me," which evokes the accidental birth motif that began with Williams' *Endymion*-style poem, tells us that the speaker was delivered involuntarily to "here." But the "protectingly" is ambiguous, applicable for the protection both of the speaker and the one who "flung" him. In both cases the flames are good and the poet wants them to coexist harmoniously. Also significant, while in "The Ordeal" the collective narrator "us" implied Bill's world, this "Appeal" is made by Bill alone: "This is my song."

Also illustrative of temperature balance, and belonging to *The Tempers,* is "Crude Lament." The speaker laments to the spirit of flame, "Mother of flames," because he was not with the young men "that went ahunting" (*CPI* 7). Not wanting to remain a boy, he wants to be among the men, who are now asleep in the snow but had "raised the heavy spears." The desire to be with them, to be a man, is great, but he is also ambivalent about leaving because the Mother of flames is the one who has kept "the fire burning." She is heat, and the men now sleep in the snow. The young wives, who have fallen asleep without their men, have doused their flames and now sleep with "wet hair." The boy, grateful for the maternal "fire" passed on to him, is torn by a desire to be the Mother of flame's warmed, dependent son (Carlos) and an independent man among the men in the snow (Bill). The only remedy for him would have been the same as that for the lost prince, that he be sequestered, without having to decide:

> O Mother of flames,
> You have kept the fire burning!
> Lo, I am helpless!
> Would God they had taken me with them!
>
> (*CPI* 8)

(The "Lo" smacks too much of a pun to be overlooked: "Low, I am helpless." That "low" can refer to his condition of being a boy, his sadness.)

The short poem "Fire Spirit" (which Williams grouped with *The Tempers* in *Collected Early Poems,* but that Litz and MacGowan place in a loose grouping of poems written from 1909–1917) keeps up the heat/cold motif in a short monologue in which the speaking persona is in flames and yet his/her core is cold:

> You warm yourselves at these fires?
> In the center of these flames
> I sit, my teeth chatter!
> Where shall I turn for comfort?
>
> (*CPI* 58)

The importance of the autobiographical inferences of heat and cold images in *The Tempers* is indirectly confirmed by Williams' description to Heal of the period during which he wrote *The Tempers:*

I was conscious of my mother's influence all through this time of writ-ing, her ordeal as a woman and as a foreigner in this country. I've al-ways held her as a mythical figure, remote from me, detached, looking down on an area in which I happened to live, a fantastic world where she was moving as a more or less pathetic figure. Remote, not because of her Puerto Rican background, but also because of her bewilderment at life in a small town in New Jersey after her years in Paris where she had been an art student.[5]

Elena and her Puerto Rican background were what Williams implicitly understood as heat images, while the area in which he "happened to live" implied a temperature the opposite of hers. Williams even employs the same word that he used in the title of one of the poems to describe the contact between those opposites: "ordeal." For ultimately Elena was not merely flame, but the "Mother of flames" in "Crude Lament." According to Litz and MacGowan, John C. Thirlwall's annotated copy of *Collected Early Poems,* which was read and commented on by Williams himself, has the word "Mother" glossed "R.H.R.," the initials of Elena's names, Raquel Helene Rose. This confirmation from Williams himself sustains the inter-pretation that the implicit son of flames was Carlos, the son seeking snow or relief was Bill, and *The Tempers* symbolized William Carlos Williams.

An important variant on the heat and cold alter images are the seasons. Williams regularly compared spiritual environments to seasonal cli-mates; hence his depiction of the literary scene as his "weather," which was cold and inhospitable to Carlos. Bill was a "creature of the weather" because Williams created him to survive in the cold. When Williams wrote as Carlos, he wrote "Against the Weather." When they collaborated, they produced *Spring and All* and *The Descent of Winter* because spring was the balance, the *temper.* Spring imagistically resolved Williams' "agony of self-realization."

Owing to the facile counterpoint of literary symbols that he made of his parents, with Elena symbolizing Spanish (and therefore the tropics) and William George symbolizing the English (and therefore a colder cli-mate), it would appear that Williams' seeing spring as an alter image came from the union of his parental symbols. His poem "La Belle Dame de Tous les Jours" leaves us with this predictable impression. Elena stares out the window, dreaming of the tropics because her life in the cold north has deadened "it," her neutralized self, which has lived

> against the snow
new-fallen beyond
the tropic windowsill

(CPI 407)

But in fact Williams inherited a consciousness of seasonal balance from both parents. Elena, we recall, had represented the totality of the world to Williams in embodying at once refinement and crudeness. In a parallel manner, her hatred of winter was actually a raw expression of a profounder sensitivity to climate (certainly related to his keen sense of literary "weather") and natural cycles. In *Yes, Mrs. Williams,* to illustrate, appears a poem in Spanish by Elena, "(Her only poem!)," titled "Por mi ventana" ("From My Window"), in which she reveals a balanced sense of the seasons, a sense from which evidently Williams received his own penchant for seeing things in a cyclical context. Here is the first of two stanzas along with Williams' translation:

[sic]Mira mira como vuelan!	Look, look how they fall
Son las hojas destacadas	They are the dried leaves
del inexorable Otono [sic].	of inexorable Autumn.
No hay porque [sic] aflijirse	No need to be sorrowful
ellas volveran [sic]	they will relive
en la radiante Primavera, . . .	in the radiant Springtime . . .

(YM 123)

Similarly, Williams' father was a model of seasonal balance, an externally cold Englishman who internally strove "to emulate his Spanish friend / and idol—the weather!" (*CPI* 408). As noted earlier, this probably was Williams' elegant image for William George's sexual adventures abroad, but his father's emulation of the tropics externally expressed itself in his wanting to return to the warm climate of his Spanish-language office or to Latin America. In Williams' adopting spring, therefore, he also aspired to emulate his father, another kind of seasonal balance, with his Anglo Bill facade possessed of an inner warmth.

In summary, from all sides, he would identify with spring, the fecund season:

> Spring days
swift and mutable
winds blowing four ways

```
hot and cold
shaking the flowers—
. . . . . . . . . . . . . . . . . .
The owner of the orchard
lies in bed
with open windows
and throws off his covers
one by one
```
                              ("St. Francis Einstein of the Daffodils," (*CPI* 415)

In *In the American Grain,* spring symbolizes the American spirit. The Puritan was a winter of logic and blandness:

> *True they had their magnificent logic but it was microscopic in dimensions—against the flamboyant mass of savagery. . . . The Puritan, finding one thing like another in a world destined for blossom only in 'Eternity,' . . .*

                                                                              (*AG* 113)

In contrast, the New World is summer:

> *Contrary to the English, Rasles recognized the New World. . . . It is a living flame compared to [the Puritan's] dead ash.*

                                                                              (*AG* 120)

Midway is springtime, the true American spirit, a flowering:

> *Already the flower is turning up its petals. . . . It is the sun. In Rasles one feels* THE INDIAN *emerging from within the pod of his isolation from eastern understanding, . . .*

                                                                              (*AG* 121)

As an alter image of fusion and balance, therefore, spring's temperate climate is implied in his idealized country yet to be discovered, a synthesis of his *tempers,* "The United States":

```
The government of your body, sweet,
shall be my model for the world.
There is no desire in me to rule
that world or to advise it. Look
how it rouses with the sun, shuts
```

> with night and sleeps fringed by
> the slowly turning stars. I boil
> I freeze before its tropics and its
> cold.

(CPII 111–112)

But Williams' temperate spring was an ideal, like his America, like the balanced William Carlos. Williams therefore also writes of a compromised spring, the simple warmth that is the only alternative to the deadening of winter, bringing on *The Descent of Winter*. That spring is the warmth implied when Williams was forced to choose between it and a spiritually cold season. In the play *Tituba's Children*, the Parris' "half-Carib, half-Negro slave" Tituba longs for the warmth of her people:

> *I wish I could take her far away in my own country—where the sun shines good all day. Away from this cold weather and these hard people. . . .*

(ML 235)

Williams was aware that of his two spiritual temperatures, Carlos' hot spirit was what made "warmth" possible. Carlos, for this reason, is often interchangeable with that realistic spring's "warmth," allowing the otherwise cool Bill to produce the spring of the poem. Bill was the writer in him, but Carlos was the poem:

> I am moved to write poetry
> for the warmth there is in it
> and for the loneliness—
> a poem that shall have you
>   in it March.

("March," CPI, 138)

But to say that Carlos' warmth made possible the spring of the poem is also to say that Carlos as spring was synonymous with Williams' female principle. This chain of associations comes alive in "The Shadow," where to express the arousal of his inner self in spring there emerges the image of a warm woman who "closes me in" over the cool earth:

> Soft as the bed in the earth
> where a stone has lain—

> so soft, so smooth, and so cool
> Spring closes me in
> with her arms and her hands.
>
> *(CPI* 50)

Once we identify the female principle, however, the chain of associated images instantly grows. Women are like spring because they give birth, as poets do, but they are also an important component of Williams in that they are all spiritually Helen, the classical ideal, and by extension Helene, Elena, the source of Carlos' warmth:

> All women are not Helen,
>   I know that,
> but have Helen in their hearts.
>   My sweet,
>   you have it also, therefore
> I love you
>   and could not love you otherwise.
>
> ("Asphodel, That Greeny Flower," *CPII* 316)

The epitome of his woman images, embodying all versions of his female principle and his ideal season (Carlos-woman-Elena-spring), was his inspiring "Kore":

> *I am indebted to Pound for the title. We had talked about Kora, the Greek parallel of Persephone, the legend of Springtime captured and taken to Hades. I thought of myself as Springtime and I felt I was on my way to Hell (but I didn't go very far).*
>
> *(IWW* 29)

The idea of spring as regeneration, removed from associations of seasonal temperatures, generated the alter image of the flower:

> A flower, at its heart (the stamens, pistil,
> etc.) is a naked woman, about 38, just
>
> out of bed, worth looking at both for
> her body and her mind . . .
>
> ("Asphodel, That Greeny Flower," *CPII* 323)

Referring to his poem "Sub Terra," Williams spoke to Heal of his sense of himself as a flower:

Why did I use the Latin title Sub Terra *for this poem? . . . I thought of myself as being under the earth, buried in other words, but as any plant is buried, retaining the power to come again. The poem is Spring, the earth giving birth to a new crop of poets, showing that I thought I would some day take my place among them, telling them that I was coming pretty soon. . . . When I spoke of flowers, I was a flower, with all the prerogatives of flowers, especially the right to come alive in the Spring.*

(*IWW* 21)

In the flower image Williams saw the lost prince who is born acciden-tally, subject to fortune and the weather, like the reviving plants "By the road to the contagious hospital":

> They enter the new world naked,
> cold, uncertain of all
> save that they enter. All about them
> the cold, familiar wind—

(*CPI* 183)

"The Flower"'s many petals, blown by the wind, are like his own time-swept components:

> One petal goes eight blocks . . .
>
> . . . .
> . . . to the small house
> in which I happen to have been born.
>
> . . . .
> Another petal reaches
>
> into the past, to Puerto Rico
> when my mother was a child bathing in a small
>
> river and splashing water up on
> the yucca leaves to see them roll back pearls.

(*CPI* 324)

(Drops of water on the large yucca leaf bead up milky white.)

As a flower, Williams reiterated his being a "creature of the weather," but stressing cycles; his hot and cold spirits were inner seasons, only "not in fixed order." The flower inside indicated through what season he was passing, whether "in a few weeks or in hours," as the cycle of blossoming or wilting always remained "of a piece":

The gross summer of the year is only a halting counterpart of those fiery days of secret triumph which in reality themselves paint the year as if upon a parchment, giving each season a mockery of the warmth or frozenness which is within ourselves. The true seasons blossom or wilt not in fixed order but so that many of them may pass in a few weeks or hours whereas sometimes a whole life passes and the season remains of a piece from one end to the other.

(*I* 82)

"Asphodel, That Greeny Flower" is about this continual process of seasonal and balancing interaction between natural forces, within and without. In Book III, Williams writes of a man in the subway who reminded him of his father. In the man's face Williams saw his own. By the time the man exited the subway, the man had become all humans:

>   With him
>   went all men
>   and all women too
>   were in his loins.

(*CPII* 329)

Then Williams combines all the pieces of "it," the scene, into the image of the flower:

>   Fanciful or not
>   it seemed to me
>   a flower
>   whose savor had been lost.
>   It was a flower
>   some exotic orchid
>   that Herman Melville had admired
>   in the
>   Hawaiian jungle.
>   Or the lilacs
>   of men who left their marks,
>   by torchlight,
>   rituals of the hunt,

> on the walls
> of prehistoric
> caves in the Pyrenees—
>
> *(CPII* 329)

"It" has as its antecedent the whole experience, but "it" also strongly suggests that procreative and thus regenerative thing between the man's legs. By arousing poetry in Williams, the man was himself a flower, likened to the orchid that inspired Herman Melville to create, or to the "lilacs / of men" who drew pictures of their killing for food. They are "all of a piece."

The flower is finally the image in which, on diverse interpretive levels, many of Williams' themes converge. The flower embodies sexuality and regeneration, the accidental birth, the frailty to the *tempers,* and the fusion of the present with a chaotic, unrecorded past into a beauty that replenishes our imagination with poetry:

> Are facts not flowers
> and flowers facts
> or poems flowers
> or all works of the imagination,
> interchangeable?
>
> *(CPII* 333)

But by its beauty's creative power, the flower also defines the opposite of procreative generosity, "the world's niggardliness," which caused his "fate" of having to suffer the "deaths" that "began in the heads / about me" (*CPII* 320). Those deaths included Carlos' dying over and over in the heads of others while Williams had been blind to the world's spiritual "niggardliness":

> I lived
> to breathe above the stench
> not knowing how I in my own person
> would be overcome
> finally.
>
> *(CPII* 321)

The apparently redundant "in my own person" refers to how the niggardliness had divided him, and therefore suggests "as one."

That niggardliness, represented by the impersonal "*they,*" undid Darwin's work. Compared to Darwin's opening "our eyes / to the gardens of the world" (*CPII* 323), which he did off the coast of Ecuador, *"they"* closed our eyes so we would not see its many different kinds of flowers. Earlier still (Williams is working backward in a pattern of rebirth), that same meanness ruined the hope of that other flowering that began with Columbus, in the fate of whose voyage "I myself am so deeply concerned":

> Or take that other voyage
> which promised so much
> but due to the world's avarice
> breeding hatred
> through fear,
> ended so disastrously;
> a voyage
> with which I myself am so deeply concerned,
> that of the *Pinta,*
> the *Niña*
> and the *Santa Maria.*
> How the world opened its eyes!
> It was a flower
> upon which April
> had descended from the skies!
> How bitter
> a disappointment!
>
> (*CPII* 323)

The avarice and niggardliness that started back there were the beginning of his many deaths, which is to say his many rebirths. Columbus' failed voyage was the seed of his inner drama of cycles:

> In all,
> this led mainly
> to the deaths I have suffered.
>
> (*CPII* 323)

But, consistent with this poem's cycle theme, Williams' fate of having to accept the many deaths of Carlos (and the Carloses of the world) also caused his having to imagine new ways of keeping that complete self alive. Deaths produced rebirths, sadness produced the joy of poetry, winter ends in a new beginning. Thus "Asphodel"'s final "Coda" celebrates cycles, light and dark, imagination and death, imagination and love, which are really, like himself, "all of a piece." It is the cycle of life about which Williams had written often, from the early "Hymn to Love Ended," in which he celebrated lost loves that have seeded great poems, to his much later "Two Pendants: for the Ears":

> Now it is spring
> Elena is dying

(CPII 207)

By embodying that cycle, the flower also teaches a frightening lesson of beauty in death:

> *The wintry landscape is a museum of dried vegetation, bearing much the same resemblance to the verdant wealth of summer that a mummy does to a living human being, yet with the difference that the vegetable mummy often retains the most graceful elegance; and this it is to be feared, can scarcely be said of any Egyptian princess, however distinguished in her time. Indeed I may go so far as to assert that some plants are positively more elegant as mummies than they were when the sap circulated in all their vessels.*

(I 297)

Lastly, Williams' consummate alter image was poetry itself. Poetry embodied his fusion, his "United States," his *tempers,* both the lost Spanish prince and the Anglo wanderer, which is also to say that in poetry a common idiom flowered from his many discordant and accidental languages: earth-words, Spanish, art, English. Poetry translated those voices—inside him but foreign to each other—into a "fierce singleness." In other words, in order to *be,* Bill was continually translating Carlos, his Kore, into English. In the act of writing, Williams was an incessant translator.

Chapter 4
Translations, Imaginary and Real

I have always wanted to do some translations from Span-
ish. It was my mother's native language as well as one
which my father spoke from childhood.

(*The Autobiography* 349)

This is the language to which few ears are tuned. . . . Thus
to say that a man has no imagination is to say nearly that
he is blind or deaf. But of old poets would translate this hid-
den language into a kind of replica of the speech of the
world with certain distinctions of rhyme and meter to show
that it was not really that speech.

(*I* 59)

So I began to invent—or try to invent. Of course I had the
advantage of not speaking English.

("The Basis of Faith in Art," *SE* 177)

In "El Hombre," Williams converted the etymology of key words into a metaphor of his background. On other occasions, imagery of his background is pushed to the foreground, as in the title *Al Que Quiere*. In either case, whether to subdue his foreignness or to highlight it as newness, Williams was responding to the "catalogue"'s holding that other America in unprestigious regard, an attitude that branched out of the history of this culture's perception of Spanish things in general. In literature, except for Lorca, until the emergence of Neruda, Parra, Borges, and others near the end of Williams' life, the only Spanish-language work widely known was the *Quixote*, although even it was rarely assigned in literature classes.[1] Spanish culture itself has been stigmatized in the United States by a long history of antipathy. As the arch-competitor in the enterprise of discovery, conquest, and worship, in the Protestant consciousness Spain was the country of cruel and rapacious monarchies, Papists, and the Inquisition. Spanish itself was also racially and geographically obnoxious, a Mediterranean language with close proximity to Moorish African savagery, spoken by a people whose blood was mixed with Arab, Jewish, and (in the Americas) African and Indian blood: any way you grabbed it, you came up with sensuality and sinfulness. A language of a people so dark, impure, and physically expressive could produce nothing spiritual and even less intellectual.

In this aspect Ezra Pound exhibited every sign of what Williams perceived as a Puritan attitude toward Spanish. Despite Pound's facility with languages and his literary concern for the voice of the tribe, he disdained Spanish. His giving Williams the first two volumes of a four-volume set of Spanish poetry amounted to a symbolic insult. He had no use for it; it spoke to Carlos. Williams knew this and added it to a quiet *jaiba* ledger sheet. In his essay "A Letter" to Reed Whittemore, Williams included the parenthetical remark "(read your Spanish lit.: 'just savages' E. P.)" (*SE* 239).

Pound's attitude toward Carlos' cultural roots, of course, also expressed itself toward Elena Hoheb. When visiting the Williams home, his conversation was only with "the Englishman," harboring no curiosity about Elena: "He let her live," Williams writes in *The Autobiography*. Pound's remark to Williams to place less stress on his mother's influence and more on "the Englishman" was not literary advice. Pound was simply urging Williams to purge that half of him that Pound disliked. Imperialism and colonialism are towers erected on a foundation of such attitudes. It would be difficult to imagine Pound's Fascist leanings without its basic ingredients:

> Is Germany's bestiality, in detail
> like certain racial traits,
> any more than a reflection of the world's
>
> evil? Take a negative, Ezra Pound
> for example, and see
> how the world impressed itself
> there.

("The Mirrors," CPII 139–140)

Pound's arrogance toward Elena and her heritage can be measured by the degree to which it compelled Williams to beat him out and prove him wrong, which he ultimately did with the help of the very Spanish poetry that Pound had cast off in the two volumes he gave Williams (see Chapter 5).

Williams' resentment of Pound for his deprecating attitude comes out in appropriately Spanish *conceptista* ploys. In *The Great American Novel,* he invented a vindictive conversation with "Aemilius," in which Spanish is used as a symbol:

> *Now then Aemilius, what is European consciousness composed of?—Tell me in one word.*—Rien, rien, rien! *It is at least very complicated. Oh very.*
>
> *You damned jackass. What do you know about Europe? Yes, what in Christ's name do you know? Your mouth is a sewer, a cloaca.*
>
> (*I* 174)

"Aemilius," derived from the Amelian Way that leads northwest from Rome, is Ezra Pound, who is being dished out what he had served. Williams rhetorically asks to know "in one word" a definition of European consciousness, then sardonically provides the answer in a morphologically ambiguous word: *rien,* which can be read as French, "nothing," or as Spanish (minus the accent), "they laugh." Making the two languages inseparable in this context, of course, is intended to make Pound's esteeming one over the other look foolish. The ambiguous "It" is indeed "at least very complicated." To sustain the insult, Williams then asks "What do you know about Europe?" This was his riposte to Pound's rhetorical question in his letter (reacting to *Al Que Quiere*) that Williams had earlier published in the prologue to *Kora:* "And America? What the h—l do you a blooming foreigner know about the place" (*I* 11). Finally, Williams comes to the end of this counterattack with another morphological ambiguity, calling Pound's mouth a "sewer," then adding the redundant "cloaca," a word simultaneously English and Spanish, from the Latin, biological jargon denoting *the posterior part of the intestinal tract of some animals.*

Williams knew that Pound's prejudice merely reflected the broader mainstream consciousness, which placed Hispanic culture outside the "catalogue." In a spirit of rebellion, he therefore brazenly flaunted Spanish in his early books. Among these the most brazen was *Al Que Quiere! A Book of Poems* (1917), written during or immediately after the years that

Williams (Kore) was in "Hell." (Williams' title *Kora in Hell* was obviously also influenced by Rimbaud's title *A Season in Hell*, as one can also find stylistic parallels and a similar intention to announce a break with a former life. The fact of Rimbaud's influence would not be contradicted by acknowledging that Williams also read into the title his own private metaphor.) Besides the bilingual title, the epigraph was in Spanish, by Rafael Arévalo Martínez:

> *Había sido un arbusto desmedrado que prolonga sus filamentos hasta encontrar el humus necesario en una tierra nueva [sic]. Y cómo me nutría. Me nutría con la beatitud con que las hojas trémulas de clorófila se extienden al sol; con la beatitud con que una raíz encuentra un cadáver en descompositión [sic]; con la beatitud con que los convalecientes dan sus pasos vacilantes en las mañanas de primivera [sic], bañadas de luz; . . .*
>
> *(Al Que Quiere!* n.p.)

> *It had been a wasted shrub that stretches its filaments until it finds the necessary humus in a new land. And how it nourished me! It fed me with the beatitude with which tremulous chlorophyll leaves extend to the sun; with the beatitude with which a root finds a decomposing cadaver; with the beatitude with which those who convalesce take their halting steps on spring mornings bathed in sunlight; . . .*

The epigraph celebrates Williams' discovery of a poetic "new land" in which his bicultural, subterranean soul can flower—as Bill explained to Heal about the poem "Sub Terra," but without alluding to his bicultural soul. That "new land" was a zone of balance between his two spirits, an image that evokes his own private image from *corazón*/Kora-zone, from which flowered both his American ideal and his poetic style. Once that shrub finds the "necessary humus," Kora emerges, endowing new life.

Several poems in *Al Que Quiere* have titles in Spanish, among them "El Hombre." Years later, in an interview with John W. Gerber and Emily M. Wallace, Williams explains that poem's title, confirming the spirit of rebellion in which it was chosen:

> *"El Hombre," because I was sick and tired of French titles. You know how the arty person loves to talk French? . . . Whether he can talk French or not, he always has to use a French term, that shows that he's smart, I suppose. Well, in order to change that around, I thought*

Spanish was a good language too, a very much neglected language
since Longfellow and well, . . . Washington Irving! Yes. Irving in his
"Alhambra" and Longfellow, they started off in Spanish.

(Wagner 23–24)

Not mentioned here, of course, as demonstrated in Chapter 1, is that the
title "El Hombre" also signaled a duplicity that Williams preferred to encode. But it is significant that he forthrightly declares Spanish "a good
language too," and explicitly justifies his using it, exhibiting an attitude
that wholly contradicts the posturing in his portrayal of his linguistic formation in *The Autobiography.*

According to Bill, as he grew up Spanish indeed did surround him, but
did not actually touch him:

Spanish and French were the languages I heard habitually while I was
growing up. Mother could talk very little English when I was born,
and Pop spoke Spanish better, in fact, than most Spaniards. But Pop
spoke English too, and as time went on one of my happiest memories
of him was when he would sometimes read to us in the evening. Those
were the marvelous days!

(*A* 15)

After saying that "Spanish and French" were the languages he "heard
habitually while growing up," he quickly sidetracks the reader to Pop,
"who spoke English too," and whose skill at Spanish represented an
achievement and not a stigma. Also noteworthy, "Mother" (whom in at
least one letter he addressed as "Mamy," an Anglicized spelling of the
Spanish "Mami"), is only indirectly identified as the speaker of both Spanish and French. Throughout *The Autobiography,* Elena's language is assumed, as if generally understood from her "foreigner" origins, the details of which are also revealed circuitously. Exemplary of his handling of
Elena, here Bill tangentially informs us that she spoke "little English,"
then proceeds to focus on his father, heightening the distraction with the
temporarily deceptive syntax suggesting that he spoke Spanish even better than she: "and Pop spoke Spanish better, in fact, than most Spaniards."

But by telling us the languages he "heard" at home, Williams was
bending the facts; the household was Spanish-speaking. In *Yes, Mrs. Williams,* Carlos rectifies:

My father spoke Spanish quite as easily as he spoke English; . . . Spanish was the language spoken in the household except by Mrs. Wellcome, my father's mother, . . . So that as children my brother and I heard Spanish constantly spoken about us. A steady flow of West Indians, South Americans, and other speakers of the Spanish language came to visit us, to stay sometimes the entire winter if it so fitted their fancy or the necessity of the case.

(*YM* 4)

That steady flow of Spanish-speakers included people with surnames like Hazel and Dodd, whose names in *The Autobiography* suggest they were purely English, but who were actually Caribbean bilinguals like his father. Even his grandmother, who we were told spoke a "pig Spanish" and who symbolizes Bill's English legacy in *The Autobiography* and "The Wanderer," over the years began to manifest a confluence of her dual cultural histories. As previously noted, after the better part of a lifetime in the Spanish Caribbean, her Cockney accent mixed with Spanish, so the final order to her grandson to stop inquiring about her past was made in Spanish: "*Cessa!*" Spanish obviously was not a symbolic language in Williams' past; it buzzed vitally around him from his birth, and through much of his life. Williams quotes her to imagistically encode once more his true linguistic background.

We recall that in his interview with Gerber and Wallace, published in 1950 and thus predating *The Autobiography*, Williams had already suggested that in fact Spanish was his first language as a child in a Spanish-speaking home of a newly arrived immigrant family:

We've dropped it in our day, curiously enough, but my parents spoke Spanish, preferable to English, and my brother and I heard it and understood it because they said things in Spanish that they didn't want us to understand.

(Wagner 24)

Again, the characteristic contradiction: "We've dropped it" suggests the entire family did, when he immediately tells us that his parents continued to speak it, "preferable to English." The "We" referred to both Williams and his brother, but ambiguously also repeats his penchant for circumventing the "I." So what he was saying is that after his initially speaking the household language, he adopted the local language, the pattern in keeping with children from bilingual households in the United States. For, once the pieces of Bill's politic, diffuse, artful biography are rearranged, his upbringing simply reflects the generic linguistic experience of generations of U.S. Latin Americans.

William Carlos perceived the incompatibilities of his two cultures as epitomized in their antagonistic attitudes toward sex. Against the squeamish sexuality of his Anglo American identity, his Latin American identity offered an antithetical openness toward the human body. Consequently, Williams' personae imaged and advocated competing sexual attitudes, a counterpoint most sharply manifested when Bill was at his most ingratiating. In "Adam," we recall, William George was depicted as a cultured gentleman tempted by the base, sensual Latin world through which duty supposedly dragged him, and in conversations with Heal, Bill portrayed himself as someone too prudish to actually touch. On the other hand, in *The Autobiography* his namesake uncle is characterized as having "an amorous disposition" (*A* 314). Elena, we are eventually told, was a flirtatious woman who attracted admiring men and "enjoyed telling one or another of the salty stories" (*YM* 36) connected with Quevedo. In "Against the Weather," to illustrate that Spanish literature confronts reality squarely, Williams highlights Quevedo for his scatological and sexual directness.

Again, as with his biculturalism, Williams' use of sexual attitude as a cultural demarcator is not peculiar to him, that border being a commonplace routinely joked about among non-European "others"—U.S. Latin Americans, African Americans, and immigrants from Latin America and the Mediterranean—when comparing themselves to Northern Europeans and Anglo Americans. Conversely, the Anglo's stereotypes of European Latins, Africans, and Latin Americans are, in the main, equally characterized by sexual hyperbole. In a 1988 interview in *Vanity Fair*, to illustrate, John Updike exhibited a Puritan atavism when he admitted to James Atlas of his awareness of the "vitality" of "these others":

> *Updike's protagonists have never had a lot of patience for blacks and Jews and women (and Roger Lambert is no exception). "I'm aware of race," Updike says. "I'm aware of myself as a Wasp who sees himself being drowned by the vitality of these others."*[2]

Updike, of course, was implicitly appealing to the sexual stereotype of "those others," whose vitality and visibility must also apply to the writings through which in part, since the sixties, "those others" had become nationally visible. That new non-mainstream literature had as an antecedent Williams' own celebration of the spoken idiom, a root that flowered in the Beats, who had also taken much from African American oral tradition. Despite that literary framework, minority writings were popularly associated with raw energy and performance art. Worse yet, the "politically correct" notion that true minority voices spoke *from the gut,* exclusively in spontaneous street talk, established a neo-romantic, doubled-edged standard that also provided a subtle basis for censorship of minority writing *from the mind,* which the left viewed as politically suspect and compromised, and the right continued to see as irrelevant to the general literary discourse.

At the heart of this latter-day convention were the contrary sexual attitudes by which Anglos and Others defined each other in this pluralistic society. This attitudinal counterpoint within Williams translated itself in the innocent, moral Bill's associating sexual imagery with "Spanish" or using sexual imagery to encode some contribution from his "Spanish" roots. In *Paterson,* for instance, except for a reference in the context of the Spanish Civil War, Williams' allusion to Lorca focuses sexually on the young girl in the play *The Love of Don Perlimplín:*

> —the first phase,
> Lorca's *The Love of Don Perlimplín,*
>   the young girl
>   no more than a child
>   leads her aged bridegroom
>   innocently enough
>   to his downfall—

—at the end of the play (she was a hot little bitch but nothing unusual—today we marry women who are past their prime, Julie was 13 and Beatrice 9 when Dante first saw her).

Love's whole gamut, the wedding night's promiscuity in the girl's mind, her determination not to be left out of the party, as a moral gesture, if ever there was one

(P 208)

In Book Five of *Paterson*, Gilbert Sorrentino's quoted letter, describing
his experience in a Spanish-speaking land, continues this sexual motif:

> ... *The whores grasping for your genitals, faces almost pleading* ...
> *"two dolla, two dolla" till you almost go in with the sheer brute desire*
> *straining at your loins, the whiskey and the fizzes and the cognac in*
> *you till a friend grabs you* ... *"no* ... *to a real house, this is shit." A*
> *reel house, a real house?* Casa real? Casa de putas?
>
> (*P* 214)

In the story "The Sailor's Son," the Spanish-named Manuel is a young
man who is caught literally "in the hay" with a nameless male friend
whom he had "known from the other side" (*FD* 21–25). And from that
same collection, even more telling is the transparently autobiographical
"A Descendant of Kings," whose title evokes the prince in "Philip and
Oradie" and underscores the heritage theme. In this story, the protagonist
Stuart (as in the kings) or "Stewie" (as in "stew") was an imagined rebirth
of Williams. Opportunely his mother "died following his birth" and he
was raised by his English grandmother. Williams' own maternal grandfather, whom in *Yes, Mrs. Williams* Elena describes as a great dancer, is
evoked in Stuart's possessing "a great sense of rhythm," which allowed
him to pick up a ukulele left behind by "the summer people," a suggestion
that these people were of a hot kind. But the story separates Stuart's
"rhythm" from his "Scotch" mother, whose only contribution is said to be
that she "endowed the boy with the frame of a bull," an image echoed in
Stuart's run-in with a real bull. Thus, Stuart's maternal inheritance is
compared to the Spanish symbol of sexual power, the bull.

In addition to its sexual prowess, his body possessed a sense of rhythm
and "long powerful fingers" that soon learned to play both the ukulele
and the bodies of women, the uke being a small guitar, another Spanish
symbol. (By contrast, his English grandmother, implicitly the antithesis of
Spanish, kept the girls at bay.) His father, from his speaking Spanish, possessed "a *simpatico*—in dealing with Spanish-speaking peoples," a detail
with no other function in the story except that it summarizes William
George and symbolically endows Stuart's father with Spanish sensuality.

Stewie's mastering the musical instrument led to his discovering his
ability to master his sexual one. The "girls" came to him and, of course,
"they came":

*The girls almost pulled him apart. He had a room of his own back of
the main shack now and his door was open day and night, figuratively
and literally. . . . I don't think it would be possible to exaggerate the
number of girls of all ages that prostrated themselves before, about
and beside Stewie in those years. A magnificent physique, skill to
dance, swim, sing and nothing in the world to worry about. Let them
come. And they came, a hundred or more as time went by.*

(*FD* 66)

Learning to play the uke, he barely survived a winter at his grandmother's
summer resort until saved by a "Jew lawyer" named Mr. Stone, who convinced Stuart to leave his grandmother's freezing home and come to his.
(Note Bill's playing the ingratiating anti-Jew, balancing his need to recreate Carlos in Stuart.) There, as Latins are Williams' caretakers of heat,
Stuart "cared for" Stone's furnace. "To sum it up, he had come through.
And he had come through with the mastery of the ukulele to his credit"
(*FD* 65). He had survived his "weather" with his sensuality intact, a sense
of triumph that parallels the one in *Kora in Hell.*

Stuart's story extends the chain of things, beyond heat and sexual
prowess, that Williams associated with Spanish. The ukulele, a variant on
the lyre, here symbolizes music, which Williams also equated with poetry.
The story, then, only reiterates what Williams told Heal, that poetry and
sex were "allied" in his mind:

*If poetry had to be written, I had to do it my own way. It all happened
very quickly. Somehow poetry and the female sex were allied in my
mind. The beauty of girls seemed the same to me as the beauty of a
poem. I knew nothing at all about the sexual approach but I had to do
something about it. I did it in the only terms I knew, through poetry.*

(*IWW* 14)

Where Williams could be said to have been confused about his identity
was in not knowing how to present himself as a sexual being in the world.
Bill was self-conscious about possessing a demonic sexual drive that
shamed him, that was figuratively and literally *foreign* to him. Unable to
freely explore and touch the magnetic female beauty, he resorted to
translating his desires into poetry. That at least was how Williams wanted
us to see he had reconciled his conflict, a picture open to question, coin-

ciding as it does with his equally unconvincing Puritan picture of William
George as a sexual abstainer. Bill as the model of abstinence also serves
to vindicate Bill the secret cyclical sinner and penitent (Bill publicly moralizing to Carlos about his kind).

In his subsequent reiteration to Heal of his sex/poetry equation Williams struggles to find a balance between saying all he sexually feels and
keeping what he says within Bill's literary parameters:

> *Two dominating forces had ruled, were still ruling me: the need to
> learn all I could about poetry, and the need to learn all I could about
> life which isn't any more poetry than prose.*

> *This was a period in my life when I was tremendously interested in
> women. I had never been a roué and women remained an enigma; no
> two had the same interest for me; they were all different. I was conse-
> quently interested in too many of them and trying to find out about
> them all. What made them tick? It was a fascinating experimentation. I
> would draw back from them and try to write it down. When you think
> of the people dead from the neck up, ossifying life for themselves, not
> daring to call their lives their own, keeping up a continual lie. Not in-
> terested in sex—oh yeah? All I can say is man is only* hors de combat
> *if he is such a poor specimen he* couldn't *be of interest to* anyone. *I'll
> die before I've said my fill about women. I feel I am saying flattering
> things about them but they won't take it. After all there are only two
> kinds of us, men and women, the he and the she of it, yet some antago-
> nism, some self-defense seems to rise out of a woman when a man tries
> to understand her. I am so terribly conscious of a woman—I become
> self-conscious—too aware that she is there ready to tell me I've got her
> all wrong. But let's talk about poetry!*

>   (*IWW* 64–65)

Whether or not Williams did indeed contain his sexual drives to vent
them in writing, in trying to explain his equating of poetry and sex he
begins to speak in two conflicting voices that elbow each other to remain
in the foreground. The earthy remark about being dead from the neck
down is cleansed ("from the neck up") and left confused:

> *When you think of the people dead from the neck up, . . . keeping up a
> continual lie. Not interested in sex—oh yeah?*

Bill's prudish reasoning, of course, says more than it intends: to identify poetry with sex also justifies one's translating sexual experiences into
poetry, and that truth would appear to be Williams' true conflict, reflected
in his shifting voices. The point here is that Williams' struggle with sexuality was another expression of his Bill/Carlos dichotomy. As manifes-
tations of his two personae, the two dominating forces in his life were
therefore "allied" in his mind, meaning fused into one composite force.
Poetry, then, was for Williams what the uke was for Stewie, synonymous
with his penis, the key to the mysteries of the female. That means that
because Carlos was his Dionysian drive, then too Carlos was poetry, ever
lusting after the beauty of the female sex, which included its epitome,
Elena and her sensual spirit, whose house was Spanish. Ultimately Spanish too was synonymous with the essence of poetry. To write his poems in
English, then, Williams had to allow the ever-aroused dark Carlos to secretly incite the pink-faced Bill's imagination, then just as secretly have
Bill translate Carlos into English.

That a chapter in *The Autobiography* is titled "Translation" attests to
translation's contributing to the person "we ourselves have been." According to that chapter, Williams' first attempts were "rather upon prose
than the poems." The prose in question was most likely his collaboration with his father in translating Rafael Arévalo Martínez's story. He
also translated, for example, Lope de Vega's verse drama *Nuevo Mundo*.[5]
He also says he he that he "tried" to translate a few poems from the "El
Romancero":

> ... *there are lyrics in the* Romancero *of distinguished beauty. We have
> scarcely touched them. I tried to bring over a few when I was just be-
> ginning to find myself, but I was not ready for them.*

(A 349)

These translations, published in the original edition of *The Tempers*, pre-
served the rhyme and were essentially imitations of English romantic poetry. Two of them were reworked and later published with two new translations from "El Romancero" in *Adam & Eve in the City* (1936).

The "Romancero" originals were from the two volumes that Pound
had given him, *Poesías Selectas Castellanas,* edited by Manuel Josef Quintana, part of a four-volume history of Spanish poetry, the same one that
Williams told Edith Heal was an anthology of "Spanish Romantic Poetry."

Judging from the underlined words (in pencil) and glosses in the margins,[4] he read the two volumes assiduously. That of the breadth of poetry in Quintana's anthology he chose those poems is significant. The four original translations, important because Williams "was just beginning to find" himself, were pastorals, and intoned Williams' sense of isolation, of being "unfused" from mainstreams, whether urban, artistic, or cultural:

> Although you do your best to regard me
> With an air of seeming offended,
> Never can you deny, when all's ended,
> Calm eyes, that you *did* regard me.

("I," *CPI* 12)

> Through never a moment
> I've known how to live lest
> All my thoughts but as one pressed
> You-ward for their concernment.
> May God send chastisement
> If in this I belie me
> And if it truth me
> My own little green eyes.
> Ah, Heaven be willing
> That you think of me somewise.

I"II," *CPI* 13)

> Each of you is telling
> How evil my chance is
> The wind among the branches,
> The mountains in their welling
> To every one telling
> You were happy to see.
> Now I am absent from you
> All are slandering me.

("III," *CPI* 14)

The fourth sounds like an imaginary dialogue of the poet with the fleeing lost prince:

> Although thou with a sleep art wresting
> 'Tis rightful though bringst it close,

That of the favour one meeting shows
An hundred may hence be attesting.
'Tis fitting too though shouldst be mindful
That the ease which we lose now, in kind, full
Ere they take thee sleeping;
Be up—away, my treasure!

("IV," *CPI* 15)

In retrospect, Williams spoke of them (to Heal) as having little merit. In the "Translation" chapter of *The Autobiography*, therefore, the specific poems from "El Romancero" pass unmentioned. He does go on to mention, however, his translations of the Arévalo Martínez story, Quevedo's novella *The Dog and the Fever*, and "poems from Loyalist Spain," which he also does not specify. These were Miguel Hernández's "Sentado sobre los Muertos" and the ballads "Juanelo de Laviano" by Rafael Beltrán Longroño and "Juan Montoya" by Mariano del Alcazar, the latter two appearing in the anthology . . . *and Spain Sings Fifty Loyalist Ballads Adapted by American Poets*.[5]

"Translation" also contains a paragraph on Lorca and Góngora, curious to be found there because Williams never translated either poet. One discounts, of course, an occasional line Williams might have translated to borrow. In "All That Is Perfect in Woman," for instance, he addresses Lorca, subsequently using the Spaniard's famous refrain from his "Llanto por Ignacio Sánchez Mejías" ("Lament for Ignacio Sánchez Mejías"), which lamented the bullfighter's death in the ring *a los cinco de la tarde*, "At five in the afternoon" (*CPII* 218). Williams' discussion of Lorca in this translation context, then, was not intended to mean that Williams had rendered Lorca's work into English. In his 1939 essay "Federico García Lorca," Williams had already announced a kinship with Lorca, whom he saw as descending from Góngora, a serious early influence on Williams himself; Lorca was also thus an inheritor of Góngora's "line."

So when in "Translation" Williams argued that by learning from Lorca and Góngora "an almost ideal opportunity" exists "for trying out new modes," what he meant was the translating of their techniques and spirit into English, a translation of structures as well as idioms. His claim to having done "nothing yet to carry this work on" is therefore ambiguous and open to interpretation. He hadn't, as noted earlier, literally translated these two specific poets into English, but in the sense of translating their structures—or their spirit—he had done considerable, because translation from the Spanish was an ongoing activity in his hidden core/Kore. To begin with, translation saved Williams from *sounding* foreign-hearted to his country. For, according to his own sense of things, what made his heart foreign had nothing to do with citizenship or nationality. Williams equated identity with language; foreignness signified being informed by a language other than English. To this point, Linda Wagner's observations concerning his stories are also applicable to his life:

> *For Williams, any person's identity rested on his spoken language.*
> *Many of his short stories open with a character speaking: we hear the*
> *words with no introduction or setting given.*
>
> (Wagner xiii)

In *The Autobiography,* for example, he summarizes his stopover at Ciudad Trujillo, Dominican Republic: "Here only a moment. Spanish again" (*A* 314). Because language was the key, his father, who refused to become a U.S. citizen, was never problematic as a "foreigner," despite the occasional allusions to his being foreign, English, and cold. Elena, on the other hand, was congenitally foreign, despite the Jones Act of 1917, which imposed U.S. citizenship on Puerto Rico and, by extension, her. Beyond the paperwork that both his parents had to negotiate as legal residents and beyond his own natural birthright as an American, the single most important thing that liberated Williams' consciousness from the stigma of Carlos' foreignness was Bill's English, which was synonymous with possessing his country:

> *When I was inclined to write poems, I was very definitely an American*
> *kid, confident of himself and also independent.*
>
> (*IWW* 14)

Insofar as he spoke English and had dropped Spanish as a child, he would write as an "American," which by convention relegates non-Anglo cultures to being *heritages,* residing in a mythically reserved place in the past even though they continue to inform the present.

By distancing himself from Spanish, characterizing it as "romantic," Bill invoked that convention. Simultaneously, of course, he also characterized himself as the antithesis of romantic. Near the end of his career, despite his several adopted Latin alter images and life experiences that proved the contrary—Gris, Picasso, Quevedo, the Spanish Civil War,

Lorca, Spanish realism (as celebrated in "Against the Weather"), and his own recognition of Elena's shocking, graphically descriptive side— Williams as Bill was still repeating his stock line (to Edith Heal) that "Spanish still seems to me synonymous with romantic" (*IWW* 17). Consequently, he also gave as the source of the "Romancero" translations in *The Tempers* an anthology of Spanish "Romantic" literature:

> *Ezra found an old copy of lyrical poems, out of Spanish Romantic Literature, and knowing that Spanish was spoken in my home, gave them to me. I think most of them were anonymous, the folklore sort of thing.*
>
> (*IWW* 16)

Although by now Williams' memory may have been slipping, his answer was a gross distortion of his contact with that anthology, one of the most influential events of his career (see Chapter 5). But this distortion was in character with the reasons that he gave in the chapter "Translation" for his interest in translating from the Spanish. There he framed his attraction to Spanish in the justification that it was a "relief from the classic mood of French and Italian":

> *I have always wanted to do some translations from Spanish. It was my mother's native language as well as one which my father spoke from childhood. But more than that the language has a strong appeal to me, temperamentally, as a relief from the classic mood of both French and Italian.*
>
> (*A* 349)

Williams had also translated from the French poems by Nicolas Calas, and Yvon Goll's "Jean Sans Terre" (*CPII*), but he didn't think of himself as intimately involved with French or of its significantly contributing to his formation. This explains his overlooking those translations in *The Autobiography*. Spanish was his other language, but its importance to him had to be tempered by a gesture of only casual interest, as is evident in the chapter "Translation," in which he preambles the brief summary of his translations from Spanish with an expression of deference to Anglo sensibilities on the superiority of English:

> *Spanish is not, in the same sense to which I refer, a literary language. . . .*
> *It isn't as rich as English in the multiplicity of its achievements, . . ."*
>
> (*A* 349)

And yet Spanish "has a place of its own, an independent place very sympathetic to the New World":

> *This independence, this lack of integration with our British past gives*
> *us an opportunity, facing Spanish literature, to make new appraisals,*
> *especially in attempting translations, which should permit us to use our*
> *language with unlimited freshness. In such attempts we will not have*
> *to follow precedent but can branch off into a new diction, adapting*
> *new forms, even discovering new forms in our attempts to find accu-*
> *rate equivalents for the felicities of the past. That at least has been my*
> *thought—especially in attacking Spanish poems.*

(A 349)

All this zigzagging simply to extol Spanish also distracts from another "conceptualist" discourse going on, hinging on a nuance. For in Williams' proffering that his interest in Spanish resulted less because it "was my mother's native language" and more as a relief "from the classic mood of French and Italian," he was revealing only to conceal: while the search for "a relief" may also be true in the sense of respite, Spanish afforded him the opportunity to *stand out* in relief. For at some point between his childhood "dropping" of Spanish, his picking it up again in order to read the Spanish poets in the Quintana anthology, and his beginning to translate, Carlos began to see his foreign heart as a fountain of originality and Bill began to admit to himself that he too was in some measure a translation. This is essentially what Williams was saying to his architect brother in a conversation recorded in "The Basis of Faith in Art."[6]

> *I always knew that I was I, precisely where I stood and that nothing*
> *could make me accept anything that had no counterpart in myself by*
> *which to recognize it. I always said to myself that I did not speak En-*
> *glish, for one thing, and that should be the basis for a beginning, that I*
> *spoke a language that was my own and that I would govern it accord-*
> *ing to my necessities and not according to unrelated traditions the*
> *necessity for whose being had long passed away. English is full of*
> *such compunctions which are wholly irrelevant for a man living as*
> *I am today but custom makes it profitable for us to be bound by them.*
> *Not me.*

(SE 177)

The above citation also contains an ambiguous rhetorical device that is a key Williams signature. What began as a Carlos-admission that "I" did not speak English (or at least not the English that everyone else spoke because he spoke "a language that was my own") is converted into the *English English versus American English* dichotomy. If that latter distinction was what he originally had in mind, then he really couldn't claim an advantage over any other American speaker of English. We must read this "conversation by design" for its unity: his personal sense of starting out foreign-tongued, literally or figuratively, gave him an insight into the Americanness of American English and the degree to which it would be choked by English English's literary traditions. Against that stifling European line, America's spirit had to shine through, if his country was also going to absorb his unique interpretation of its language, a translation of himself. His being a translation gave him that mingling advantage over those so-called Americans whose minds and hearts were still in Europe, who conserved English's divisive "compunctions which are wholly irrelevant for a man living as I am today." Those compunctions and traditions—"the necessity for whose being had long passed away"—ambiguously refer to both literary traditions and the social tradition of not mingling, with the reference to "for a man living as I am" actually meaning *for me*. So that William Carlos may thrive, a truly American English had to first win out because "nothing could make me accept anything that had no counterpart in myself by which to recognize it."

The personal point that Williams was making in "The Basis of Faith in Art," a point characteristically *interknit* with a broader aesthetic proposition, was that only art could properly translate into timeless and universal imagery the ephemeral particulars of his background. Thus the "best designer" possessed such a profound insight into lives as to be able to *interpret* that vision into technique:

> *He with the most profound insight into the lives of the people and the widest imaginative skill in its technical interpretation—or any part thereof.*

(*SE* 195)

His having to be a translator of his biculturalism afforded Williams the opportunity to become a "best designer": in a wondrous mingled America in which purist, latter-day Puritans were mere ethnic tourists, he trans-

lated the true American spirit into an idiom understood by those mis-
guided Americans. In other, more personal terms, through his "best design" Williams intended to make his "townspeople" see in his work the
very ingredient that their conventions about his Carlos background made
them presume it lacked: themselves.

Williams' translation of deep structure, the poem under his poem in English, is what he called an imaginary translation. That epithet, which he
only used once, in the appropriately parenthetical subtitle to his poem
"Hymn to Love Ended (*Imaginary Translation from the Spanish*),"[7]
makes visible a stealth technique that Williams used often.

The curious subtitle "*Imaginary Translation*" raises the question of
why he called the poem a translation from the Spanish, as it is simply
another of his poems whose central metaphor is spring:

> As from an illness, as after drought
> the streams released to flow
> filling the fields with freshness
> the birds drinking from every twig
> and beasts from every hollow—
> bellowing, singing of the unrestraint
> to colors of a waking world.

                                                                                (*CPI* 392)

The Spanish in the subtitle appears to be Bill's justification for the poem's
pastoral, romantic quality (which it shares with his "El Romancero"
translations), and equally to underscore his stress on the sexuality of
regeneration:

> Through what extremes of passion
> had you come, Sappho, to the peace
> of deathless song?

The birds and beasts and "all / who will besides" (note the pun on will),
who are enervated at springtime, thus belong to "this company" of Villon,
Shakespeare, Dante, Goethe, Li Po—all poets who were revitalized to
translate into poetry their sadness when "love is ended" (*CPII* 392).

The "*Imaginary Translation*" subtitle also suggests that because
"Hymn" (a *conceptista* pun, *him* to love ended) appears to be just another
of Williams' poems, we can infer that some of his other poems that seem

to have nothing to do with Spanish are, in some manner or to some extent, also imaginary translations. This reasoning is further supported by another poem explicitly introduced as a translation, "Translation." As in "Hymn to Love Ended," the "Translation" in the title acts as a lens through which we should read the poem, signaling and justifying the poem's being romantic, and therefore telling the reader that Carlos is the culprit who brings it out of him. Unlike "Hymn," however, the title "Translation" is also thematically warranted, as the poem is literally about translation, specifically of unspoken love words into "loving performance," which the poem equates to the giving of a flower's fragrance and ultimately to the writing of the poem:

> There is no distinction in the encounter, Sweet
>   there is no grace but perfume
> to the rose but from us, which give it
>   by our loving performance.

(CPII 198)

In this performance the "caresses" are a translation of "a word spoken":

>   By them
> the violet wins its word of love, no mere
>   scent but a word spoken,
>
> a unique caress. . . .

Thus a gesture of warmth is equivalent to a word. We are, of course, not told outright that the word is in Spanish; we simply know it is a word in the language of sexuality.

Because one act of love is essentially all acts of love and the genital flower all flowers, one's translating a word to performance releases in gesture love's essential "fragrance," from all flowers. They include, in backward rebirth, Williams' wife-flower Florence, the "violet" Viola Baxter, and the "rose," Raquel Helene Rose. Extending the conceit, this single essence in different erotic loves is the essential fragrance of poetry itself, which is captured in translation:

> That is the reason I wake
>   before dawn and crush my pillow:
> because of the strangeness of that flower
> whose petals hide from me

more than should be spoken, of love
   uniting all flowers beyond
caresses, to disclose that fragrance which is
   Our Mistress whom we serve.

(CPII 198–199)

A lingering question does remain: who is the "Sweet" whom he is addressing? Florence or Elena? That "Sweet" appears to be all encounters in one and therefore ultimately the true "Mistress," poetry itself. It is her sweetness, extracted by translating the unspoken word to caresses, the idiom of sexuality, which the poet then translates into language. In Williams' consistent lexicon, however, we know that the language of sexuality was Spanish, which through an act of imaginary translation he wrote in English.

"The House," an earlier poem, is another imaginary translation, giving every appearance of having been generated from the salutation in Spanish, "*Estás en tu casa*" ("You are in your house"):

The house is yours
to wander in as you please—

  . . . .
  . . . .
  . . . .

the whole house
is waiting—for you
to walk in it at your pleasure—
It is yours.

(CPI 340–341)

The visual imagery draws a highly evocative house, which has been made new, rebuilt, an external manifestation of the transformation that "we" have undergone since standing "penniless / by the hogshead of crockery." Now they have the currency and therefore possess a "new / hotwater heater and a new / gas-stove. . . ." (*CPI* 340).

The pennilessness of the owners can be interpreted as their lacking the currency (language) as they stood by a U.S. measurement (hogshead) of earthenware. Thanks to the new currency, the house itself was rebuilt with new heat sources in its core. This newly warmed American house exists to "please," a word said twice and in the allomorph "pleasure,"

hinting at its offering sensuality. But the dominant pleasure is one of fusion, the wholeness of the house, as well as the fusion of the owner with
the readers invited to walk through it and the poem at their pleasure. For
the poem is the house that is yours, and you the reader are its guest, a
house's purpose being not unlike a poem's. In a conversation with his
architect brother in "The Basis of Faith in Art," Williams reiterates this
parallel:

> *Houses are to live in, that's one of the finest things about architecture.*
> *You build houses, for people. Poems are the same.*

(SE 177–178)

"The House" translates into word images the "fragrance" of fusion that
the poem must have, that America must have. That's why the house had
to be rebuilt, with a new furnace and gas stove, to effectively warm it
against the Puritan winter.

In sum, the imaginary translation technique is intrinsic to Williams'
style. Entire poems, as noted above, may have been conceived in translation, while transient, less elaborate performances of imaginary translations are evident in isolated moments of writing, in words such as the
previously discussed neologism "disman" or "interknit." The neologism
"interknit" could have been a variant on the flat "interweave," but more
likely appears to have sprung from a novel transliteration of *entretejido*,
literally *entre* ("inter-") and *tejido* ("woven" or "knitted"), one of whose
more common denotations in Spanish is to insert words into another,
separate text. Thus, this imaginary translation illustrates the poem's point
about Williams' relying on secret sources: "interknit with the unfathomable ground / where we walk daily. . . . (*CPII* 68).

Williams' most extensive work of imagery translation is *Yes, Mrs. Williams,* which as discussed earlier from an artistic perspective, is a composition on the influences of Elena's speech on Williams' writing style. In
that book, we find examples of Elena's accented spoken translations (her
imaginary translations), his own narrative explanations (his imaginary
translations), his aural recreations of her Spanish, and, finally, of her suspect English, suspicious in that we cannot tell for certain if it had been
conceived and spoken as English or rendered as English by Williams.
Even Williams' narrative, for example, while appearing to be his, is a hybrid of his English and Elena's English or his translation of it, samples of
which Williams adjusted in order to extract some imagistic value or

simply to bring it closer to his English. In summary, in that book one
cannot tell which samples of language were originally spoken or written
in English and which in Spanish—by either Elena or Williams.

On the other hand, defining each voice is really unimportant, as it
would seem that Williams' intention was the creation of a single composite voice, a style rooted in the recreation of her speech, which was graphic
and deceptively simple:

> *No. I don't want to. Once when I was a girl they told me that if I*
> *cleaned my teeth with a cigar it would make them strong and white.*
> *So I took a cigar and rubbed them with it. Well, before breakfast.*
> *Chah! I was sick as a dog after.*
>
> *The Spanish have a saying—I must have told you,* Haciendo de tri-
> pas corazon—*that is, when you have no heart for anything, make it*
> *from your bowels.*

> (*YM* 90)

In this example, one questions if Elena's explanation of the saying is actually hers. Williams nevertheless has it flow directly out of her story to
blur the differences between subject and narrator. Similarly, one detects
that Williams has intervened when he has Elena saying things that
change the point of view: "In Puerto Rico, the natives call it *hablando
caballo*—horses' talk" (*YM* 70). What natives? She probably said *los jíba-
ros*, a distinction commonly made between the gentry and the country
folk. She might also have said "we call it." Williams suppressing Elena's
identification with Spanish in the first person is a strange pattern in the
book. For example, in another section he quotes her as saying, "Like the
Spanish say: They didn't have a place to drop dead" (*YM* 79). The common Spanish saying is accurately rendered in English, although we cannot tell if by Elena or Williams. One suspects that "Like the Spanish say"
was translated from either "*como se dice en español*" or "*como decimos en
español*," respectively "as is said in Spanish" or "as we say in Spanish."
Again, that Elena should impersonalize her translation is suspect—especially given that she hated English and identified with her language so
fiercely. On the other hand, Williams' putting in the words "Like the
Spanish say" is consistent with the editorial interventions he makes
throughout to selectively impersonalize Elena's utterances.

Other sections patently don't sound as if Elena had uttered them in

English at all, and instead appear to have been smoothly translated by Williams into English and put into her mouth:

> *I smell the stew. It makes me think of Mrs. Hope. She never could understand why Pop objected to the smell of cabbage cooking—in the house. She liked it. It smells so good, she said.*

> (*YM* 69)

Becoming Elena's mouthpiece through literal or imaginary translation was not something Williams first did in *Yes, Mrs. Williams. Kora,* early in his career, has such moments. Years later, "Elena," the second section of "Two Pendants for the Ears" (another fruit of the long period of gestation before Williams was ready to write *Yes, Mrs. Williams*), consists of a dialogue in which the two are fused in one voice—not this time in the sense of their voices being indistinguishable, but in that what Williams selects of what she says (or his translation of what she says) are lines that sound like him:

> Let me clean your
> glasses.
> They put them on my nose!
> They're trying to make a monkey
> out of me.

> (*CPII* 212)

Elena's lines above ring suspiciously as having been translated from the Spanish, but others in that poem are provably so. Notably, the diminutive in "There's a little Spanish wine" is a literal translation of "*un vinito español,*" which actually refers not to an amount but to the speaker's sweet memory of it ("*vinito*"). Williams offers us his English translation only to set up Elena's pronouncing the wine's name in Spanish, which then permits another ambiguity:

> There's a little Spanish wine,
> *pajarete*
>
> p-a-j-a-r-e-te
> But pure Spanish!

His separating the letters by hyphens doesn't quite reproduce her probably breaking down the word into phonetic syllables, but does allow for a visualization into his English letters, making a fresh image. This in turn loads the subsequent line. By using her translated "But pure Spanish!" from what was most likely her original *"Pero puro español!,"* he created an ambiguity that both plays on her saying *pajarete* in "pure Spanish" and encodedly tells the reader that this "pure Spanish" was all written in pure English. In this devious fashion, then, we are really hearing Williams' voice much more than we think, in the kind of duplicitous translating that he expanded into book form in *Yes, Mrs. Williams,* his overdue tribute to the influence of Elena's Spanish on his work.

Owing to this influence, and as demonstrated in a few instances in *Yes, Mrs. Williams,* Williams' use of translation as a writing technique was not limited to imaginary translations from Spanish to English. Elena's use of Spanish and, less often, French to either punctuate a thought or because her English failed her at the moment also worked its way into Williams' psyche, to the extent that it became a part of his style. Thus, the obverse of saying "pure Spanish" in English was the device of translating purely English thoughts into Spanish. In "Man in a Room," for instance, the solitude of the man reaches its maximum expression in the Spanish ejaculation *"Ay de mi!"* (*CPI* 123). In "January Morning" the poet pauses to observe the irony of the ferry's name:

> —and the rickety ferry-boat "Arden"!
> What an object to be called "Arden"
>
> (*CPI* 102)

Williams read the Latin etymology of the English name through the Spanish: *arden* is the present tense, third person plural form of the verb *arder* ("to burn"), so *"Arden"* means "they burn." The immediate irony of a ferry that proudly announces that its passengers burn can be taken as an allusion to crossing the river Styx, or as a private sexual joke having something to do with those who take the ferry from New York. (Manuel in "The Sailor's Son [*FD* 21] knew his New York friend from the hotly ambiguous "other side.") What is noteworthy is that Williams calls the reader's attention to the irony, presuming that his reader understands Spanish.

   This example also addresses another aspect of Spanish as an intrinsic element of his style. As noted already, Williams' aural Spanish was written exactly as he heard it in English. Whether this was intentional is difficult to assess. His father, we recall, spoke Spanish better than "most Span-iards," and became "furious" over the typos that appeared in the Spanish in *Al Que Quiere*. Was Williams' resistance to becoming literate in Spanish yet another form of rebellion? Did he aesthetically intend to sound heard and not spoken, a concession to Carlos without capitulating? Whatever the underlying motivation and his limited grammatical skills in speaking or writing it, a component of Williams' struggle with balance was his cog-nizance that Spanish remained important to him and was destined to be "interknit" into his writing language. A graphic paradigm of this kind of weaving is a segment of *Kora in Hell*, in which Williams uses both Spanish and its phonetic counterpart in English:

> *Baaaa! Ba-ha-ha-ha-ha-ha-ha!* Beba esa purga. *It is the goats of Santo Domingo talking.* Beba esa purga! *Bebeesapurga! And the answer is:* Yo no lo quiero beber! *Yonoloquierobeber!*

(*I* 75)

The difference between Spanish and Spanish as phonetically trans-lated into English forms an image that reiterates the meaning of the pas-sage. The "goats" pun on "ghosts," spirits of a Caribbean past, and liter-ally are such ghosts in memory. This pun may have been something that Elena, entranced, once said in her accented English. The goats/ghosts of Santo Domingo (the figurative, and perhaps literal, place of Williams' conception) order him to *Beba esa purga,* "Drink that purgative." Another image of the cultural "cure"? Are his Latin ghosts telling him to come clean, purge the Bill persona? But Bill doesn't glean the sense; he hears in English: "Bebeesapurga!" His answer, impersonalized as "the answer," is "I don't want to drink it," said in ungrammatical but intentionally real Spanish and then repeated phonetically in English: "Yonoloquierobeber!" The poetic result is strange new imagery, an image of the raw stage of translation through which Bill puts Carlos in order to produce the poem in English. Through this linguistic imagery, Williams translated into po-etry the interaction in himself of the sounds of his dual cultures.

That example should also clearly leave imprinted that Spanish was important to Williams as something more than ethnic symbolism. As a language of the "other," in its contrapuntal English context Spanish in-herently offered freshness, new imagery, and, as he explores in the para-graph that introduces the goats/ghosts piece, an insight into metaphysical balance:

That which is known has value only by virtue of the dark. This cannot be otherwise. A thing known passes out of the mind into the muscles, the will is quit of it, save only when set into vibration by the forces of darkness opposed to it.

(*I* 75)

This prefatory paragraph abstractly explains the concept behind the linguistic play in the goats/ghosts piece that follows it. But here Bill is foregrounded, and he obliquely admits that he is most conscious of who he is "only when set into vibration by the forces of darkness." Carlos, of course, and Spanish implicitly are the "forces of darkness" that "set into vibration" other *sub terra* evocations in *Kora in Hell.* But this involvement of Spanish happens subliminally, beyond consciousness, Bill tells us: a known thing, a lived experience, is dissolved in the anatomy and the "muscles" so that the conscious "will" (once more, a pun on "Will") is separated from the experience, which is now unconscious and distinct from Bill. What returns the experience back to consciousness, to be "known" again, are "the forces of darkness," or Carlos.

More than just new images, then, Spanish afforded a wholly different epistemology. Spanish titles therefore signal another semantic dimension to Williams' English-language poems. "Mujer" (*CPI* 78), a poem about his cat mating, also celebrates his associating Spanish with sexuality. "Con Brio" (*CPII* 11), an imitation of Quevedo, celebrates Lancelot's sexual prowess (Lance a lot). "El Hombre" encodes his hidden core, another layer to the poem. The poem "Convivio" (*CPII* 199), from the (here unaccented) preterite third person form of the verb *convivir* ("to live together"), appeals for unity among the "brotherhood" of those whose first concern is "the words," while its Spanish title implicitly adds the excluded poet Carlos, as well as other members of the "brotherhood" excluded from the "catalogue."

The title "Convivio" also encodes Williams' awareness that his Latin half heightened the liability of his being a literary outsider, leaving him exposed to the kind of *ad hominem* body blows that Pound stooped to in constantly accusing him of being a "foreigner." On the other hand, Williams' use of Spanish was emblematic of his determination not to be held back or dictated to; in his mind he wedded his foreignness and his literary newness, justifying the former by his campaigning for the latter. This marriage is discernible from his explanation to Heal on the origins of the Spanish title to his book *Al Que Quiere!:*

> *My translation of the phrase* Al Que Quiere! *is "To Him Who Wants It," and I have always associated it with a figure on a soccer field: to him who wants the ball to be passed to him. Moreover I associate it with a particular boy, older than myself, at school with me in 1898 at Chateau de Lancy near Geneva, Switzerland. He was a fine soccer player and he took me under his wing, got me on the varsity team. His name was Suares, a Spaniard, and as I was half-Spanish, there was a bond. He gave me his school cap when he left, a great honor. The phrase made me think of him, wanting the ball on the soccer field, and of myself. I was convinced nobody in the world of poetry wanted me but I was there willing to pass the ball if anyone did want it.*

> (*IWW* 19)

Williams here confesses to a preoccupation over the literary world's not accepting his poetry both for its being aesthetically different and because of its Latin cultural consciousness. One also can infer from the anecdote that, even though as Bill he played his due role in the proper circles, his own intimate awareness of being a translation of a foreign psyche is what kept him feeling foreign-hearted and on the margins of the mainstream. This very idea of his own "living together" with that other consciousness is also contained in the original Spanish title "Convivio."

So while defiant in his use of Spanish, his innate dependence on imaginary translation also left Williams concerned about being rejected for extraliterary reasons, a nagging preoccupation that was part of his "agony of self-realization" and also generally infiltrated his work. Three years before writing "Convivio," to illustrate, a similar intervention of his bilingual consciousness was the premise of "At Kenneth Burke's Place." Both poems condemn the "murder" of poets, in "Convivio" by orthodoxy, in "At Kenneth Burke's Place" by the "plotted murders" in "anthologies." "Convivio" appeals to the "brotherhood" that should come first "no matter what / our quarrels" (*CPII* 199), the surface differences provoked by the "catalogue." "At Kenneth Burke's Place" therefore attacks the "catalogue" and defends those poets glibly hated for racial ("the colored") or cultural reasons ("those who speak a private language").

But the earlier poem, containing no Spanish or the appearance of translating anything into either language, best reveals the extent to which Williams' Spanish-language consciousness and its accompanying preoccupation operate *sub terra*. In other words, the concerns vented symbolically in the Spanish title "Convivio" had already been argued in greater imagistic detail in "At Kenneth Burke's Place." While at that "place," Williams echoed the others who "glibly" said that they hated "the 'Esoteric' . . . ,'" the younger generation, "the colored (unless marketable)," and the "'private language.'" In the second stanza, however, he reflects on his posturing while being, also figuratively, *at Kenneth Burke's place* and rectifies:

> But
> the earth is also a 'private language'
> . . . .
> . . . .
> Catalogues are not its business.
> Its business, its business is
> external to anthologies, outside the
> orthodoxy of plotted murders.

> (*CPII* 107)

The poet's performance is what most matters under the skin. Like Eve, Williams offers the reader an apple, which is the earth, that "green apple smudged with /a sooty life that clings." The earth too has a "private language," and that language is "the esoteric to our dullness." And he knows of a basketful of green apples, strange other worlds, apples that are "half rotten" and yet vital and full of long-lost taste under the skin, of whose pleasures the "catalogue" had glibly deprived itself:

> There is a basketful
> of them half rotted on the half rotten
> bench. Take up one
> and bite into it. It is still good
> even unusual compared with the usual,
> as if a taste long lost and regretted
> had in the end, finally,
> been brought to life again.

> (*CPII* 107–108)

This defense of the rotten apples was, of course, a defense of himself, and by extension his secret Spanish from which he often found himself stealing to translate into his own "private language."

In both poems, then, Williams interpreted personal mission and social preoccupations in imaginary translation: in one by compressing an appeal in English for openness into a Spanish title, in the other by translating the structure of Carlos' Spanish-feelings into English. Tellingly, both poems were written soon after World War II: "At Kenneth Burke's Place" in the final months of 1946 (*NW* 516), and "Convivio" in 1949 (*CPII* 199). Thus, they both came after what Litz and MacGowan call the "turning point in his poetic life" (*CPII* xvii), the year 1939. Although Litz and MacGowan do not specify, that year marks the defeat of the Spanish Republican forces, the painful defeat that set off in Williams a second phase of reflecting on his identity.

Also in the background, in 1945 began the post–World War II Puerto Rican immigration and the backlash against it, which was daily sensationalized in the newspapers. Moreover, a postwar restlessness against segregation in the South had begun. In other words, during those years from all around Williams was aware of the divided national mood. This consciousness also signified that in his secret heart Williams, who had sided with "the others" in the Spanish Civil War, was fully cognizant of being a voice of "the other" at home. Thus no explicit Spanish-related imagery was needed in "At Kenneth Burke's Place" for us to discern that in that poem he had performed an imaginary translation into English of his visceral response to the national condition epitomized by the restlessness in the South or the treatment of Puerto Rican immigrants.

Williams' sense of himself as a translator of essences from Spanish to English and vice versa naturally contributed to his seeing the possibilities of translating into poetry the techniques of other artistic media. His opera libretto on the life of Washington is one example:

> *There is no other way than music. With recollection taking the action immediately clear of a preconceived notion of plodding fact—the mere historicity of events—an audience will be liberated to follow something else. It will look for the meaning, in a nonsequence, automatically. And this disembodied drama the music must enforce; it is the music.*
>
> (*ML* 306–307)

Painting, however, was the medium with which Williams identified: "Music doesn't mean much to me. . . . Painting is much more my meat" (Wagner 53).

Williams' interest in art expressed itself early. When thinking of a career for himself, he always thought he would be a painter. At the University of Pennsylvania, where he studied medicine, his closest college friends were either artists themselves or, like Pound, steeped in the art of their day. Christopher J. MacGowan underscores that the criticism loses sight of this incipient influence by focusing on the 1913 Armory Show as if it were the beginning, and not a continuation, of Williams' thinking as an artist:

> *Discussion of William Carlos Williams' interest in the visual arts tends to begin with the impact of the 1913 New York Armory Show upon the poet. But . . . he did not attend the show; his interest in painters and his adaptation of painterly ideas to his poetic strategy are evident in his writings before 1913; and Ezra Pound's letters of news of London remained an important influence upon his work beyond that date. A more accurate and useful sense of the visual arts background to Williams' early poetry is gained by putting aside the red herring of the Armory Show, and starting with his earliest poetry and his important early relationships with his brother Edgar, Charles Demuth, and Pound.[8]*

But Williams' artistic role models even predate MacGowan's list. To speak of Williams' earliest proclivity toward art as a career is to say that he was emulating Elena, the failed portraitist and erstwhile commercial landscapist, whom MacGowan's book does later credit in passing. James E. Breslin, who didn't see Elena's influence as creative, did attribute to Elena her son's turn toward painting:

> *Into a largely sterile environment, Mrs. Williams introduced an early and important impetus toward artistic activity. Because of her, Williams was at first interested in painting.*

(Breslin 6)

By *painting* words, Williams both evoked Elena and tried to reach her with his poetry (which she never did like), hoping to communicate with the "old woman" (from the affectionate form of address in Spanish, *vieja*):

All this—
    was for you, old woman.
I wanted to write a poem
that you could understand
For what good is it to me
if you can't understand it?

                ("January Morning," *CPI* 103)

Two other childhood models are also worth mentioning. First, there was Elena's cousin Ludovic Monsanto, also a painter, with whom she lived when studying in Paris. The Monsantos lived in Brooklyn and were one of the "steady flow" of Spanish-speakers who passed through the Williams home. Second, there was the family friend Dr. Henna, who at some point sat on the board of the Metropolitan Museum of Art. Henna, as discussed, figures in *The Autobiography* as a somewhat silly family acquaintance from the island days, despite the fact that his name serves as the title of a chapter in the story of the person "we ourselves have been." While Bill's depiction of Henna suggests that his contribution was limited to Williams' medical career, one can hardly believe that Henna's interest in art did not spill over into conversations with the Williams family. Furthermore, as Monsanto and Henna were both Spanish-speakers, they were also symbols of foreignness and tributaries to the central symbol that was Elena—and all three were Puerto Ricans who had studied in Paris.

These direct (Elena) and indirect (Monsanto/Henna) models, who influenced Williams' earliest proclivity to art, also contributed to his associating art with his Spanish-speaking half and the people in his life whom he also associated with translation. His associating painting with translation was also important because whereas Elena, Monsanto, and Henna symbolized foreignness, in the context of art they became speakers of a more universal language of visual images; painting translated these foreigner-symbols in a way that universalized them. Understandably, then, if Williams desired to be a painter to unconsciously emulate his mother, he also gravitated toward painting because it offered an alternate language that they could fluently speak to each other, thus bringing him closer to her. Furthermore, painting resolved the problem of his having to choose between writing about the foreignizing particulars of his life, the stuff of narration, and the universals that would make those particulars of secondary or no importance. MacGowan, intending no reference to painting's having anything to do with Williams' identity drama, did see in his early poems the struggle to understand the relationship between his autobiographical particulars and the universalizing concept that those particulars evoked:

> *These [early, 1909] poems constantly insist upon a dichotomy between the ephemeral particulars and the timeless universal, but in Williams' later work this dichotomy is resolved.*

(MacGowan 5)

In painting, then, Williams found a language with which to translate his public and secret languages into a single system of symbols, a fusion that became the hallmark of his mature style. Thus, Breughel's "Self-Portrait" is also of Williams, reborn as the blond Bill:

                         a

     man unused to
     manual labor unshaved his
     blond beard half trimmed
     no time for any-
     thing but his painting

(*CPII* 385)

Several books on painting's influence in Williams' work have already elaborated on that tributary in Williams' career and amply demonstrate its outcome in still-lifes, landscapes, and portraits translated into poetry.[9] These attest to a variety of artistic influences—his early relationships, such as with his architect brother and Demuth (MacGowan), and the effect of the Arensberg group (Marling) or of Stieglitz and his circle (Dijkstra)—with at least Dijkstra making a case for intellectually environmental influences that Williams himself may not have been aware of: for example, that Stieglitz shared his ideas with many artists who in turn wrote ideas that Williams read later on without connecting them to Stieglitz. Rather than join that colloquy, however, our present interest is to demonstrate that in adopting painterly techniques Williams was implementing the lessons in communication that he had learned from his bilingual upbringing: that discursive *ideas* were stigmatizingly culture-specific, while *things* were objectively universal.

As his critics have amply argued, over time Williams was probably influenced in his visual techniques by several sources from both the American and European art scenes, but as illustrated by his adopting Juan Gris as an alter image, the style in which he most vividly saw himself expressed was cubism. Like himself, cubism was a hybrid born from a Spanish and French imagination. Also, as Williams himself did, cubism enjoyed African tributaries that addressed the exhaustion of European art and that also made cubism the fruit of a mingling, therefore wholly American, spirit. This new art, then, even though European, carried on a conversation that he subliminally understood as being about him. Behind Williams' enthusiasm for Gris, as noted in the previous chapter, was this sense of himself as a collage by Gris, pieces of a life identifiable both as themselves and as participants in the unity of the composite.

On the other hand, the new aesthetic augured a social revolution, an opening of the American imagination so that it would be capable of entertaining an entirely different perception of reality, an American revolution that would allow Williams' full identity its freedom:

> *the greatest characteristic of the present age is that it is stale—stale as literature—*
>
> *To enter a new world, and have there freedom of movement and newness.*

$$(I\ 134)$$

In that New World, thanks to the new imagination, he would not have to misrepresent himself with the mask of Bill.

Owing to this ability to transform a stale, narrow America to his ideal America, cubism specifically and the new art in general composed an alter image of the ideal William Carlos Williams. A measure of how much importance Williams gave to painting as his alter medium is his turning his analyses of art into essays on the aesthetics of his own work. In an unpublished "Preface" to a book on the art of Fernando Puma, Williams' discussion on Picasso's having translated his *objet d'art* to another medium is simultaneously an apologia:

> *Picasso quit painting to take up ceramics, something you can hold in your hand. He quit the painting which is, after all, only some pigments on a piece of canvas stretched over a frame. But a vessel to hold water is an* objet d'art *no matter how crazily you treat it. Whatever you do to it* [sic] *still remains an "object."*[10]

Writing about the Argentine Puma and the Spanish Picasso inspired Williams to illustrate his point by playing with Spanish:

> *So what? Put the painting aside and seek the object again, the thing, the olla. It is a cure. And when they are cured? Then what?*[11]

The important thing was to "seek the object again," whether you called it an *olla* or a "pot." Changing the medium does not change the object. That is the "cure," which we understand as "solution," which in turn allows Williams to play with the ambiguity "And when they are cured?" The word "cure," of course, suggests both the curing of the painters of their problems and the curing of the ceramic vessels. But this "cure" pun has more nuances. Its coming immediately after *olla* suggests that Williams was also engaging in imaginary translation. The painters, who had a problem, sought a "cure"; an odd-sounding usage here that immediately turns the painters' aforementioned problem into a figurative malady. But because that is unsupported by the context, we instead accept "cure" to mean "solution." The Spanish word *remedio,* however, colloquially means both "cure" and "solution." Williams' positioning "cure" after *olla* suggests that the pun came to him by mentally translating *remedio,* which instantly renders the pun. Reed Whittemore's biography[12] devotes a chapter to "Stealing," and this private manner of word play was one manner in which Bill stole from Carlos. Even more important, the "cure" also refers to Williams' *remedio* for fusing the universal in the object. In sum, his ostensible defense of Puma and Picasso was actually a defense of his own technique. Translation, whether from painting to ceramics or *remedio* to "cure," was simply another device available to Williams' imagination so that it might generate poetry.

By means of such mental translations, words, whether as evoked image or unique morphology, could be perceived as visual objects. That possibility allowed Williams to discover that "poetry, like painting, can give the inmost concerns of man a tactile reality,"[13] which obviously included the inmost concerns in his hidden Kore. Visual images, moreover, work without the subjective narrative of language, eliminating those elements that stir the emotions alone, which only distort perception, so that the object-image appeals to the eyes and the intellect:

The true value is that particularity which gives an object a character
by itself. The associational or sentimental value is the false.

(I 14)

A perceived object stripped of narrative allows the viewer to focus on
it and reflect on the tension in it that attracted the viewer. The word-
made-object is then an object twice, as a word and as the thing it paints
in the imagination. As the word "translation" in titles of poems provides
new lenses through which we read additional semantic layers, so too
this "painted poem" with its tension compressed in the word-object
awaits the right pair of eyes that will understand that the poem has been
translated, so that it must be visualized, both on the page and in the
imagination.

In the early poem "Pastoral" (*CPI* 70–71), for example, Williams
paints sparrows that "hop ingenuously" over the pavement as they quar-
rel "with sharp voices / over those things / that interest them," not over
those things that might incite the lyrical observer. A parallel image then
depicts a man "gathering dog-lime" and his "tread / is more majestic
than / that of an Episcopal minister / approaching the pulpit / on Sunday."
Whatever that slow tread may say about the minister or about the man is
subject to interpretation, left as an undefined tension upon which the poet
does not intrude. The framing final lines remind us that those images,
created in words, really touched off something that was beyond language:
"These things / astonish me beyond words." And so, in this imaginary
translation of a poem to painting the traditional narrative of the "Pastoral"
is rewritten into one that is "Past Oral," a "conceptualist"'s *concepto* that
Williams repeats in all his five poems titled "Pastoral," which all play with
the idea of things experienced beyond words.

Williams' use of imaginary translation, both into visual imagery and from
Spanish, appears to account for his creation of "The Red Wheelbarrow"
(*CPI* 224). Originally published in *Spring and All* (1923), this poem shares
images with "Brilliant Sad Sun," a poem that Williams placed among
"Collected Poems 1934" in *The Collected Earlier Poems,* but that had ac-
tually appeared in *The Dial* in 1927 (*CPI* 513) and that whose writing,
from the reasoning to follow, actually predates "The Red Wheelbarrow."
As with Williams' other early poems, "Brilliant Sad Sun" also contains

some painterly techniques, but nothing quite like those in "The Red Wheelbarrow" (the title that by convention has been given to this originally untitled poem). In fact, although published first, "The Red Wheelbarrow" appears to be the result of an experiment in imaginary translation that Williams performed on "Brilliant Sad Sun," translating it from a narrating representational painting to an abstract minimalist one.

"Brilliant Sad Sun" opens with a visual representation of the signs around an outdoor eatery:

> Lee's
> Lunch
>
> Spaghetti   Oysters
> a Specialty   Clams
>
> (*CPI* 269)

These contrast with Elena's nostalgic chatter that prompts her brilliant sad son to ask "what good" is her escaping from sharply defined reality by speaking "thoughts / romantic but true. . . ." For her benefit, he projects a visual image of her in the third person so she may appreciate its concreteness: "Look! / from a glass pitcher she serves / clear water to the white chickens," adding "What are your memories / beside that purity?" But his mother, the empty pitcher "dangling / from her grip," simply continues talking about old memories she has kept alive for years, set in France and Puerto Rico:

> her coarse voice croaks
> *Bonjor'*
>
> And Patti, on her first concert tour
> sang at your house in Mayaguez
> and your brother was there
>
> (*CPI* 270)

So much of what was important to Williams depended on Elena, and she poured out her vitality in nostalgia to escape his reality as an American and an artist. But Bill accepts her doing this as part of a tragic natural order, she being Latin and thus romantic by nature. Her pouring water to the chickens imparts a measure of life to him by producing sadness, which yields the fruit of another regeneration, the poem itself. Thus the poem celebrates the pathetic fallacy: around them is "Spring!" and from his sadness emerges the brilliant sun/son in the form of Kore.

To arrive at "The Red Wheelbarrow," Williams translated the relationship between Elena, the poet, and her physical surroundings into visual images. The soul-dead Elena, who held in her hand the empty pitcher from which she had poured out the regenerative vitality of water, is compressed into the idea of something on which so much *pende* ("hangs"). The original "dangling," a (suspected) Nordic word that means "hang from," was thus translated into the parallel Latinate "depends." The "Spring!" around them and the sustaining image "she serves / clear water" in "Brilliant Sad Sun" are condensed into "rainwater," and this image is also reinforced by the atmosphere suggested by white chickens walking out in the rain. A melting of the "glass pitcher" into "glazed with rain / water" conserves the shining quality of the original "pitcher." Eliminated is the circular interaction of metaphors in the first poem: spring, restaurant, winter done to a turn, water, chickens, sadness, regeneration, spring. The new images, no longer metaphors, are the objects that the words paint in the imagination as well as the words themselves: cubist-style, the words "wheel / barrow" and "rain/water" are artificially broken, emphasizing the plasticity of the words, making us conscious of them as visual objects.

But from what element in "Brilliant Sad Sun" did Williams get the "red wheelbarrow"? From an imaginary translation from the Spanish. In Spanish, to know things by heart or to do something by rote can be described by the phrase *de carretilla: hacer de carretilla* or *saber de carretilla*. The image evokes carrying around the knowledge using a small cart. Colloquially, one can refer to someone's habitually prattling on about something as bringing back one's *carretilla*. And *carretilla* also literally denotes "wheelbarrow." On that afternoon, Rose was prattling nostalgically *de carretilla*, so the *carretilla* was Rose's, *la carretilla de Rosa*, which homonymously translated also says "the red wheelbarrow."

In "The Red Wheelbarrow," therefore, the central image is still a vessel bearing water, spring rainwater that falls on an outdoor setting similar to the suggested one in "Brilliant Sad Sun," with white chickens. But whereas in the first poem the narrative explains the network of relationships between metaphors, in the second poem the centrality of that semantic chain gives way to a purity of forms and colors. In sharp contrast to the cool, white, softly round chickens, the red wheelbarrow is flaming and angular. By virtue of being cooled and glazed by rainwater, however, it simultaneously belongs beside them. The romanticizing Elena in "Brilliant Sad Sun" was the opposite of the concreteness of the chickens, and yet each was doing what came naturally: "Look! / from a glass pitcher she serves / clear water to the white chickens." But once the imaginary translation is performed, the language of the new poem produces a distinct poem that is a new "conversation by design," one whose painted images and arrangement of words broaden the implications of that on which "So much depends."

Williams, who habitually covers his sources ("But they have no access to my sources" [*CPI* 67]), of course, nowhere explicitly attests to his performing this translation. And one can argue that "The Red Wheelbarrow" came to Williams not derived directly from "Brilliant Sad Sun" but by the original experience that remained with him so vividly that over time it inspired separate poems with the same imagery. But that argument would leave the poem hollow of important semantic possibilities, flattening the dimensions of the "red wheelbarrow" while disregarding parallel instances of the kind of imaginary translation that produced that image. Such a parallel is found in Williams' preface to the works of Fernando Puma:

> But a vessel to hold water is an objet d'art *no matter how crazily you treat it. Whatever you do to it [sic] still remains an "object."*[14]

Merely invoking the great Picasso sufficed to make a case for this kind of translation. But, as observed earlier, in defending Picasso's quitting painting to capture the same *objet d'art* in ceramics, Williams was actually defending the acts of imaginary translation that he himself had performed. A closer look at his language in his essay reinforces this contention. His original subject had been Picasso's transition from painting to ceramics. The "vessel to hold water" was Williams' imaginary translation of an as yet unstated antecedent, the synecdochic *olla* ("pot") image that represents Picasso's exploration of "ceramics." But it is Williams who had introduced the pot image and limited its function to that of a vessel intended to hold water. His declaration on how crazily one can treat an object of art is really a non sequitur. One infers from this illogic that Picasso was merely a vehicle that Williams was using to point to his own techniques, that the example foremost in Williams' mind was a vessel that holds water and which, like the glass pitcher and the rain-glazed wheel-barrow, he did treat crazily.

That the imagination can perform the kind of translation that produced the "red wheelbarrow" from *carretilla de Rosa* is what makes poetry or art possible. In the picture painted by the poem we witness the power of the imagination at work, understanding by seeing, rather than being told—an example of the purity that the brilliant sad son had attempted to *tell* Elena to see. This interpretation of Williams' poem as a paradigm, of course, precedes and is independent of our knowing how the poem came to be. But the evolution of its invention does reaffirm the poem's being a paradigm of the writing of poems, and gives another reason why "so much depends" on a red wheelbarrow.

Eliminate the previously discussed leap of the imagination that produced the "red wheel / barrow" image and the poem suddenly loses a power it had gained as paradigm, as well as its signature of Williams' style, the balance of the autobiographical and the aesthetically universal: the "red wheel / barrow" was a tribute to his bloodline twice, first in cryptically evoking Elena on whom so much of his life depended, and ultimately in celebrating his artistic lineage. For the performance of imaginary translation that produced the image was also an application of *conceptismo,* specifically of the lessons that came to him through a major tributary, from whom he discovered early on how wild comparisons in the imagination can bring tremendous inventiveness to the poem on the page. That mentor was Luis de Góngora, cubism's prime literary predecessor and one of several Spanish writers through whom Williams claimed Elena's literary bloodline.

Chapter 5

Bloodline, Poetic Line

> *We in the United States are climactically as by latitude and weather much nearer Spain than England, as also in the volatility of our spirits, in racial mixture—much more like Gothic and Moorish Spain.*
>
> ("An Informal Discussion of Poetic Form," *Revista* 45)

Williams' 1941 talk at the Inter-American Writers Conference at the University of Puerto Rico discussed the contribution that Latin America can make to Anglo American writers:

> *To introduce us to Spanish and Portuguese Literature—pure and simple. And if to that literature, to make us familiar with its forms as contrasted with our own.*[1]

He then proceeded to describe what Spanish had to offer:

> *Specifically, by showing us a shorter, four-stressed line rather than the pentameter; by showing us a great dramatic talent, Lope de Vega, who did not use the iambic pentameter—gave that hint which will tend to free us to our own uses.*
>
> (*Revista* 45)

And, beside its freeing "us to our own uses," his reason for believing that the "four-stressed line" would serve Anglo Americans best was that the culture in which it thrived was "nearer" modern Anglo American culture, better "than . . . England ever was":

> *For in many ways 16th and 17th century Spain and Spaniards are nearer to us in the U.S. today than perhaps England ever was. It is a point worth at least taking under consideration.*
>
> (*Revista* 45)

These 1941 remarks on Spanish literature were taken from Williams' 1939 essay "Federico García Lorca," and were later synopsized in his 1951 autobiography. In all three cases, he wrote of Spanish as being worthy of making an as yet hypothetical contribution. But, characteristically encoded and duplicitous, his recommendations to look into Spanish literature were really an invitation to find his sources; behind his advocacy was the knowledge that through him Spanish literature had already influenced Anglo American writing.

Consistently contradictory, Williams himself, of course, was also responsible for hiding that connection. Because of the disappointments that followed his Spanish phase, notably culminating with the failure of *In the American Grain*, he foregrounded Carlos rarely; indeed, such promotions of Spanish poetry in strictly ethnic contexts (the Lorca essay, the talk in Puerto Rico, and the remarks in the chapter "Translation" in *The Autobiography*) made such talk sound occasional, symbolic, and tributary, and so fell on deaf ears. But, ever of two minds, this is also probably the way Williams wanted things to work out. For as is even true of today's literary "weather," it was only in ethnic contexts that the "catalogue" permitted taking seriously certain kinds of poets as poets. Bill knew not to cross wires unduly. When he waxed ethnic it always happened in the permitted context: his essay on Lorca was endowed with a broader interest because it tapped into the public's sympathy with the Spanish Loyalist's cause; his remarks on Spanish literature, before an audience of Latin American writers in his mother's birthplace, provided a reasonable occasion to extol a literary influence obliquely; his repetition of those ideas in *The Autobiography* were in the context of an interest in translation as a "relief from . . . French and Italian" (*A* 349).

Bill's politic respect for the protocol of the "catalogue" has achieved its purpose in misleading his critics. Mariani, in deference to the poet's characteristic attitude, treats Williams' references to Spanish literature in the Puerto Rico talk as remarks appended to an earlier talk given at Harvard, in order to win over his inter-American audience:

> *This time he studded his talk with references to Spanish literature and to the salutary influence that literature had on the American language.*
>
> (*NW* 446)

Mariani goes into some detail on the implications of the talk, alluding to Williams' "work with Quevedo," and rightly adds that Williams' accent on Spanish was "paying a tribute to his parents" (*NW* 447).

But Williams' gesture was no sentimental appendage. His debt to six-teenth- and seventeenth-century Spanish poetry was in fact information omitted from his Harvard talk; it was the Harvard talk that was tailored to please a public. Furthermore, far from being tacked on, his pitch for Spanish literature was the logical culmination of a talk that began by speaking of poetry as "related to the structural character of the age" (*Revista* 43), and that went on to define the strongest of the structural approaches to poetry as paralleling "the inventive impetus of other times with structural concepts derived from [the poet's] own day" (*Revista* 44). Again, his conviction came from experience. In the Spanish centuries he discussed, Williams had indeed discovered a poetry surprisingly more modern and relevant to the poetry of his day than the English poetry he had been reared on. From that Spanish poetry, as a young poet he took something considerably more useful to his writing than a sense of cul-tural pride: another poetic "line" that became an important root of his writing. At the time he gave that talk, for example, Williams himself was experimenting with that shorter, four-stress line in the verse passages of his play *Many Loves*, in whose opening scene Hubert (Williams) wants to teach a woman (America) his new verse form:

> HUBERT:
> > I've told you.
> I'm schooling her gradually to
> speak as I wish her to—a verse
> form that'll be modern and expressive.
> I must myself first learn how. It's difficult.
> She is most important to me . . .
>
> > > > > > > (*ML* 31)

The exact year in which Williams began to delve seriously into Span-ish literature is unclear; the biographies give scant importance to this phase. His initial brushings with it were surely his mother's Quevedo sto-ries. Mariani mentions in passing Williams' "slaving away at a translation he was doing of Lope de Vega's *Nuevo Mundo*" (*NW* 112), around 1913. Williams writes nothing about that play in *The Autobiography*, in which his trip to Spain is given a quirky treatment, buried in a chapter titled

"Paris and Italy" even though one third of the chapter is devoted to his jaunt through Spain. In that chapter, no reference is made to his having had any curiosity or interest in Spanish literature. Nevertheless, during that period in Europe (1909–1910), he did receive from Pound the two volumes of *Poesías Selectas Castellanas,* edited by Manuel Josef Quintana, from which he selected the poems he translated from "El Romancero." More than as just a source of material to translate, these two volumes proved to be a crucial contribution to the "person we ourselves have been."

In those books, now among his papers at Yale's Beinecke Library, Williams underlined in pencil numerous words throughout Quintana's preface and in the poetry selections. Those appear to be words that he looked up in a dictionary. Also, marginal vertical lines or exclamation marks highlight specific paragraphs of the introduction and, in the poetry selections, stanzas, and in a few cases, entire poems. We must assume that the markings were made by Williams because of the pattern of what was highlighted. Throughout the preface, for example, he marked off those things said by Quintana that sharply apply to Williams himself or to his "weather."

The first book begins with an "Introducción" by the editor, a brief history of Spanish poetry up to 1817, the year the book was published. The preface itself begins by describing the origins of a truly Spanish poetic voice. As Williams cites from Quintana in "Federico García Lorca" (in presumably Williams' own translation), just prior to Columbus' voyage and up to the sixteenth century, "the influence of Italy held an ascendancy" in Spain's poetry. Spain's independence and renascence came with the appearance of the *romances.* That Williams chose to translate from "El Romancero," which he retranslated over the years, more than demonstrates a keen interest in them: the *romances* were alter images, celebrating his own rebirth in his Spanish lineage. He doubtless read into Spain's breaking away from the Italian standard the disagreement between himself and Pound. This identification with the *romances* was probably brought on by Quintana's description of them in a paragraph that Williams marginally marked off:

Stripped of the artifice and violence which the imitation of other modes had required, its authors caring little for what Horace's odes or Petrarch's canciones were like, and composed more from instinct than

art, the romances *weren't as complex as nor did they attain the sta-*
ture of the odes of León, Herrera, and Rioja. But they were our lyric
poetry: in their music spoke its accent; they were what one heard at
night in the drawing rooms and in the streets to the sound of the harp
or the guitar; they served as the vehicles or incentives for loves, like
arrows . . .

(Quintana lxxx)

Because the *romances* were "composed . . . from instinct," Williams
would have identified with them a great deal. In *The Embodiment of
Knowledge,* we recall, he identifies with the autodidact Shakespeare, celebrating an unacademic "naturalism," and in *The Autobiography* he confesses to proceed instinctively, from a lack of skills:

. . . so French! To them the meaning of art is skill, to manipulate the
parts to produce an effect diametrically opposed to my own values, my
lack of skills forced to proceed without them.

(*A* 119)

One can also easily see how Williams would identify with those *romancero* poets, who wrote even though seriously occupied at other things, and
who were looked down upon by the autocratic Quintana, who was unable
to find in the *romances* "the sustained elegance and perfection of taste":

One cannot deny a good part of our authors an admirable talent, wide
erudition, and great knowledge of the ancient classics; and yet uncom-
mon in them is the sustained elegance and the perfection of taste, which
other modern authors have imbibed from the same fountains. Many
causes contributed to this. One of them is that those poets communi-
cated very little among themselves: a common center of urbanity and
taste was lacking, a literary legislature that would draw the line be-
tween swelled chests and greatness, exaggeration and strength, affec-
tation and elegance . . .

Another cause is the secondary place that poetry had in many of
those who cultivated it. They wrote verses to distract themselves from
other more serious occupations, and those who write poetry to enter-
tain themselves are not generally very careful about election of theme,
nor too polished in the execution.

(Quintana cxvii–cxviii)

Quintana must have sounded to Williams like a forebear of William George, who measured his son's work by its lack of "sustained elegance and perfection of taste," and who also saw Williams' writing as a distraction from more practical endeavors.

Similarly, also resounding with William George's dissatisfaction with his son's work, Quintana's pronouncement on Luis de León was understandably marked off:

> He isn't successful at versifying: although sweet, fluid, and graceful, he lacks gravity, and falls flat not a few times owing to a lack of quantity and fullness. To this defect another is added, more serious in my opinion, which is that no one has less poetry when the ardor fades: then languid and prosaic, he neither touches, nor moves, nor enraptures, and all he has left is the merit of his diction and style, which are always sound and pure, even when deficient in life and color.

(Quintana liii)

Among the poets in Quintana's overview, Luis de Góngora clearly most excited Williams and, of course, Quintana's words on Góngora were duly highlighted:

> ... Believing that the language of poetry was losing its vitality and surrendering naturalness to poverty, purity to grossness, and facility to abandon, he aspired to extend the limits of the language and of poetry and devoted himself to inventing a new dialect, to extol the art of humble simplicity, to which, according to him, he had been reduced. This dialect would distinguish itself by the novelty of the words or their use, by the rarity and the dislocation of the phrase, by the daring and abundance of imagery: and not only did he write in it his Soledades and his Polifemo, he uglified in the same way almost all of his sonnets and songs, splashing some of that language on considerable passages of his romances and letrillas ...
>
> If to the excellent talents he possessed Góngora would have added the education and good taste he lacked, if he would have turned his writing into the profound investigation of Herrera, and meditated on the resources of the language, heeded its character, wealth, and harmony, perhaps he would have achieved what he wanted, and he would have been the restorer of the art, and not the ignominious corrupter of it.

(Quintana xcv–xcvii)

In Williams' praise of Góngora in his essay "Federico García Lorca," he again quotes Quintana (once more presumably in Williams' translation), but does so out of context so as to distort Quintana's intended conservatism. The words, which originally complained of the Spanish poet's having broken down the language, are subverted to affirm Góngora as the liberator of Spanish:

> *"But curiously enough in a few years this revival of a taste which popularized poetry, and rescued it from the limits of imitation to which the earlier poets had reduced it, served also to make it incorrect and to break it down, inviting to this abandon the same facility as in its rehabilitation." Góngora was the man!*

(*SE* 224)

Góngora as an alter image of Williams himself was indeed "El Hombre," which is why Williams proceeds enthusiastically:

> *It was Luis de Góngora who as a lyric poet brought the new adventure to its fullest fruition and then attempted to go away, up and beyond it—to amazing effect.*
>
> *Góngora is the only Spanish poet whose inventions, at the beginning of the seventeenth century, retain a lively interest for us today, one of the few poets of Spain of world reputation and lasting quality of greatness.*

(*SE* 225)

The most important Spanish writer after Cervantes, Góngora was called by Lorca "the father of modern poetry," a praise borne out by Góngora's broad influence on Lorca, W. H. Auden, García Márquez, Mallarmé, and Pablo Neruda, among many others. As Quintana has noted, Góngora had earned a reputation by writing popular *romances* and *letrillas*. Like the works of his contemporaries, his poems were built on the *concepto*. Equivalent to the English Metaphysical "conceit," the Spanish *concepto* extracted figurative relations of things to the limit of the language, enciphering the poet's wit so that, in order to enjoy it, the seventeenth-century reader was expected to decode the poem for its network of meanings. Word play, puns, and homonymic associations extended a conceit on several linguistic planes. Among the *conceptista* poets, one school emphasized intricate interactions between the poem's ideas, while others specialized in witty displays of the artificiality of poetic language. The former style appealed to the intellect, the latter to the senses, involving an over-embellishing with metaphor, witty use of prosody, literary allusions, and even gratuitous inventiveness. This flashy, "cultured" style was called (both seriously and satirically) *culterano,* meaning "cultured," but also a play or an anti-Protestant spin on Lutheran, *luterano* (Luther/anus). It eventually came to be called *gongorismo,* after Góngora, the most loved and hated master builder of this complex poetry.

In his later works, Góngora elevated the cultured style to yet another plateau of complexity. Imitating Latin, an inflected language with an unfixed syntax, Góngora translated that freedom into Spanish, which although inflected does have a conventional word order. To that freedom he added hyperbaton, an even greater disruption of natural word order, such as between article and noun. The result was that, besides the artificial breakup of lines in a poem, the Spanish sentence itself was violently fractured, much like a cubist painter fractures/composes an object into/from the sum of different parts and points of view, or at first glance, certain kinds of today's "language" poetry. Góngora also extended his *conceptos* by using periphrasis, a circumlocution that allowed for protracted elaboration of an image. Lastly, Góngora's metaphors, which mainly appealed to the eyes, sometimes made leaping comparisons that verged on being completely arbitrary connections between images, solely intended to exhibit the poet's brilliance. Sheep being white, for instance, became *"Errantes lirios,"* "Errant lilies" (Barrett 350). The arm of a girl drinking from a stream became "an aqueduct carrying liquid crystal."

Williams saw in Góngora's style an aesthetic that allowed for an illogical conversation, like El Greco's "tortured line" (El Greco being, of course, a Greek with Spanish sight):

> *When Góngora found himself confined by the old, unwilling to go back to the borrowed Italianate mode, he sought release in an illogical, climbing manner, precursor of today . . .—so he went up! steeply, to the illogical, to El Greco's tortured line.*

(*SE* 225)

Góngora's fracturing of images in reordered syntax, and the juxtaposition of images with unexpected twists, were a "conversation as design," the thinking of a mystic, a spiritualist, or a cubist. Góngora was in fact Picasso's "favorite poet."[2] In 1948 Picasso published *Góngora*, a book of illustrated sonnets. In the introduction to the translated reprint of that book, John Russell commented: "And, in point of fact, the supposedly impenetrable sonnets of Góngora were as important to Picasso as they were to Federico García Lorca."[3]

Williams read Góngora's poetry either during or before 1911–1913, when he had also made the "Metropolitan Museum of Art and the New York art galleries regular stops on his frequent visits" to New York (*NW* 106). Whether or not he missed the Armory show, as Flossie adamantly insisted (*NW* 107), Williams was already justified in believing that the new art of Picasso, Braque, and Gris, as well as that of other new American artists, whether in the Stieglitz or Arensberg circle of artists, descended from an aesthetic ancestry very much like his own. Góngora was indeed the "man" whose career ambition, to confer on Spanish poetry the perfection and prestige that Latin was afforded throughout Europe,[4] paralleled Carlos' ambition to infuse his own unprestigious spirit into English. Furthermore, Góngora's inventive violence was not just directed at poetry but at the language itself. Arguably, then, Góngora's illogical metaphors and his daring to break down the language inspired Williams to perform the kind of translation that would turn Rosa's nostalgic escapes into *carretilla de Rosa* and then back to a wholly different image, a "red wheelbarrow." Góngora was an antipoet who aptly vindicated Carlos' heritage to Bill, whose culture, as represented by Pound, understood nothing about how much Carlos' culture had to offer.

One masterpiece of *gongorismo* was an unfinished *Endymion*-like pastoral epic named *Las Soledades*. No one is sure about the significance of the title, literally *The Solitudes*, implying different states or, by imaginary extension, sites, of solitude. Góngora's poem is about a brokenhearted "errant youth," also referred to as *peregrino*, or "pilgrim." In keeping with Góngora's penchant for oxymoron and paradox, *Las Soledades* fuses counterpoints; the poem is both epic and pastoral, and interweaves nature and urban imagery. The narrative itself is rambling and fractured, with an objective that is never made clear, except that in the course of its rambling the poet invents striking images of country scenes and people in the youth's wanderings. Confusion intentionally reigns: Góngora's invented genre, the *soledad confusa*, unifies by con-fusing contradictions and dichotomies. Trees become "edifices," the countryside is tyrannized "usefully," a "gaze speaks hushing":

> Muda la admiración habla callando,
> y ciega un río sigue, que luciente
> >   de aquellos montes hijo,
> con torcido discuros, aunque prolijo,
> tiraniza los campos útilmente;
> orladas sus orillas de frutales,
> quiere la Copia que su cuerno sea
> (si al animal armaron de Amaltea
> >   diáfanos cristales);
> engazando edificios en su plata,
> >   de muros de corona,
> rocas abraza, islas aprisiona,
> de la alta gruta donde se desata
> hasta los jaspes líquidos, adonde
> su orgullo pierde y su memoria esconde.[5]

> Mute his gaze speaks hushing
> and blind pursues a river that, brilliant
> >   offspring of those hills,
> with winding discourse, while scintillating,
> the countryside tyrannizes usefully;
> its banks so heralded with fruit,
> Plenty desires it for a Horn
> (as if diaphanous mirrors materialized
> >   the beast Almathaea);
> garlanding edifices with its silver,
> >   itself it crowns with walls,
> encircles rocks, confines islands,
> from the high grotto where it lets itself fall
> down to the liquid jaspers where
> pride it drowns and memory it conceals.

Góngora draws a textual map of the scene, so the lines themselves become a "winding discourse." The river "tyrannizes usefully" in its fertilizing (exerting its potency over) the countryside. The "beast Almathaea"

was the goat who suckled Jupiter's infant, whose horn was the Cornuco-
pia. The reference to the "diaphanous mirrors"' materializing the "beast"
is a metaphorical comparison between the river's winding and the goat's
curling horns. Finally the "liquid jaspers" is a subdued metaphor of
the sea.[6]

The river's "winding discourse," in addition to evoking the Passaic,
also evokes Williams' use of translation as image, the synonymy of act and
discourse, as in "a word spoken, / a unique caress" ("Translation," *CPII*
198). But not only because of the river, or that Góngora's wanderer comes
across a wedding scene, or that even the entire premise of *Las Soledades*
patently evokes "The Wanderer," should we suspect a direct influence
from this poem. Besides the similarities that, as a pastoral, *Las Soledades*
naturally has with *Endymion* and other poems about youth searching in
the countryside, in "The Wanderer" we also encounter specific resonances of Góngora's tone and identifiable syntactic twists:

> Even in the time when as yet
> I had no certain knowledge of her
> She sprang from the nest, a young crow,
> Whose first flight circled the forest.
> I know now how then she showed me
> Her mind, reaching out to the horizon,
> She close above the tree tops.
> I saw her eyes straining at the new distance
> And as the woods fell from her flying
> Likewise they fell from me as I followed
> So that I strongly guessed all that I must put from me
> To come through ready for the high courses.
>
> (*CPI* 108)

Williams' stylized syntax in "I know now how then she showed me" dis-
rupts the natural parallel between "now" and "then" ("Now I know how
then she showed me" or "I know now how she showed me then"), and
has resonances of Góngora's attaining an unexpected emphasis by strain-
ing the syntax. In the same vein, "As the woods fell from her flying"
shares Góngora's illogic in "Mute his gaze speaks hushing." Another example of this twisted logic appears in "The Wanderer"'s next stanza:

I had been wearying many questions
Which she had put on to try me:

(CPI 108)

The strained pun on *wear/grow weary of* is typically *conceptista*, and the logic of "questions / Which she had put on to try me" most clearly imitates Góngora's metaphor-making, which packs with several simultaneous ideas: the youth's grandmother asked questions that tired him, that were "put on" him in concern for his welfare (like making him wear a sweater), which he also wore because she wanted to see if he could pass a test ("to try me"), because the questions he carried around were what made him really hers. *Gongorismo* indeed.

"The Wanderer"'s having an ancestry in *Las Soledades* explains Williams' subtitling his own poem "A Rococo Study," an encoded tribute. Williams told Heal that "The Wanderer" was written "before the other poems" (*IWW* 25) in his book *Al Que Quiere*, in which it was originally published in 1917. An earlier version was published in *The Egoist* in March, 1914 (*CPI* 477), which means that he wrote it in the same period that he wrote *The Tempers* (1913), when he was also translating the "Romancero" and mining Quintana's anthology. When asked by Heal why he gave "The Wanderer" the subtitle "A Rococo Study," he answered, "Why Rococo I don't know except it was one of my mother's favorite words" (*IWW* 25). But "Rococo" fits too well to be so spontaneous and unplanned. In art, rococo descends from the baroque, refining its heavier plasticity and its profounder effects of light while heightening the decorative in color, form, and linearity; it was a softer baroque. *Gongorismo* was, of course, exemplary of *baroquismo* in Spanish poetry. Williams' poem, whose "Study" in the subtitle signals that the poem is an experiment, is rococo in that it departs from Góngora's sensuous imagery and complex conceits while still emulating his twisted syntactic lines, softened by the limits of English's more rigid syntax.

Another important poem by Góngora that appears to have had major resonances in Williams' work was *La Fábula de Polifemo y Galatea,* a retelling of a mythological fable from Ovid's *Metamorphoses,* XIII. In it, the giant Cyclops Polyphemus falls in love with the sea-nymph Doris' daughter Galatea, who loves the young Acis. After being captured, they both try to escape, but the Cyclops sees them and causes a large rock to crush Acis. Galatea beseeches the gods, who compassionately transform Acis' limbs into a current of water flowing to the sea (Doris):

> Sus miembros lastimosamente opresos
> del escollo fatal fueron apenas,
> que los pies de los árboles más gruesos
> calzó el líquido aljófar de sus venas.
> Corriendo plata al fin sus blancos huesos,
> lamiendo flores y argentando arenas,
> a Doris llega, que, con llanto pío,
> yerno le saludó, le aclamó río.
>
> (Góngora, *Poesía* 106)

> His limbs being hardly
> by the fatal rock oppressed,
> the tallest trees wore as shoes
> the pearly liquid from his veins.
> Flowing silver finally his white bones,
> laminating flowers and plating sands,
> he reaches Doris who, bounteous with zeal,
> a son-in-law embraces, proclaims him river.

In "The Wanderer," Williams himself becomes a son of the Passaic by rewriting in the first person the scene of Acis' becoming a river:

> And so, backward and forward,
> It tortured itself within me
> Until time had been washed finally under,
> And the river had found its level—
> And its last motion had ceased
> And I knew all—it became me.
> And I knew this for a double certain
> For there I saw myself, whitely,
> Being borne off under the water!
>
> (*CPI* 116)

It is also arguable, of course, that Williams was familiar with the original fable. On the other hand, he was notoriously and admittedly unbookish, "natural," and picked up much of his knowledge from experience and other people, people being the greatest influence on him. Pound, for ex-

ample, contributed the idea of Kore. That he for a time should uncharac-
teristically have devoted so much attention to Spanish writing was an indicator of its importance to him. Given the lack of evidence that Williams
read Ovid or Greek mythology, and factoring in his tribute to Góngora in
"Federico García Lorca," the argument is tenable that the Acis story as
told by Góngora inspired Williams' identification with a river.

Another influence on Williams came in the course of his researching
Góngora. Góngora's obscure style generated a controversy among his
writing colleagues, as his detractors complained of his indirectness and
syntactic excesses. The poet Juan de Jáuregui wrote a critical "Antídoto"
("Antidote") to Góngora's *Soledades.* Among that poem's defects, Jáuregui
complained of Góngora's exaggeration:

And just seeing a young man's making a strong leap brings on all this:

> Garbed in cold marble his gaze,
> hardly could he arch his brows,
> his envy wore ice-hard shoes,
> stiff he stays, etcetera . . .[7]

Quevedo took several satirical swipes at the *Soledades* in particular
and at Góngora's cultured style in general, always underscoring that *gongorismo* was really just a facile formula based on the overworking of
some words and devices: *"Esto es más fácil que pedir prestado"* ("This
thing is easier than asking for a loan") (Góngora, *Poesía* 114). His most
famous critique of Góngora is the poem "Receta," a "Recipe" on how to
write in the Gongorine style, a poem that also serves as a thumbnail
stylistic analysis. Quevedo, for example, devoted twelve of the poem's
twenty-one lines to listing the words and phrases on which Góngora's
style overdepended (a few of which, critics observe, Quevedo himself had
overworked). Furthermore, Quevedo illustrated Góngora's syntactic extremes by inventing one example of hyperbaton that Góngora had yet to
perform. Centuries before E. E. Cummings, Quevedo imbedded a phrase
between two syllables of a word:

> Quien quisere ser culto en sólo un día,
> la jeri (aprenderá) gonza siguiente:[8]
>
> He wishing to be cultured in a day,
> the ensuing gib (he should learn) berish:

Lope de Vega (with the help of others, it is believed) also contributed to this controversy with his ironic "Letter to a Friend" (Góngora, *Soledades* 168), written in reaction to *Las Soledades*. That letter prompted Góngora's "Letter in Response" (*Soledades* 170), his only defense in prose of his obscure style, in which he flatly states that his poem was written only for learned readers, those willing to take the trouble to "remove its bark." This response was in turn answered by Lope who, among other things, disputed the merits of Góngora's boast that *Las Soledades* had reached the heights and perfection of Latin, arguing that the Roman's language was the instrument of a vulgar and homogenizing empire. Their respective views don't neatly parallel Williams' and Pound's, but the letters resonate with the tone and subject matter of the latter-day competition. Moreover, as occurred in that modern exchange, owing to the importance of the participants in the *gongorismo* controversy and how much that controversy contributes to our appreciation of Góngora, critics invariably add to their anthologies and treatments some selection of at least Quevedo's (although usually also others') criticism on Góngora.

Góngora's legacy, then, is a composite of his work and his detractors' satirical responses. Thus one can reason that from researching Góngora, a step absolutely necessary when one reads this poet, Williams must have also picked up a lesson on the double-edged function of other poets' criticism of him, seeing in it the possibility of applying the cubist principle of simultaneism. In his "Prologue" to *Kora in Hell*, Williams applied this principal by making himself the center of a controversy, citing critical letters from Wallace Stevens, H.D. (Hilda Doolittle), and Ezra Pound (to be discussed in greater detail in Chapter 7). By incorporating those letters into his text, he subverted their language so that it performed an unintended function, in the same way that, in his essay on Lorca, he later subverted Quintana's critique of Góngora. Once quoted, the words of others became his own and, thanks to their detailed description of him, enhanced his total portrait. The same device figures in *Paterson*, in which Marcia Nardi's letters criticizing him are quoted extensively. By criticizing she voices Williams' own genuine passion for writing, and his isolation, as well as his frustration with the literary scene. Similarly, in Book Five of *Paterson* Williams quoted from a television transcript in which an interviewer asks him if a text by E. E. Cummings is in fact poetry. The interviewer, who is actually questioning modern poetry, becomes another voice of Williams, his own self-questioning expressed in this contrary point of view. To summarize, in absorbing his own critics' words, Williams took possession of another dimension of his writing and fused it into the totality. This was a way of grasping reality, as reaffirmed by the simultaneism of cubism, an idea he had earlier stumbled across in both reading and researching Góngora.

But even though Williams praised Góngora as "the man," and Góngora was doubtless an alter image of Williams as poet, this elevation was also a diversion, another effort to control the keys to his sources. The poet who was even closer in temperament to Williams as both man and poet was the other great *conceptista,* Quevedo. As an alter image, Quevedo embodied the fusion between Williams the writer and his cultural bloodline through Elena, whose anecdotes of Quevedo made him palpably part of Williams' heritage. But Williams postured, playing down Quevedo:

> *When Mother and I began to translate* The Dog and The Fever, *I knew no more of Quevedo than the bawdy reports reputed to him which had come down the two hundred years after his death even to Mayaguez and so on to me.*
>
> (*YM* 21)

That he knew no more about Quevedo than the "bawdy reports" was untrue; Quintana described him in his anthology. Even though, oddly, in Quintana's preface the paragraphs on Quevedo are not marked off, Williams would not have lost the opportunity to learn more about this writer whom he associated with his mother and about whom he had been hearing all his life. Besides, Quintana described Quevedo in a way that Williams undoubtedly imagined were the very words his own detractors used to describe him:

> *For others . . . his spirit, . . . instead of being festive, is indecent railing; he has impoverished the language, depriving it of infinite modes of saying that, formerly noble and decent, are now and because of him cheap and crude; and if he ever entertains it is because of the inventive foolishness of his ravings.*
>
> (Quintana vi)

> *The same impropriety and bad taste one finds in his style, composed of high and noble phrases and expressions, joined to others trivial and*

low, is evident in his images and ideas, which are thrown together
without economy, good sense, or a sense of decorum.

(Quintana ciii)

Francisco Quevedo's legends have always preceded his poetry, which
also suffered from his legendary versatility. He was, as Jorge Luis Borges
noted, "less a man than a vast and complex literature."[9] The premier
craftsman of Spanish letters, his diverse works, periods, and tones produced sterling religious, contemplative, lyrical, scatological, satirical, and
love poems. He also wrote the classic, perhaps ultimate picaresque novel
La Vida del Buscón, about a rogue pure and simple, with Quevedo's stamp
of prosaic wit and brutal realism. But this brilliance only contributed to
what Borges, drawn to enigmas, observed: that because of the range of
his talent, he lacked a focused identity; no central images represented
him. Instead we associate Quevedo with the wealth of his conceits. Quevedo was the master of that school of *conceptismo* that appealed to the
intellect more than to the senses, forsaking excesses for their own showy
purposes, in order to attain a surface simplicity that was actually charged
with subtle, unexpected encodings of wit. Whether or not Williams owned
up to it, while Góngora's aesthetics enervated and freed him, Quevedo's
encoded stylistic simplicity in both prose and poetry imparted a durable
model for his own encoding in both prose and poetry.

Quevedo's *conceptista* style is well illustrated by his sonnet "Ardor Di-
simulado de Amante," which for brevity can be translated "A Lover's Dis-
sembled Ardor," although puns hover. In this poem, the poet addresses
the volcano Vesuvius, which is turned into a fertility symbol by being
metaphorically compared to a phallus that masturbated over Pompeii.
The volcano's name, which in Spanish is *Vesubio*, occasions a strained
pun that plays on the verbal forms *ve* ("he sees") and *subio*, (*subió*, "it
rose" or "stood"):

> Salamandra frondosa y bien poblada
> te vio la antiguedad, columna ardiente,
> ¡oh Vesubio, gigante el más valiente
> que al cielo amenazó con diestra osada!

(Quevedo 131)

No translation of this sonnet would serve our exegetic purposes, as any
effort would only compromise too many rich possibilities. In just the

stanza cited above, whose salamander image may or may not have been the model for Williams' deity in "The Ordeal" and "Appeal," Vesuvius is addressed as a salamander, which both invokes the mythical power of the animal to survive fire and compares the volcano to a kind of coal-burning stove known as a *salamandra*. The *salamandra* is *frondosa* ("lush/leaf-filled/overabundant," and therefore "full" or even "hairy"), but also like a "sling" (*fronda*) and *bien poblada* ("packed/well-procreated/well-inseminated"). In all those ways, the second line tells us, did antiquity perceive that volcano. The contradictory possibilities of the first line also highlight a hermaphroditic quality about the volcano, which is both oven-like and phallic. Read differently, then, another semantic layer rises to the surface. *Salamandra* being a feminine noun which also signified a kind of stove, and Vesuvius being masculine and phallic, the line could be read homonymously, making the salamander a female rapist of the volcano as *te vio la antiguedad, columna ardiente* ("antiquity saw you, inflamed column") also can be read to sound like *te viola, antiguedad, columna ardiente* ("rapes you, old thing, inflamed column"). In the third line, there is the aforementioned pun on *Vesubio*, followed by another on *valiente* ("valiant/valuable") to modify *gigante* ("giant," but itself playing with *giga*, a precursor to the violin) that, in the fourth line, "menaced heaven" with *diestra osada*, an ambiguity that at first glance might more seriously sound like a rare form of *osadía* ("daring") modified by *diestra* ("dexterous"), rendering "dexterous daring." On the other hand, *osada* can still be read as a modifier ("daring") and *diestra* as its more colloquial denotation, from its original Latin meaning, which would then render the complete line as "menaced heaven with a daring right hand," i.e., a volcanic masturbation.

This final twist reflects the sense of humor that Williams himself cultivated. His "Con Brio," on the sexual nuances of "Lancelot," is in that vein. Another poem, "Smell!," however, is in fact redolent with Quevedo's direct influence from the Spaniard's (glancingly anti-Semitic) "To a Man of Great Nose":

> Erase un hombre a una nariz pegado,
> érase una nariz superlativa,
> érase una alquitara medio viva,
> érase un peje espada mal barbado;
> era un reloj de sol mal encarado,

érase un elefante boca arriba,
érase una nariz sayón y escriba,
un Ovidio Nasón mal narigado.
Erase el espolón de una galera,
érase una pirámide de Egipto,
las doce tribus de narices era;
érase un naricísimo infinito,
frisón archinariz, caratulera,
sabañón garrafal, morado y frito.

(Quevedo 150)

A nose there was on which a man had grown
a honker to out-honker all,
a spouted beaker come alive,
a fuzzily-whiskered swordfish;
a crooked sundial,
an elephant lying trunk up,
a nose headsman and scribe,
a Nasal Ovid misdiagnosed.
A floating galley's prow it was,
an Egyptian pyramid,
the twelve tribes of noses,
a Nosecism that knows no end,
a long-faced Dutch horse,
a carafe-shaped frostbite, red and fried.

Here is a stanza from "Smell!":

Oh strong-ridged and deeply hollowed
nose of mine! what will you not be smelling?
What tactless asses we are, you and I bony nose
always indiscriminate, always unashamed,

(*CPI* 92)

Curiously, the pattern of highlighted paragraphs in Quintana's preface does not correspond with Williams' markings of the anthology's selection of poems, which in these two first volumes did not chronologically get to Góngora or Quevedo. Williams underlined numerous lines, stanzas, and even entire poems, but none of these highlighted poems were from "El Romancero." (This pattern parallels the one in his choice of poems to translate: except structurally into his own poetic idiom in imaginary translation, exclusive of collaborating on Quevedo's prose, Williams never translated into English the Spanish-language poets by whom he appears to have been most influenced.) But the pattern of poems that he did underline appears to signal that the specific poems were of keen interest, although not representative of a style or poet that could serve as model or alter image. Francisco de la Torre's complete "Soneto III," for example, is noted by vertical lines along the margin. This poet's life and work did not motivate Williams to highlight him in Quintana's preface. But his sonnet is a love poem to a "Ninfa," a metaphor of poetry or the poet's muse, who calms him from inner emotional tempests, an equivalent to the nymph in Keats' *Endymion,* and an even closer parallel to, if not an ancestor of, the old queen in "The Wanderer":

> Beauty, if with the light I adore for itself,
> She quells the tempest of wind and sea.
> Beauty, if over the endurance of my sorrow,
> She restores the wonders of the celestial chorus.
>
> (Quintana 116)

> At which I answered her, "Marvelous old queen,
> Grant me power to catch something of this day's
> Air and sun into your service!
> That these toilers after peace and after pleasure
> May turn to you, worshipers at all hours!"
>
> (*CPI* 110)

Williams most exuberantly highlighted, with long fat exclamation marks beside several stanzas, the famous *Coplas, Songs on the Death of His Father,* by Jorge Manrique (1440?–1479). Here is the first stanza, which Williams noted:

> And so we see the present
> as if at some point absent
>   and finished;
> if wisely we judge,
> we'll know the not yet now
>   is past.
>
> (Quintana 17)

That stanza apparently left a deep impression on Williams. Years later he either recalled or returned to it, in the course of writing *Paterson*, for a section that was also published separately as "The Descent" in *Pictures from Brueghel*, a poem that evokes Manrique's tone and rhythm as well as his metaphysical irony:

> The descent beckons
> > as the ascent beckoned.
> > > Memory is a kind
> of accomplishment,
> > a sort of renewal
> > > even
> an initiation, since the spaces it opens are new places
> > inhabited by hordes
> > > heretofore unrealized,
> of new kinds—
> > since their movements
> > > are toward new objectives
> (even though formerly they were abandoned).
>
> > > > > > > > > (*P* 77)

Another long exclamation mark appears beside Manrique's best known stanza, also metaphysically ironic, that compares lives to rivers that flow to an inexorable sea of death:

> Our lives are the rivers,
> whose courses run to the sea,
> > what dying is;
> there run the noble lords
> forward to end
> > and be consumed;
> there the great rivers,
> there the others, medium-sized
> > and the smallest;
> put together, they are the same,
> as those living by their hands
> > and the rich.
>
> > > > > > > > (Quintana 18)

This poem could very well have awakened in Williams a vision of the Passaic he didn't have before, or reaffirmed his identification with the river in Góngora's *Polifemo* or *Soledades.*

Williams also read and researched other Spanish anthologies and critics, as is evident from "Against the Weather," an immersion that left him with a different impression of Spanish than the romantic one that his Bill persona claims he always had. The second part of "Against the Weather" lauds the tradition of realism in Spanish literature, as well as the models it offers for our time, as exemplified in *Poema del Cid* and *El Libro de Buen Amor* by Juan Ruiz, the Archpriest of Hita. But Carlos' challenging of Bill's Anglo-minded association of Spanish with romantic is only one way in which this essay goes against the "weather." For this "A Study of the Artist," its subtitle, is also about his experimenting with his Carlos persona's wholly authoring an essay, something he hadn't done since the unsuccessful *In the American Grain.* Williams' objectifying his subject, a study of "the artist" is a rhetorical device equivalent to his use of "we" for "I" in other contexts, but the essay is really a summary of Williams' self-realization in his Spanish literary roots, a search couched in a broader discourse on the artist.

That framework camouflages Williams' questioning of the Anglo American literary consciousness that catalogues, quarantines, and discriminates. In contrast, he underscores, the *Poema del Cid* reports its story "without preconception" about the *other:*

> The poet saw a sword flash! It lit the field. He did not see a CASTILIAN sword flash or a MOORISH sword flash. He saw a SWORD flash. The effect of that flashing did not immediately concern either Spain or Arabia, it concerned a man. The sword rose or it fell and the work was done or missed. The poet recorded it with a power that took it out of the partial, a power which derived from his passion as an artist to know, in full. This is good.

(SE 200–201)

Because for Williams fusion was a measure of goodness, he perceived the very writing of a poem as goodness itself. The poem fuses things that in life are separate, author and readers, to begin with, also those fusions impossible in reality, such as the unity that the Archpriest Juan Ruiz can attain in his *Book of Good Love* by showing the essential goodness of the love of God and human expressions of love, both spiritual and physical. But that "good" love was also a product of Ruiz's literary "weather," Williams notes, a time and place that nurtured unity and fusion:

> *He came, this amorous archpriest, of a time when Moslem, Christian and Jew mingled, as it has been said, in one great fraternity of mirth and pleasure, whatever ends each otherwise was also seeking. They mingled without prejudice, a resemblance to the conditions of art. They mingled and* El Libro de Buen Amor *took it up and lives.*
>
> (*SE* 201)

Williams identified in the Archpriest Ruiz an alter image and one of the roots of his own passion for mingling. His warm feelings for Ruiz were the same that he evinced for the Catholic Church in *In the American Grain,* for its openness to touch and become America. Williams had received that Latin spirit, passed on through Columbus, Cortez, Ponce de León, through his mother's blood, as well as from the American lands, which drank Spanish blood and received its violating sperm. The parallels between Ruiz's moral spirit in *The Book of Good Love* and the spirit idealized in *In the American Grain* lead one to conclude that the Archpriest's ambiguous play on love that is *buen/bueno* ("morally good/proficient") is a direct antecedent of Williams' frequent use of "good" to describe the mingling *Nuevo Mundo* had to offer.

Ruiz's fusing spirit also produced the poetry of Federico García Lorca, to whom Williams was attracted owing to that spirit and a number of other motivations. Lorca was a poet whose work enjoyed a popularity few poets have known. His poems were steeped in the speech rhythms of the unlettered and unschooled, with whom Williams felt closest, as both a "natural" artist and doctor. Because of his popularity, Lorca symbolized the Spanish Republican side in the civil war, with whose symbols and ideals Williams deeply identified. Lastly, Lorca's literary lineage was one that Williams felt he too had inherited. This explains why Williams' essay "Federico García Lorca" is actually half devoted to Lorca's genealogy— the *Cid,* Juan Ruiz, Juan de Mena, Fernando de Herrera, Fray Luis de León, Saint Teresa, the anonymous *romances,* up to Luis de Góngora—so that in writing about Lorca, Williams was displaying his extensive exploration of his own genealogy. Spain's cultural bloodline, born in *El Cid*, nurtured by Ruiz, epitomized in Góngora, and passed on through the centuries, descended to Lorca and William Carlos Williams.[10]

That bloodline had also given the world the mysticism of Saint Teresa and the "tortured lines of El Greco." According to Williams, the supreme value of its legacy was the "illogic" that would allow the Spanish poet to discover new forms and remain free from European cultural dominance. Williams cites the philosopher Miguel de Unamuno:

> *"I proceed," Unamuno says still in the twentieth century, "by what they call arbitrary affirmations, without documentation, without proof, outside of modern European logic, disdainful of its methods."*[11]

Williams cites Unamuno again, partly to define this Spanish illogical temperament, but as well to underscore its being non-European:

> *. . . the upward sweep into the sun and the air which characterized the aspirations of St. Teresa, of El Greco and the Góngora whom none understood or wished to understand in his day, the "obscurities" which Unamuno embraces with his eye toward "Augustine, the great African, soul of fire that split itself in leaping waves of rhetoric, twists of the phrase, antitheses, paradoxes and ingenuities . . . [Ellipses by Williams] a Góngorine and a conceptualist at the same time. What makes me think that Góngorism and conceptualism are the most natural forms of passion and vehemence."*
>
> (*SE* 226–227)

El Greco's "tortured line," then, referred not just to his artist's line, but also to the illogical, unsyllogistic psyche of the Spanish bloodline. As he did when discussing his own background, turning his identity drama into literary discourse, Williams identified Lorca's bloodline with his poetic line. Through that genealogy, Lorca inherited the eight-syllable assonanced line in which the popular *romances* were written:

> *It is of sixteen syllables assonanced sometimes for long periods on the same vowel. The line, divided in half as usually written, becomes the basis for the* romance *or ballad, many of the* romances viejos *being, in all probability, as old as* Poema del Cid *itself or even older. It was a*

*form much used by Lorca whose reassertion of its structural line, un-
changed, forms the basis for his work.*

(*SE* 220)

Williams proceeds to tell an anecdote of when Lorca heard "the old
meter" in the words of a *copla* Lorca himself had written, but that was
being sung by an illiterate guitarist in a wine shop in Seville, "syllable for
syllable in the mode of the twelfth-century epic." Illogically, Williams immediately juxtaposes an account of his own experience of being in Toledo
and "listening in" on a group of men drinking as one sang to a guitar.
Williams was "a young man not very familiar with the language and an
obvious stranger," which made the men self-conscious, so he left. Lorca
had been listening to the man sing the lyrics of one of his poems; Williams, on the other hand, felt like an outsider. But the juxtaposition of
these two events conveys what Williams realized: that as Lorca recognized his poetic line being song, Williams had been hearing his own
"line" in the guitarist's (undescribed) song. Because even though Williams wrote in English, he could still possess the Spanish "line," both as
spirit and the "eight syllable, four-stress line" that in 1941 in Puerto Rico
he offered as an alternative to the iambic pentameter. That symbolic
"line," his legacy from *El Cid* to Lorca, could inspirit English with the
mingling essence of Spanish and therefore nurture a culture that is more
unified, more American.

Williams' background, as noted earlier, was "Spanish" only in the loose,
popular sense that generalizes that anyone connected to the Spanish language is "Spanish." What "Spanish" culture he received from his mother
was in fact Puerto Rican, whose distinct characteristics were probably
unknown to both of them. Furthermore, even though during Elena's for-
mative years Puerto Rico was still a Spanish colony, she surely felt no
more Spanish than the separatists Henna and Betances felt they were
Spanish. Moreover, "Spanish culture" itself is a generalization, denoting
the geographic grouping of Iberian peninsular cultures, not all of whom
speak Spanish. This convention obstructs our appreciating that more accurately the Iberian culture sown in Puerto Rico was predominantly from
Andalusia (by way of Cádiz, the port that monopolized New World trade)
and the Canary Islands, where many Andalusian adventurers caught ships
to the Caribbean. Spaniards from Extremadura and Galicia also boarded
those ships, but the dominant cultural and linguistic influence came from

the two southernmost regions. Today Puerto Ricans who travel to Spain return expressing amazement at the kinship, the language, the spirit, the sense of humor they share with Andalusians.

Although the question of cultural legacies has historically given rise to a controversy of theories, and anthropologists disagree on how much Andalusia gave the New World of itself and how much was originally from other provinces by way of Andalusia, Williams' personality exhibited certain traits akin to that Andalusian strain, a condition that may explain his gravitating to its geography, its literature, and art. In his *A Life of Picasso,* John Richardson posits that "being Andalusian, [Picasso] was apt to be at the mercy" of his obsessions, an important one being the Andalusian's penchant for the *mirada fuerte* ("strong gaze") (Richardson 10). Richardson cites from David Gilmore's *Aggression and Community: Paradoxes of Andalusian Culture:* "In Andalusia the eye is akin to a sexual organ . . . looking too intently at a woman is akin to ocular rape." To this Richardson adds:

> *So is painting a woman, especially when Picasso wields the brush. The* mirada fuerte *is the key—the Andalusian key—that helps unlock the mysteries of Picasso's late work, and of his work as a whole. It helps us understand his recurrent references to voyeurism; the way he uses art and sex—painting and making love—as metaphors for each other;* . . .
>
> (Richardson 10)

The *mirada fuerte* is directly related to *machismo,* which kept the sense of opposite genders sharply obsessive, and turned the look itself into a form of sexual contact. Gilmore is cited once more, defining in greater detail the Andalusian custom of restraining sexual contact to channel that touch through the eyes:

> *If you mention something valuable to an Andalusian, he wants to see it, wants to eye it. To express that something is good or true, he points to his eye, tapping the side of his head . . . ; he needs to see it and in seeing to experience it, feel it. . . . When the Andalusian fixes a thing with a stare, he grasps it. His eyes are fingers holding and probing. . . .*
>
> (Richardson 10)

Picasso's making of painting and sex metaphors of each other, of course, parallels Williams' equating sex and poetry. The restrained sexuality of the *machista* society reminds us of Williams' idealization of women and of his subsequent "saving himself" from sex and for writing (a theme which Mariani makes a leitmotif in *William Carlos Williams: A New World Naked*), while being at the mercy of his voyeuristic sexual obsessions and expressing them through gazing at and writing about women. Góngora's line, "The eyes of that Andalusian are killing me" (Richardson 11), could fittingly describe the reaction of a German girl on the Ross Platz, at whom Williams stared "so intently that she had become flustered and had finally walked off" (*NW* 83). Gilmore's comment on the Andalusian's voyeurism, with eyes as "fingers holding and probing," evoke the dark confession of Williams' urges in the poem "The Ogre":

> Sweet child,
> little girl with well-shaped legs
> you cannot touch the thoughts
> I put over and under and around you.
> This is fortunate for they would
> burn you to an ash otherwise.
> Your petals would be quite curled up.
>
> (*CPI* 95)

Another of Williams' traits that echoes Andalusia was the cult of the Dionysian spirit, which according to Federico García Lorca expressed itself in the "earth-force" that Andalusians call *duende*. As Lorca noted, *duende* is universal:

> This *"mysterious power that all may feel and no philosophy can explain,"* is, in sum, the earth-force, the same duende *that fired the heart of Nietzsche, who sought it in its external forms on the Rialto Bridge, or in the music of Bizet, without ever finding it, or understanding that the* duende *he pursued had rebounded from the mystery-minded Greeks to the dancers of Cádiz or the gored, Dionysian cry of Silverio's* siguiriya.[12]

Duende, then, was what Williams also interpreted as the creative spirit or fecund earth-force by which Washington or Thomas Morton became truly American; *duende* was the Andalusian word for that Dionysian presence, the fire in the heart, that Williams identified as Carlos. Williams' recognition of this constant tribute to *duende* in Andalusia must have been a revelation: his strong gaze at this mirror-land surely penetrated deep into his own heart's dark, out of which Carlos' *mirada fuerte* stared back. So one gathers from his impressions of that experience recorded in "Asphodel, That Greeny Flower," in which he describes his trip in Granada as one of the "pinnacles," along with the previous visit to the snow-covered Jungfrau. The juxtaposition of experiences gives the poem an imagistic stasis between hot and cold alter images, the snow-covered Jungfrau and the heat of Granada. Looking at the Jungfrau's majestic beauty, Williams felt a sense of fusion with the physical world. Fusion is also implicitly evoked by the images "Interlaken" and the "Jungfrau," a young woman, a Kore. In *A Voyage to Pagany* we are told why that vision of the Jungfrau was a "pinnacle" and given another sense in which Williams associated that peak with fusion:

> *All day, since five in the morning, the struggling and rolling train had moved with the sun through valley after valley, in mountainous passes until the mountains had seemed to enter the train possessing it so that it became a mountain train, a thing belonging to the rocks and snows. All, nearly all day, the window had been pelted with these sights. Evans felt almost a mountaineer; he grew used to the melting winter of the Alps and their implications: Thus the world is and I am part of it.*
>
> (*VP* 224)

Belonging now to the world, Evans also "felt almost a mountaineer," which meant that he was feeling less foreign to the cold of the "melting winter of the Alps," and more important, less foreign to "their implications": like him, the world is a composite of cold and hot and he, "almost a mountaineer," can now claim to be a full reflection of it.

By means of the Alps Williams was also proclaiming his European lineage, through English, and thus, against the backdrop of his entire work, writing his signature of balance. Similarly, in "Asphodel" the Jungfrau scene balances the subsequent Granada episode, except that when the two are compared the latter enjoys elaborate poetic suggestiveness, bespeaking the level of artistic tension it produced in Williams:

> When I was at Granada,
>   I remember,
>   in the overpowering heat
>   climbing a treeless hill
>   overlooking the Alhambra.

> At my appearance at the summit
> > two small boys
> > > who had been playing
>
> there
> > made themselves scarce.

(*CPII* 320)

Granada variously means "prominent," "grenade," "pomegranate," or "having reached the seed stage," figuratively the stage of his formation as a writer at the time. The "I remember" elaborates on the conceit, as signifying "recollect," but is also a *conceptista* play on the word's morphology, re-membering evoking both fragmentation and reunion. In the implicitly sexual "overpowering heat" of Latin Granada, he had climbed a barren hill devoid of phallic trees, while he ignored (overlooked) "the Alhambra": while Williams was there he was still out of touch with his Spanish literary lineage. At the summit, though, "two small boys / who had been playing / there / made themselves scarce." Did they remind him of Pound and Eliot? Or were they the boys William and Carlos, whose two boyhoods, on this hill, gave way to the single dichotomous consciousness of William Carlos? For on this "barren" hill, he was reborn. Now he was "Starting to come down / by a new path":

> > Starting to come down
> > > by a new path
> > > > I at once found myself surrounded
> > > > > by gypsy women
> > > > who came up to me,
> > > > > I could speak little Spanish,
> > > > > > and directed me,
> > > > guided by a young girl,
> > > > > on my way.

(*CPII* 320)

The "gypsy women" were the embodiments of his foreign heart. From that point in his life a young gypsy girl "directed" and "guided" him on his way. She, a young version of the dark-eyed Elena, became synonymous with his dark Kore, his Carlos self.

Juxtaposed, his accounts of both pinnacles demonstrate that, although representing a balance of psyches, semantically the experiences were imbalanced. The Jungfrau (the other young woman and maternal breast, "pinnacle," seen "on a tip from one of the waitresses") did also give him imagistic rebirth, but it was more rhetorical than visceral. That northern European lineage had produced fewer important alter images. This explains why a more haunting cultural rebirth took place in Granada, in the Iberian province whose Moorish five centuries sowed seeds of cubism and whose culture, temperament, and variant of Spanish extended to the Caribbean, to Puerto Rico, to Elena, and eventually to him. Unsurprisingly, of the places he visited in Europe, Williams returned only to Andalusia, whose *duende* had also produced those kindred artists in whose "line" he recognized himself: Góngora, Picasso, and Lorca.

Chapter 6

Inherited Souls

If men inherit souls this is the color of mine. We are, too, the others.

(In the American Grain 41)

I am talking of the one thing that is permanent. Spirits.

(The Great American Novel, I 210)

In *Refiguring America: A Study of William Carlos Williams' "In the American Grain,"* Bryce Conrad focuses on Williams' female metaphor of America:

> There is essentially only one female figure in the book: the landscape itself, She, the female essence of the New World. "One is forced upon the conception of the New World as a woman" (222), Williams writes in his chapter on Poe. But it is Williams who presses that conception upon his book, patterning American history after the image that had provided him with the cover illustration for Kora in Hell: multiple spermatozoa surrounding a single ovum. Many men, but only one woman, like a continent. They gather upon her shores, and at times, like De Soto, plunge into her body, achieving the objective Williams had pursued in Contact, *and that kindled his writing of* In the American Grain: *the "implantation of the sperm."*[1]

Conrad refines this model by adding that Williams' female metaphor is not just a vessel to be fertilized by men; she fertilizes men. Williams rejected the more common idea of male poets begetting or being androgynously begotten by other male poets. That male-regenerating model was the one inherited unquestioned by Pound, who pursued in Europe the fathering traditions that would father him so he might father himself:

> ... the New World is not a passive woman upon whose body the male inscribes his narrative. She resists inscription within history—history,

*that is, as represented by the rigidly fixed literary forms that Williams
associates with the "father to father" sterility of Europe's ruling literary canons. Indeed, it is her power to rupture those forms that makes
her a supplying female, the one who fertilizes the male. That is the
founding mythos of* In the American Grain—*the birth of a poet out of
fertilizing contact with the female body.*

(Conrad 107)

The sexual mythos that Conrad perceives in *In the American Grain* is
based on his psychological interpretation of *Yes, Mrs. Williams,* which we
are told Williams was motivated to write because he was "determined to
gain some control over the lives of women in his writing" (Conrad 143),
and that by so writing he intended to "create for himself the woman who
created him." Just as Williams wrote *Yes* completely disregarding Elena's
quoted insistence that he not write about her, Conrad concludes, in *In the
American Grain* "Williams' poetics actually celebrate a ritualized violation" of the woman (Conrad 146).

Williams' writing *Yes, Mrs. Williams* was indeed another *violence* performed on a woman, the figure of speech on which Conrad's reasoning is
validly founded, but the grave immorality suggested by that metaphor ob-
scures Williams' rationale, which is also important. Williams had been
motivated to write *Yes* because he realized that through the years he had
known her, Elena had been buried alive in an unwanted life, amidst a
"barbarous" society with which he as Bill betrayingly identified. As he
wrote in "Eve," her sight was dimming when he gained the insight to
appreciate her for who she truly was. So justified, by the moral right with
which one disobeys the wishes of a suicide, he decided to write, *Yes,
Mrs. Williams,* "making you live (in a book!)" ("Eve," *CP1* 412). Given his
highly interpretable intentions, to call his ambition to rescue her against
her wishes an act of violence without some qualification is misleading.
Furthermore, the merits of Conrad's analysis notwithstanding, his quickly
jumping to analyze that act of "violence" as emblematic of Williams' attitude toward the female distorts by veering our attention away from the
particulars of this mother-son relationship. Conrad's overlooking that key
detail in order to advance his idea of Williams' need to dominate
"woman" is really yet another circumvention of the full implications of
Elena's centrality. Before Elena symbolized "woman" to Williams, she
symbolized his core/Kore, which other women symbolized only second-

arily: Elena, not abstractly "woman," was the model for his female soul in *In the American Grain.*

Of the determined women in Williams' life, only Elena possessed the tributaries of blood and spirits that evoked the pluralism that he equated with America. Like the American continent, owing to accident and circumstance, Elena too was violated by history. And America in turn images the spiritualist Elena in its being the medium of many spirits, so Williams can invoke the continent's spirits in the same manner that Elena summoned spirits that possessed her. For despite Bill's writing of his shame and fear of Elena's spiritualistic trances, Carlos ultimately believed in spirits, "the one thing that is permanent." Just as Elena in her trances spoke with the voices of others, so does America speak to him with the voices of souls of different cultural and racial colors. Thus, *In the American Grain* is a seance, with Williams himself turned medium, changing his writing voices to invoke the range of spirits in Elena-America, an alter image of Williams himself.

This historical essay, written by Carlos, neither assumed a European's idealized view of America (as Pound completely misunderstood) nor offered a radical revision of the mainstream's idea of American history. In it Williams wrote his own social autobiography to reclaim America by proving that, far from being the outsider, he descended from a heritage that was the true standard by which the reader must measure the subsequent figurative Puritans who excluded all others. By way of Hispaniola, Martinique, Puerto Rico, Williams' forebears explored the New World with the right spirit, the Spanish spirit, which although cruel and base in its material ambition was elevated by ideals of the Catholic Church, which also informed the French. That Spanish or Catholic spirit epitomized America, as Williams described in the chapter "Pere Sebastian Rasles." Different from the Puritans, the Catholics touched America:

> *If enamored of the gospel, the Puritans . . . blocked all ingress and all egress (in theory) to the tenderer humanities, the frailties in which beauty lives entangled, rendering their lives hard, unproductive of that openness which would have been to them as a flower to the stalk; so the Catholics to the north, equally lost, would achieve the same end of escape by the equivalent of a blow to the head at the start, that relieved them of responsibility. Thus stunned and benumbed to terror, the Church comes at least with gentleness to aid. So that they could ap-*

proach the Indians who, if they were lost, *still had their apt sensual touch which the Puritan occluded.*

(*AG* 129)

Williams' last sentence ambiguously reiterates his association of images when speaking as Carlos: "the good" with "the sensual touch." The antecedent to "they" can be either Catholics or Indians, who could both be "*lost*" (spiritually, geographically) and were both capable of an "apt sensual touch." "Catholic" throughout the book, however, is synonymous with the Latin linguistic strain that spiritually fertilized him. Latin and Catholic spirits were the antithesis of William George's exterior English cold, Pound's haughty pedigree and the U.S. mainstream's hostility to Elena: "All that will be new in America will be anti-Puritan" (*AG* 120). Puritans cast their eyes on America and saw only themselves. To them, the Indian was an "unformed Puritan." The Catholics slept with, married, and ate America, which the Puritan saw as savage. While the pretext of Spanish conquest was to "civilize," which only really meant to Europeanize, the Catholic character nevertheless imposed on that plan its own saving grace. The Church, like the "earth" in "At Kenneth Burke's Place," knew nothing of "catalogues," and its vision evoked Juan Gris' art:

Nothing shall be ignored. All shall be included. The world is a parcel of the Church so that every leaf, every vein in every leaf, the throbbing of the temples is of that mysterious flower. Here is richness, here is color, here is form.

(*AG* 120–121)

Thus the Church embodied the fusing spirit, the mingling:

It is this *to be* moral: *to be* positive, *to be peculiar, to be sure, generous, brave—TO MARRY, to* touch—*to give because one HAS, not because one is nothing. And to give to him who HAS, who will join, who will make, who will fertilize, who will be like you yourself: to create, to hybridize, to crosspollenize,—not to sterilize, to draw back, to fear, to dry up, to rot.*

(*AG* 121)

For his allowing himself to be fertilized by female America does she speak lovingly to De Soto:

And if, to survive, you yourself in the end turned native, this victory is sweetest of all. Bitter the need that at Nilco will cause that horrid slaughter: You already sick, in grave danger, thinking of the men. Let them talk, my Indian: I will console you.

(*AG* 51)

And like Rasles and De Soto, the Africans were generous with their beauty and gave it abundantly to America, marrying with her and changing her forever. Like all Williams' truly American heroes, they expressed by their performance their inner ambition to be fertilized by America's fusing spirit:

Poised against the Mayflower *is the slave ship—manned by Yankees and Englishmen—bringing another race to try upon the New World, that will prove its tenacity and ability to thrive by seizing upon the Christian religion—a thing to replace their own elephant-, snake- and gorilla-filled jungles—on which to fasten for stability, blowing into it the soul of their own darkness, where, as were the Aztecs in their bloody chapels, they are founded—*

(*AG* 208)

Only certain Protestants, despite their exteriors, possessed an American spirit. These Williams highlights as dichotomous, outwardly cool, but blessed with an inner creative sensuality, implicitly a *duende* or Carlos heart, that he identified with being Latin and truly American: Washington was outwardly Puritan and inwardly sensual, Burr was loved by women, Poe "conceived the possibility, the sullen, volcanic inevitability of the *place.*" Gifted with the nobler of America's spirits, Thomas Morton cavorted with Indians:

As Morton laid his hands, roughly perhaps but lovingly, upon the flesh of his Indian consorts, so the Puritans laid theirs with malice, with envy, insanely, not only upon him, but also—one thing leading to another—upon the unoffending Quakers.

(*AG* 80)

Years later, in his essay "Against the Weather," it was this Spanish and Catholic openness to mixing the races to which Williams rendered tribute in his praise of *El Cid* and the Archpriest Juan Ruiz's *The Book of Good Love.*

But the full value to Williams of that history is diminished if one skips over Elena to focus on the generic female. Conrad does, and consequently fails to bridge his book's two major arguments. Early in his study he affirms that "the Spanish do serve Williams with a cultural paradigm that runs against the grain of the English scheme of colonization" (Conrad 55). Because Spain's mission was to make the land an extension of Spain itself, "their drive to penetrate to the very core of the New World's life is what enables Williams to ground the beginnings of his history so securely upon them" (Conrad 56). What Conrad affirms but never plainly formulates is that Williams' confidence in his American identity came from his having descended from that culture that mingled its sperm with the New World. That American identity is what Elena-America, with all that blood and all those spirits, embodied for him. A domination of her, a ritualized violation of her is indeed celebrated in *In the American Grain,* and other interpretations on Williams' perception of the female may be gleaned from this book, but no substantive reading of *In the American Grain* can circumvent Williams' underlying declaration: Elena's being Puerto Rican made him truly American, more so than Pound and his "line," which thirsted only to suckle from Europe.

By rescuing his American "line" inherited from Elena, in *In the American Grain* Williams tried to recover a history in which he could see himself imaged. In the process, of course, he challenged myths of American "others," Indian and African, with whom he identified. Understandably mainstream readers didn't identify with this call for mingling, an exercise perceived as peculiar to those "others" and exotic to Anglo American literature, which naturally never mingled either. For, as Williams himself shows, in American history the real mainstream minglers in spirit, like Boone or Houston, left no written words. In forts, both real and of the imagination, the Puritan's separatist spirit passed on writings that only rarely contemplated, daring perhaps to touch, the American experience in its totality. In critiquing that legacy, *In the American Grain* stepped outside that tradition and got lost, overlooked by mainstream literary culture and without a proper context to reinforce its vision. From today's vantage point, however, we can see that *In the American Grain* prefigured the radicalizing social revisionist writings of the sixties and seventies, most notably of the newly visible minority writers. Unfortunately, in the decades when that literary consciousness emerged to challenge the dominant legacy, few if any of those writers were aware that Williams had already written a major antecedent, a book that in the spirit of *Good Love* posited a vision as radical as the one that defined their generation.

That *In the American Grain* probably sounded strange to readers of its time was only logical because it was an imaginary translation, an attempt to interpret in the Anglo American language a consciousness that was in fact Latin American. This novelty was another encoded leitmotif in Williams' writings: "I am an American. A United Stateser," he wrote in *The Great American Novel* (*I* 175), using the literal translation of the Spanish *estadounidense,* which situates the United States in an array of American countries. That Latin American consciousness also later intervened in a draft of *Yes, Mrs. Williams,* in which "America" is lined out and changed to "United States." From Carlos' discourse, pieced together after either decoding, extrapolating, or simply isolating from Williams' writings, one can clearly identify the Americanist side of Spanish American culture, a lineage that has always challenged the competing Westernist strain, which has advocated European supremacy and incessantly monopolized the official history of the encounter between the European "civilizers" and non-European cultures and races on American soil. Williams' confrontation with the Puritan lineage in *In the American Grain* is the Northern participation in that greater controversy throughout America, whose broader context it would do well to understand if one is to appreciate Williams' Latin-hearted book.

In Latin America, the polar extremes of the great cultural competition have been most clearly articulated by many writers, among whom were the Cuban José Martí (1853–1895) and the Argentine Domingo Sarmiento (1811–1888). Sarmiento's most famous writing is the polemic-biography *Facundo: Civilización y Barbarie (Civilization and Barbarism: The Life of Facundo Quiroga,* 1845) an examination of the upbringing of a provincial dictator. On the surface the book appeals for democracy, education, erudition, urbanity, and civilization, and the other accouterments of liberalism, representative of which both Sarmiento and this book are often taught. But while liberalism affords a philosophical framework for this book, it also provides a lofty diversion from its being a racist tract. Quiroga, Sarmiento argued, grew up in the countryside, the pampas, whose natural laws engendered the Indian who, like the African, was of an inferior race, molded by natural setting to be prone to the knife and spear. According to Sarmiento, only those peoples who were white and descended from "civilization," literally cities but in practice Europe, possessed the mettle to erect a civilized society (and therefore, by implication, study and advocate liberalism). Thus, to forge civility, when he became president of Argentina, Sarmiento organized campaigns to annihilate the Indian populations and instituted programs to whiten Argentina by limiting immigration to Europeans. Other Latin Americans, corrupted by race or the influence of savagely populated countrysides, were to be excluded from Argentina. Even Spaniards, an impure mixture of European, Arab, and Jew, were undesirable.

But Sarmiento's vision was not peculiar to Argentines. It was harbored by white *criollos* even in those very Latin American countries that Sarmiento would have frowned upon. That included a country as racially dichotomous and segregationist as Cuba, which produced the poet and political leader José Martí. A lifelong revolutionary in quest of Cuba's independence from Spain, Martí wrote a great deal, producing in his lifetime three books of poetry and a body of short prose (speeches, essays, book and art reviews, magazine and newspaper articles) that fill seventy volumes. A major *modernista* poet, his work introduced to Latin America a leaner language, stripped of the romantic rhetorical devices that continued to characterize his prose. A staunch Americanist, his essays, reviews, and lectures consistently worked toward defining an American vision in politics, art, and literature. From 1880 to 1895 he resided in New York, where he wrote and carried out his revolutionary work. He arrived a strong admirer of his country, an *American* country, and ended up dismayed by the economic extremes, its materialism, racism, and social divisions. Many of his works contrast the lack of an American spirit in the United States and the emergence of it in Latin America.

In 1880, in the New York journal *The Hour*, Martí published a review of a study of Native American writing. Written in English, this piece's introduction prefigures *In the American Grain:*

> *The spirit of a people resides in the land in which they live and is drawn in with the air one breathes. One may descend from fathers of Valencia and mothers of the Canary islands, yet one feels the blood of Tamanco and Paracamoni run hot through one's veins and regards as one's own the blood of the heroic, naked Caracas warriors which stained the craggy ground of Mount Calvary where they met the armored Spanish soldiers hand to hand! It is good that canals be dug, schools be built, steamship lines organized, good that we keep abreast*

of the times and in the vanguard of the beautiful human march; but if
we are not to fail from the lack of a living spirit, or the pursuit of false
values, we must drink deeply at the springs of the Nature in which we
were born, which is strengthened and animated by the spirit of men of
all races who spring from its soil and return to it. Politics and litera-
ture prosper only when they are a direct expression of their people. The
American intelligence is an Indian head dress. Is it not yet apparent
that the blow that paralyzed the Indian, paralyzed America? Until the
Indian marches again, America will limp.[2]

Martí also prefigured Williams in calling for an American writing,
aware that such a consciousness will come about only after America's
writers discover their unique language and understand the originality of
being American:

. . . America will not produce a single immortal writer . . . unless he
reflects within himself the multiple and confused conditions of this age:
concise, poetic, pithy and shaped by supreme artistic genius. A lan-
guage formed by the mother tongue itself, and by the language now
influencing America, may bring to bear that necessary influence with
sufficient forejudgment to impress upon us what must remain fixed
from this age of genesis. . . . Such must be the language that our Dante
speaks. . . . However, we have no literature of our own. There can be no
literature, . . . unless there is substance to express it in. And there will be
no Spanish-American literature unless there is a Spanish America.[3]

In *The Great American Novel,* Williams later echoed this literary
stance, arguing that, like Cortez, the American writer must burn his ships,
face America, and not look back:

America is lost. . . .
*   And the reason is that no American poet, no American man of letters*
has taken the responsibility upon his own person. The responsibility
for what? There is the fire. What is literature anyway but suffering re-
corded in palpating syllables. . . . Why, man, Europe is YEARNING *to see*
something new come out of America. . . .
*   The danger is in forgetting that the good of the past is the same*
good of the present. That the power that lived then lives today. That we
too possess it. . . . Europe's enemy is the past. Our enemy is Europe, a

*thing unrelated to us in any way. Our lie that we must fight to the last
breath is that it is related to us.*

(I 209–210)

Martí envisioned the birth of a genuinely American identity when
there is a "merging"—what Williams would call mingling and touch—
and Americans choose generosity and affection over a European heritage
of divisiveness and exclusivity:

*Will there be an essential and blessed merging, in urgent or mutual af-
fection, of the ancient and related peoples of America? Or will there be
a division, because of belly greed and petty jealousies, into spineless,
marginal, and dialectical countries?*

(Martí, *On Art* 306)

In "Our America" (1891), an essay in which Martí warns Latin
America that denying its true self will leave it at the mercy of the rapacious United States, Martí employs a metaphor that parallels the female
metaphor in *In the American Grain* and describes a divided devotion that
eerily mirrors Carlos' care of Elena and Bill's shame of her:

*If they are Parisians or from Madrid, let them go to the Prado under
lamplight, or to Tortoni for a sherbet. . . . Those born in America who
are ashamed of the mother who reared them, because she wears an Indian apron, and who disown their sick mother, the scoundrels, aban-
doning her on her sickbed! Then who is the real man? He who stays
with his mother and nurses her in her illness, or he who puts her to
work out of sight, and lives at her expense on decadent lands, sporting
fancy neckties, cursing the womb that carried him, . . .*[4]

According to Martí, that son who tends to his sick mother, America, is
"the natural man," the one formed by his natural surroundings and life
experiences and not from bookish, imported ideas. The natural man,
abhorred by both Domingo Sarmiento and Cotton Mather, is the American, a man steeped in knowledge gleaned from discovering, touching.
Martí adds:

*That is why the imported book has been conquered in America by
the natural man. . . . The struggle is not between civilization and bar-
barity, but between false erudition and Nature. . . . Knowing is what
counts. To know one's country and govern it with that knowledge is*

the only way to free it from tyranny. The European university must
bow to the American university. . . . Our Greece must take priority over
the Greece which is not ours.

(Martí, *Our America* 88)

Martí's counterpoint between book learning and experience re-
emerged in Williams' own rejection of scholarship over "naturalism." As
one who writes from instinct, Williams, as was shown earlier, identified
with this "naturalism" in Góngora and his "grandfather" Shakespeare, in
whom Williams saw an American spirit:

There is a unique element in Shakespeare, unique that is, up until his
time, that has baffled scholarship which has been at a loss to place it, a
new element, a "naturalism" which clashed with all earlier and classic
formalizations.
. . . Shakespeare knew nothing of these things. He wrote outside the
scholarly tradition. One must make a choice in accepting his work: ei-
ther he is a menace to the best in literature or the classic mode has been
discovered by him in a fault. . . .
He, Shakespeare, occupied in relation to this world the precise posi-
tion America, a nation, occupies toward the classical culture of Europe
or the East today. We at our best (so far) are not scholars but we have
wit, alert sensibilities. Our problem before the world is precisely his:
shall we be accepted because of our species of "naturalism" or rejected
because we do not meet the qualifications of scholarship?

(*EK* 138–139)

In *Spring and All*, through the imagery of banjo jazz being played by
"Our orchestra," Williams portrays what is American as synonymous with
naturalism:

Get the rhythm
That sheet stuff
's a lot of cheese.

Man
gimme the key

and lemme loose

("XVII," *CPI* 216)

The premise of *The Great American Novel* questions the idea of the "sheet stuff" implied by the traditional novel. Aside from what seems like a narrative about car protagonists mixed in with other improvisations on literature, *The Great American Novel* is a prose poem on the pulse and rhythm of America as filtered through Carlos' continental consciousness. Its title is a pun: The Great American New. That prose poem was later translated into the essay *In the American Grain*. Both books, rooted in the American consciousness represented in Spanish by José Martí, are authored by Carlos, who brazenly drags Bill to savage regions beyond the fort of Anglo American letters.

Owing to the lack of evidence that Williams actually read Martí, the similarities between them can only be interpreted as a textual coincidence of two writers who reflected on a common American experience. But more than coincidence may account for their proximity. Williams grew up never far from Martí's ideas. Martí was revered among Cuban and Puerto Rican exiles in New York. Upon his arrival in 1880, he was made leader of the *Comité Revolucionario Cubano,* which he eventually turned into a political party. He spoke and published frequently. His ideas were spread by the community of Antillean intellectuals working to liberate both Cuba and Puerto Rico from Spain. Prominent among these was Dr. Julio José Henna:

> On 23rd Street and Third Avenue a Puerto Rican named Domingo Per-
> aza had opened up a drugstore.... It came to be known as the Puerto
> Rican Consulate in New York. It was the frequent meeting place of
> Dr. Henna, Baerga, Lisandro, Picón, Silvestre, and other compatriots
> connected to the Antillean liberation movement.

(Vega 64)

Henna's circle figured in Martí's blueprint to attain independence for both islands. After Martí's death in battle in 1895, "the Puerto Rican section of the Partido Revolucionario Cubano was founded in the home of Dr. Julio J. Henna" (Vega 77). One has to assume that in the thirty-five years between Williams' birth and the death of his father in 1918 the seething events pertinent to Henna's and Elena's homeland were discussed in the Williams household, especially with Henna in the eye of the hurricane when Martí died in battle, and later during the Spanish-American War, when William Carlos was fifteen. (Henna died in 1924.) Nor can one imagine that Henna, during Williams' internship at the

French Hospital, would have failed to bring up the respected Martí, and that he was an excellent poet whom Henna knew personally. In sum, while we have no textual connections to verify Williams' having read Martí, the channels existed through which Williams would have repeatedly heard Martí's ideas.

As inheritor of the Americanist side of Latin American culture, Williams also inherited its un-European attitude toward race. Martí had observed:

> *There can be no racial animosity, because there are no races. The theorists and feeble thinkers string together and warm over the bookshelf races which the well-disposed observer and the fair-minded traveler vainly seek in the justice of Nature where man's universal identity springs forth from triumphant love and their turbulent hunger for life.*
> (*Our America* 93–94)

This Americanist attitude may not coincide with the impression one receives when, speaking as Bill, Williams uses racist epithets. But Williams appears to have used racist words as part of his characterization of Bill, to consolidate him with the mainstream reader, as well as for shock value, texture, sound, spontaneity, and local flavor. In the prefatory note to his translation of Luis Palés Matos' poem, for example, while actually introducing a poem that celebrates the racial composition of the Caribbean, Williams as Bill observes that some of the language cannot be rendered in English, not even in "American nigger talk" ("Prelude," *American Prefaces* 156). On close examination, those terms reveal themselves to be blatant signals of Bill's inconsistent posturing, proving hollow in Carlos' broader democratic context. That context more often celebrated a spirit of fusion, touch, and generosity, all which implied oneness, a perception of beauty in the "other," including features of race.

For Williams' family background naturally inculcated a view of race that contradicted the racial attitudes of the "catalogue." His parents grew up in a strongly African region of the Americas. In that steady stream of Spanish-speakers who flowed through his house, some descended from that "Enriquez" side that was partly the source of racial uncertainties in Williams' mother's bloodline. *Yes* also records his mother's gentrified fascination with the African customs among the servants. As for his father, one gathers from how he made his living that William George was attracted to dark beauty. He was also an avid reader of at least one African-

American poet. Among Williams' first contacts with poetry in English, we are told in *The Autobiography,* was his father's readings of Paul Laurence Dunbar's poetry:

> *But Pop spoke English too, and as time went on one of my happiest memories of him was when he would sometimes read to us in the evening. Those were the marvelous days!*
>
> *I remember now his readings of the poems of Paul Laurence Dunbar, and I can to this day repeat many of the refrains he made familiar to me then. It was he who introduced me to Shakespeare. . . .*

(A 15)

This early contact with Dunbar, which the criticism has disregarded, seems suspiciously of utmost literary significance. Dunbar was revolutionary in writing serious poetry in the kind of language white people joked about:

> Dey had a gread big pahty down to Tom's de othah
>   night; Was I dah? You bet! I nevah in my
> life see sich a sight; All de folks f'om
>   fou' plantations was invited, an dey' come,
> Dey come troopin' thick ez chillun when dey
>   hyeahs a fife an' drum.[5]

Patently the merits of the spoken voice and its imagistic possibilities were first heard by Williams, aside from Shakespeare's dialogue, in the poetry of Dunbar. Being one of the culture's "nonentities," however, Dunbar was invisible to critics of mainstream literature, a situation that expunged his possible contribution to Williams from any serious consideration. But that Williams mentions Dunbar in his autobiography is significant, especially juxtaposed alongside his beloved Shakespeare. Even more significantly, Dunbar *precedes* Shakespeare in order of importance in Williams' recollection. The suggestion is strong that Bill was encoding his debt to the great "nonentity" poet, an influence that, had he elaborated upon it, would have been out of character with Bill and that his readers wouldn't have likely understood or appreciated. In the context of his fuller autobiography, completed by the addition of *Yes, Mrs. Williams,* Dunbar's being a secret tributary makes complete sense.

For Williams' moral rejection of supremacist racial attitudes was inevitably also visceral. Besides the consciousness gleaned from the racial question hovering in his own background, throughout his life supremacy and bigotry had affected his mother and, as also suggested in *Yes*, her familial happiness. Supremacy and bigotry, Williams knew, were what the "catalogue" was all about; they were the paired dogs trained to attack his foreign freshness and novelty, his Latin heritage, and any other naked or unmasked sign of his being also "the other." As Carlos knew all too well, an "American will not serve another man . . . ," which here really means the "other":

> *Instead of that, we have "service," the thing that Rabindranath Tagore so admired, telling us we did now know we had it: Sending supplies to relieve the cyclone sufferers. . . . It is a passion. But to serve another, with a harder personal devotion is foreign to us. . . . Do not serve another for you might have to* TOUCH *him and he might be a* JEW *or a* NIGGER.

(*AG* 176)

In that same chapter, "Jacataqua," Williams tells an anecdote that also alludes to his own sense of being the "other." A white woman "accused of having had intercourse with the apartment's colored elevator boy" was abandoned by her husband and later it was discovered that "there had been a darky in *his* family six generations before." This evokes the implied mingling that took place when his grandfather Sol Hoheb married Williams' grandmother from Martinique, as well as that hazy link to the "Enriquez" brothers. Williams punctuates his anecdote with the exclamation, "There's the dénouement for every good American!" This *conceptista* remark is quite loaded: true Americans should discover this mingling in the final scene of their lives; that discovery would also be both to undo (*denouer*) and untie (thus liberate) "good" (Puritan) Americans. This emblematic celebration of his own mingled blood gives his final admonition a satirical, autobiographical application: "Be careful whom you marry!"

The chapter "Advent of the Slaves," then, was also more than an exercise in history writing. In it, Williams advanced the qualities that Africans contributed both to America and to himself. Drawn to their beauty, he praised African-American culture:

> *For purity of religious devotion, in the simplicity of their manoeuvres, they exceed our greatest application. Personal cleanliness becomes*

them with an oriental grace before which our ablutions pale to
insignificance.[6]

(*AG* 211)

He then cites briefly from his poem "Apology," from *Al Que Quiere.* That
poem both apologizes and is an apology for his having been stirred "today" to write about the beauty of "our non-entities," whose dark polished
faces he compares to "old Florentine oak." He is addressing the "leading
citizens," whose white faces, here called "set pieces," also stir him, "but
not / in the same way" (*AG* 210), a comment that is left up to the reader
to interpret. Another riddle here is the ambiguity of the word "today." Did
black faces inspire him on a given day, or was this a description of his
consciousness at that stage of his life? If the latter, he was genteelly expressing the same feelings that, years later, he put into the mouth of Tituba in the play *Tituba's Children:* "These are not my people. You all got
white, hard faces" (*ML* 235).

Consistent with his identifying with "the other," Williams also confessed to a strong sexual attraction for the dark woman. Although this
attraction also makes him given to stereotypes of her as more sinful and
passionate, for his time this public confession of weakness for the mag-
netism of the dark she-demon reveals Bill at his most daring and liberated. The poem "XXVII" in *Spring and All* enthrones the "Black eyed su-
san." Sounding like a Spanish conqueror enraptured by his conquest, he
voices his love for the "savagery" that he perceives in her. The "white
daisy / is not / enough" (Florence was a white flower), attracted as he was
to the "dark woman," which of course included the black-haired gypsy
girl in Granada:

> But you
> are rich
> in savagery—
>
> Arab
> Indian
> dark woman

(*CPI* 236)

"The Colored Girls of Passenack—Old and New" describes the difference in intensity between the heat given off by the white woman and the
"furnaces of emotional power" he experienced in the woman of color:

I've seen tremendous furnaces of emotional power in certain colored women, unmatched in any white—outside, perhaps, the devotional females who make up "society," and whose decadent fervors are so little understood. There, in the heat of "entertainments," of pleasure perhaps, the Negress can be matched. Perhaps the fervent type is more accessible in the colored race because it is not removed to socially restricted areas. I don't know. But I do know that I have had my breath taken away by sights of colored women that no white woman has equalled for me.

(*FD* 55)

The "furnace" here evokes the one in which he destroyed "Philip and Oradie," the furnace Stewie took care of, and the gas stove in "The House," all symbols of the heat with which Williams also associated Latin sensuality. Because of their heat, women of color are spiritually American.

A kindred celebration of dark beauty was one of several things that Williams found appealing about the poetry of the Puerto Rican poet Luis Palés Matos, whom he imitated in a few poems. In the 1941 "The Gentle Negress," for example, Williams subtly emulated Palés' technique of portraying a black person as an embodiment of overlapping times and spirits. The titular gentle negress intrigues Williams because of her quiet way, her listening for the "more / than can be seen" while she is "Unresistant to go / down down quietly." What she hears, Williams imagines, are sounds of her African past:

No other such luxuriance: the
elephant among bending trees,
the grass parting and
horned head through!
. . . .
Listening; more
than can be seen! Listening to
the shriek of monkeys that hides
a deeper tone—under.

(*CPII* 47)

Several such simian images are found throughout Palés Matos' poems, but that elephant image most explicitly echoes the one in Palés' poem "Numen":

> and the powerful elephant
> halving jungles with each step
> pounds a path toward the farthest
> and eternal ancestral numen.[7]

Aside from that borrowed image, "The Gentle Negress" is actually modeled after a combination of two other poems by Palés, "Pueblo Negro" and "Kalahari." In "Pueblo Negro," the names of African cities, "Mussumba, Tombuctú, Farafangana," evoke in the poet a black town "of dream," in which

> The compact hippo submerges
> in a succulent mud broth,
> and the fat and ivory elephant
> chews his vague dream under the baobab.

> (Palés Matos 155)

This dream town, however, only exists as the song of a muse, a black woman whose sensual song spreads in the poet's imagination:

> It is the black woman singing
> her sober life of a domestic animal;
> the black woman from sunbaked zones,
> who smells of earth, of game, of sex.
> It is the black woman singing,
> and her sensual song spreads without bound
> like a clear atmosphere of bliss
> in the shade of the palm trees.

> (Palés Matos 155)

"Kalahari" is also about the evocative power of a name, this time of the desert region from which slaves were brought to Puerto Rico. The hungover poet describes the morning and the previous night's brothel where, he recalled, things "became distant" and he heard someone say "Camel, a drink, a drink." Then that morning, while reading a magazine, the word simply popped into his head:

Don't know why, but my thoughts without rudder
cast anchor in a bay of cameoed palm trees
with monkeys, monkeys by the hundreds
braiding a wild crisscross of leaps.

Why now the word Kalahari?
It has surged unexpectedly, inexplicably . . . [sic]
Kalahari! Kalahari! Kalahari! . . .

(Palés Matos 157)

Williams' "The Gentle Negress" is also a catalog of images evoked by a name, "Lillian":

Hiding
and waiting: a luxuriance,
a prominence. Unresistant to go
down quietly, in a violence of
half spoken words! Lillian!
Lillian!

(*CPII* 47)

Three years later, in 1944, Williams published another "The Gentle Negress," this one translated into his own voice, stripped of Palés' African imagery, although still retaining the animal imagery in the suggestion that the poet and Lillian were two cats: "Wandering among the chimneys / my love and I would meet" (*CPII* 94). But, reminiscent of Palés Matos' love poem to a symbolic mulatta, Williams' new love poem still underscores the complement of his "pale skin" ("white skin" in the earlier version) and hers "brown as peat." This pairing of dark and light, of course, also respects Williams' stylistic grammar, in which dark is always the deeper color. So the woman's implicitly black eyes have "a longing hard to fathom." Equally hard to fathom are the final loaded two lines, "as I sat to comfort her / lying in bed," which have three possible meanings: only she was lying in bed, he was lying in bed with her, or they were telling love lies to each other in bed.

Besides being a kindred admirer of dark women, Luis Palés Matos represented an important component of Williams' identity, about which he showed signs of becoming obsessed during the Spanish Civil War. Two years after the defeat of the Spanish Republicans, he attended the Inter-American Writers Conference where he received Palés Matos' book

Tuntún de Pasa y Grifería (*Tomtom of Kinky Hair and Black Things,*
1937), subtitled *Poemas Afroantillana* (*Afro-Antillean Poems*), a collection
of poems for which the Puerto Rican had become known throughout Latin
America. The timing was optimal for Williams to come in contact with
this poet from Elena's homeland, because Palés Matos instantly occupied
the empty gap in a literary genealogy that Williams had been interweav-
ing into his work since his Kore was first in "hell."

Luis Palés Matos (1898–1959) grew up in the distinctly African coastal
town of Guyama, where his parents' black maids often took him by the
hand into their world. Like other Latin Americans who emulated new
European movements before realizing that what Europeans "discovered"
they had already known in their respective cultures,[8] during a Dadaist
phase Palés Matos became interested in black speech for its sound value.
He discovered, however, that much of that language had really become
part of the island's standard speech. He realized as well that this language,
whose humor and African-derived words no serious writer would have
dared to use, also made possible a poetry that spoke in a novel and truly
Caribbean voice. Eventually Palés' tightly Gongorine "Afro-Antillean"
poems (Palés was another brother in Williams' "line") inspired other
Latin American poets, both black and white, to discover the unprestigious
lexicon in their own societies, thereby spawning a movement. Over time,
unfortunately, his work was wrongly compared to the poetry of black
poets, compared to whom Palés Matos appeared to exploit rather than
celebrate black culture, prompting his being dismissed in the sixties as a
racist.

But Palés Matos was not a maker of black masks: his subject was the
spirit. *Tuntún de Pasa y Grifería* (Palés Matos 146) records his evolving
consciousness, from stereotypical invocations of the white explorer's Africa to satires of black Caribbean colonial imitators. Every poem was an
exercise in defining the *numen* or spiritual essence of the Caribbean, and
ultimately affirmed an American vision that paralleled Williams' in *In the
American Grain.* With the extinction of the native Taínos and Caribs, Palés
argued in his essay "Hacia una poesía afroantillana" ("Toward an Antillean Poetry"), the island's Africans, who had found in the Caribbean an
emerald copy of their original geography, took possession of the landscape, becoming the new natives. While the whites, dreaming of Europe,
owned and materially exploited the New World, the African, who worked
it, gave the land its character:

To cure themselves of the tedium of the islands—that unfathomable te-
dium that not adapting produces—the well-off colonials take trips to
the mother country. Others, less fortunate, console themselves by
dreaming of Galicia and Andalusia. Thus, in the original process of
our psychological formation, we found ourselves with two competing
cardinal forces: one, the Hispanic posture, fleeting, unresigned, resis-
tant; another, the black stance, firm and confidently claiming a stake
in the new environment.

(Palés Matos 221)

In the face of the Yankee intruder trying to impose Anglo culture on his people, and island intellectuals who in reaction became disciples of the exiled Spaniards Juan Ramón Jiménez and Pablo Casals, who locally dominated the cultural scene, Palés Matos boldly posited that while the Caribbean's roots were half-Western, its defining spirit was African, which also informed its inhabitants, whatever their color. Moreover, what European culture remained was exhausted while African culture contin- ued to impart its vitality, as expressed in the island's cult to sensuality. This sensual *numen* both gave distinction to a people who would other- wise be bland colonial imitations of Spain, and guaranteed that Puerto Rico would never be annexed by the United States, as the Yankee will always mercifully disdain a nigger, sinful and savage. "Shake it," exhorts a refrain of a later poem:

> While you dance, no power on earth
> can transform your soul and spunk.
> Neither turncoats from down here,
> nor Misters from up there.[9]

In sum, from Palés Matos' poetry radiated the Dionysian *duende*, and in him Williams had found a truly American spiritual brother, from his mother's homeland no less, who understood that the spirit of a culture resides in the local idiom, the popular speech, and not in a remotely rele- vant European literary language. Thus, in the prefatory note to his trans- lation "Prelude in Boricua," Williams elevates Palés Matos, concluding with words that in a U.S. context also applied to himself:

Luis Pales Matos is a Puerto Rican, probably one of the most important
poets of all Latin America today—though many would contest this
from a conventional viewpoint.[10]

Judging from that note, Williams met Palés Matos, a poet in whom he instantly perceived something of himself. A bit of Uncle Carlos' life resides in the cultured family that Williams describes and, like William Carlos, Palés Matos was in need of a translator:

> He is a man of about forty, one of five children, brothers and sisters, of two very remarkable people. The elder Matos was a distinguished writer in his own right, his wife the same, and all the children are writers. It is said to be a marvelous treat to hear any one of them read any of the family productions. It is said of the father, who was an ardent atheist, that he dropped dead in a theatre while reading one of his poems embodying a violent attack of the Creator. Luis Palés Matos, the son, is in crying need of an American translator or, at worst, interpreter.

> ("Prelude," *American Prefaces* 156)

The note also leaves clear that one key detail about the translated poem ironically escaped Williams' understanding. Williams thought that the titular "Boricua" was a "corruption" of the indigenous name for Puerto Rico, "Borinquen." While derived from "Borinquen," "Boricua" is an indigenous word synonymous with "Puerto Rican," as Yankee would mean U.S. American. So the title "Preludio en Boricua" means a "prelude" (literally intended as "before the play") in the language of the "Boricua," or the Puerto Rican idiom. Williams' explanation, however, proved felicitous because the more accurate title would have senselessly claimed that the English translation was in another language. On the other hand, Williams was indeed aware of the impossibility of translating the "musical sense" of Palés' poems, which was why he acknowledged that he did not pretend to actually translate the poem:

> This not-to-be-called translation of Matos' introductory poem from the collection Tuntún de Pasa y Grifería is offered with profound apologies to the poet. It is no more than an approximate translation which makes no attempt to give the musical sense of the original. Some of the words cannot be rendered in English at all, not even in American nigger talk. The mood is West Indian, as are the words which portray the mood.[11]

His rendering is, as he admits, approximate, but more important, Williams takes possession of the poem, making it express the ideas in *In the*

American Grain and *The Great American Novel*. The two opening lines reveal the consciousness with which Williams translated the poem:

> Tuntún de pasa y grifería
> y otros parejeros tuntunes.

> Mixup of kinkhead and high yaller
> And other big time mixups.

(CPII 45)

The onomatopoetic "tuntún" imitates a drumbeat ("tomtom"). The word has another idiomatic application, *al tuntún:* "off the cuff, off the top of one's head," but would not translate as "Mixup." Williams' choosing to translate it "mixup" did stress the poem's general theme; it also expressed his own favorite theme of American mingling:

> From her jamboree, taking the trail,
> Flies Cuba, all sails set
> To gather on her haunches
> The golden tourist Niagara.

> (Tomorrow they'll be shareholders
> In some sugar mill
> And take over with the money . . .)

> And in whatever corner—lot, bay,
> Pier or cane-field—
> The negro drinks his cold portion
> Consoled by the melody
> That springs from his own bowels.

> Jamaica, the heavy tub-of-guts
> Switches her lingo to guts enough.
> Santo Domingo dolls herself up
> And with imposing civic gesture
> Stirs her heroic genius
> To a hundred presidential odes.
> With her tray of penny candy
> And white magic eyes
> Comes Haiti to the market.
> The Windward Islands are made up

Of overwhelming disgusts
To astonish the cyclones
With their fly-swatter palm trees.

And Puerto Rico? My burning island
For thee all has indeed ended.
Among the shambles of a continent
Puerto Rico, lugubriously
You bleat like a roast goat.

(*CPII* 45–46)

The tossed salad of island images in that poem obviously filled lacunae of his father's and mother's background, especially the memories of his father, who traveled through the region. Furthermore, Williams must have read into the poem the healing power of the imagination. In the Spanish original the "*negro*" is more literally "intoxicated" by his inner music; Williams has him "consoled."

Although "Preface in Boricua" was the only poem Williams translated from *Tuntún*, as seen in the poem "The Gentle Negress" others from that book were of special interest to Williams. In "Mulata-Antilla," a poem about a mythic mulatta, Palés Matos celebrates his finally accepting that his American culture is not the purely Spanish one dreamed by his society, but something new, half Spanish and half African, symbolized by the mulatta:

In you now, mulatta,
I cling to the lukewarm sea of the Antilles.
. . . .
. . . .
. . . .
in your womb both my races conjugate
their essential, affable juices.

(Palés Matos 171–172)

This poem culminated a process that had begun with Palés Matos' poking fun at black culture as he adventured in its popular speech. Now, he sees his own spirit defined by that culture: "In you now, mulatta. . . ." Thus, she was Palés Matos' counterpart to Williams' black-eyed Jacataqua "in whom showed the best traits of her mixed French and Indian blood" (*AG* 186); Palés' Mulata-Antilla embodied the mingled Caribbean *numen* or genius, as Williams' Jacataqua and She-metaphor embodied America. Around this pivotal idea, Palés Matos' diversity of poems written in different phases, in a variety of tones and postures, form a book-long declaration of love to his Caribbean islands, however unprestigious before the world. This regional focus of *Tuntún de Pasa y Grifería* obviously had much to offer Williams who, as he told Edith Heal, had been wanting "to write a long poem" but didn't know what to write about until he hit on the "idea of a man identified with a city," an "idea" that happened to coincide with the idea of Palés Matos' persona, a man identified with a geographical region. Williams told Edith Heal that the final concept of *Paterson* came to him in 1941, which also happened to be the year of the Inter-American Writers Conference in Puerto Rico:

> *I had known always that I wanted to write a long poem but I didn't know what I wanted to do until I got the idea of a man identified with a city. . . . Looking around, the idea came to me in a leisurely way. I had written a poem called* Paterson *as far back as 1926. . . . However, the early poem did not touch on my later theme for the long poem. You have seen, however, that by 1941 the idea was there. . . .*
>
> *(IWW* 71–72)

Williams' reference to 1941, of course, could have been merely coincidental. The Inter-American Writers Conference took place in April of that year, so it is also possible that the "later theme" came to Williams in the months preceding the conference and *Tuntún* at best only confirmed the concept's merits. But Williams had another marker to help him remember the importance of that year: his translation of "Prelude in Boricua" (published in 1942), a poem that conveniently articulated, in a Caribbean context, the "later theme" of his epic. Besides the translation itself, another indicator that Williams in fact felt indebted to Palés is the tribute to him found in Book One.[12] It is introduced by a prose segment on the importation of Irish women to Barbados "to be sold as slaves," signifying the procreation of more mixed blood:

> *Forced by their owners to mate with the others these unfortunates were succeeded by a few generations of Irish-speaking negroes and mulattoes. And it is commonly asserted to this day the natives of Barbados speak with an Irish brogue.*
>
> *(P* 13)

The "mingling" and mulatta theme thus introduced, the following poem, about a *National Geographic* photograph, echoes Palés' poems with images of an imagined Africa:

> I remember
> a *Geographic* picture, the 9 women
> of some African chief semi-naked
> astraddle a log, an official log to
> be presumed, heads left:
>
> Foremost
> froze the young and the latest,
> erect, a proud queen, conscious of her power,
> mud-caked, her monumental hair
> slanted above her brow—violently frowning.
>
> (*P* 13)

The "remember," as in "Asphodel," is a *conceptista* image, "re-member," suggesting fragmentation and composition, a memory that integrates itself with him once more. Here he remembers a "*Geographic* picture," which although set in an exotic region, contains images that are global, *geo-graphic*, not *National Geographic*. Williams' "African chief," with nine mudcaked wives, imitates an image in Palés' "Elegía del Duque de la Mermelada" ("Elegy on the Duke of Marmalade"), in which the Duke is said to have "five wives smelling of mud and the jungle" (Palés Matos 166). Williams' image of "the young and the latest" wife, also "mudcaked," is a replica of Palés' "Black Majesty," in which the goddess Tembandumba materializes on the Caribbean street when invoked by black dances:

> Culipandeando la reina avanza
> y de su inmensa grupa resbalan
> meneos cachondos que el gongo cuaja
> en ríos de azúcar y de melaza.
>
> (Palés Matos 156)

> Curvaceous behind, the Queen advances
> as down her huge rump drip
> sexual jiggles the conga curds
> into rivers of cane juice and molasses.

The neologism *culipandeando,* translated here as "Curvaceous behind," makes the line especially memorable in Spanish because it onomatopoetically evokes the cadence of Tembandumba's gait. This is significant because Williams cloned the original rhythm, while transforming the image of the "proud queen"'s rear end to a column of other wives "Behind her":

> Culipandeando la Reina avanza,
> y de su inmensa grupa resbalan
>
> Behind her, packed tight up
> in a descending scale of freshness

                                                                    (*P* 13)

By this imitation in *Paterson* Williams rendered tribute both to his Puerto Rican heritage and to Palés Matos for giving him the conceptual framework for his own autobiography in poem. Thus Palés joined the other Spanish-language tributaries to the person "we ourselves have been," along with Ruiz, who contributed a sense of good fusion, Manrique and Góngora, who together contributed the river, the *conceptismo* of both Góngora and Quevedo, who also contributed the wit, and Lorca, who contributed a sense of continuity. For, even though a contemporary, Palés Matos, also in the "line" of Góngora, was Williams' necessary New World link that completed the genealogy of the structure through which he expressed his struggle. That completed Spanish-language genealogy forms the deep structure of the poetic history of the son of a Latin-rooted *Pater*—

> telling by how dark a bed
> the current moves
> to what sea that shines
> and ripples in my thought

                                              ("A Flowing River," *CPII* 66)

—and over that dark bed runs the river on whose surface shine the visible reflections of *Paterson.*

Tributes, whether encoded or explicit, were intrinsic to Williams' style, a structural acknowledgment that his writing possessed collaborating spirits. Allusions, including the alter images, are the most obvious tributes, but the same double service can be performed by any trope, translation, or encoding (Góngora's strained syntax in "The Wanderer," Quevedo's sense of humor in "Con Brio," and the imitation of Palés Matos in *Paterson*), a way of adding to his surface self-portrait, a deep-structure self-characterization. Certainly Pound must have contributed to Williams' interest in this sense of "tribe" as another measure of identity. But Pound was selective about who made up the members of the tribe. While advocating a universal tribe, in practice he excluded Carlos and Elena. Pound's personal divisive attitude must have readily provoked Williams to define for himself "the tribe" whose tale poetry is supposed to tell. In so defining, Williams personalized the tribe concept, seeing the American tribe in his own image, a composite like himself, of spirits converging from many origins.

Williams' most elaborate tribute conceit is, of course, the Passaic River. Historically his antecedents traveled long distances by means of water tributaries, which were the avenues of native tribes, Spanish tribes, English tribes, French tribes. Rivers threaded the diverse American bloodlines, as mingled as his own heritages. Thus the river was the perfect multilayered metaphor of American pluralism and of his own multistreamed life. And he had read Jorge Manrique's *Coplas* in Quintana's anthology, in which he marked off enthusiastically: "Our lives are the rivers / whose courses run to the sea / . . . ." But, whereas Manrique's eyes followed the current toward a figurative death, Williams developed his metaphor by looking back toward its origins and its life:

> *I took the river as it followed its course down to the sea; all I had to do was follow it and I had a poem. There were the poor who lived on the banks of the river, people I had written about in my stories. And there was the way I felt about life, like a river, following a course. . . .*
>
> *The poem begins with general observations of the conditions of life in the area, "the elemental character of the place" as I said in the Author's Note. A stream has to begin somewhere; that somewhere seemed to me important. The concept of the beginning of a river is of course a symbol of all beginnings.*
>
> (*IWW* 73–74)

Williams' river was more like Góngora's, which "tyrannized the countryside usefully," creating valleys, fertilizing, and allowing cities to flourish: a maker. In *A Voyage to Pagany,* the Arno is described as gathering "tribute" and is compared to the "makers" of Florence and France:

> *It was the Arno, before Florence, gathering tribute from the fields—a*
> *workaday river—countryman, maker, poet—poetic river. River, make*
> *new, always new—using rain, subterranean springs to make great*
> *bounty.*

(VP 96)

What Williams saw in the Passaic was a perfect reflection of himself: the product of tributaries and the maker. And like him, the Passaic reflected to the world images of his immediate world while the countless, remote legacies from its tributaries were mixed unseen in its murky depths. The challenge was to pull "the disparate together to clarify" what would otherwise be murky and "compress" into the dimensions of a poem:

```
. . . a mass of detail
to interrelate on a new ground, difficultly;
an assonance, a homologue
                              triple piles
pulling the disparate together to clarify
and compress

the river, curling, full . . .
```

(P 20)

The lines' river-like structure, especially in Williams' combining the river's flow with rhetorical imagery, evokes Góngora's "winding discourse" that made an image of the texture of the text.

Imitations, of course, are forms of tribute because influences are synonymous with tributaries. Where simple *influence* differs from *tribute* is that in the latter Williams intends to make the connection visible or resonant in some way that is identifiable, even if just to himself. Admittedly, distinguishing between unconscious influence, encoded tribute, and outright tribute can come down to interpretation. The presence of Góngora, for example, in the quoted winding image of the river is far more subtle, perhaps even questionable, than an allusion to Shakespeare or Gris. But the *concept* of tribute remains fundamental to both Williams' sense of himself and his style, which means that in reading him one has to *assume* tribute, even if one has to seek it out. The tribute, in other words, is merely a tropical (excuse the pun: from *trope*) manifestation of what Louis Simpson succinctly defined as Williams' single discourse, his autobiography:

> *With other writers, we must be on guard against thinking that they are writing about themselves—with Williams the reverse is true: almost everything he wrote is autobiography.*[15]

Williams employed the *tribute* to acknowledge those *tributaries* that rendered inspiriting *contributions* to his writing, and therefore his being. A tributary was a medium through which Williams inherited another soul or spirit, and paying tribute reaffirmed or celebrated membership in that spiritual *tribus,* resulting in a rebirth and a kinship. *The Autobiography,* for example, is composed of tributes to those who "contributed" to the making of the writer; *Paterson* reiterates the same tribute idea but with the central image of the river, whose disparate details are tributaries. In this vein, all his poems addressed "To" someone or something are tributes that are intended to affirm, in either a subdued or explicit fashion, a spiritual tributary. Only two of his poems, however, actually have the word "Tribute" in the title, but these serve as paradigms of Williams' application of the concept.

Rebirth and kinship are ideas explicitly delineated in "Tribute to Neruda the Poet Collector of Seashells." Speaking about Neruda as if he were dead at the time of the poem's writing, Williams speaks to his mother on her treatment in heaven of the Chilean poet.[14] Punning on "see/sea," Williams compares Neruda's sea/see-shells with the imagination:

> Now that I am all but blind,
> however it came about,
> though I can see as well
> as anyone—the imagination
>
> has turned inward as happened
> to my mother when she
> became old: . . .

(CPII 357)

Poems, see-shells, are a turning inward, which the shell collector Neruda certainly did often, to write from within. According to Williams, the "changeless beauty" of the varieties of seashells—the varieties of ways to turn inward—contributed to Neruda's lines' possessing "the variable pitch / which modern verse requires" (*CPII* 358).

Williams' sense of kinship with Neruda, however, was not just rooted in a common appreciation of modern verse. Indeed, Neruda was a truly world class poet from Latin America, making him a vindication of Carlos. More specifically, they shared the same cultural-spiritual-poetic *tribus*. Thus Neruda was a figurative brother: "Be patient with / him, darling mother" (*CPII* 358). Also, like Lorca, Neruda affirmed the continuity of their "line," which also reaffirmed Williams' sense of himself. And because Neruda *contributed*, Williams rendered *tribute* in kind. Conversely, through this tribute, Williams is reborn in Neruda as a Spanish-writing poet, the son of Elena, who never cared for her son's modern poems.

In "Tribute to Painters" Williams writes to those painters who contributed to the evolution of the new aesthetics, in whose perception of reality his own personal and literary illogic makes complete sense. The poem traces the chronology of painters who had made their offerings to the modern search for "the cure," that favorite word that implies a malady and which here alludes to painting's moribund condition at the turn of the century. But this *cure* was also a *remedy* for his personal condition of being a divided self with a fragmented life, a condition understood by the new art. Thus the poem simultaneously pays public and private tribute to the therapeutic effects of the new art.

This "cure" began with Arabic art, which was conceptual, appealing to the intellect with geometric riddles:

> The cure began, perhaps,
> with the abstractions
> of Arabic art

(*CPII* 296)

Arabic art, one of the antecedents of cubism, was also another tributary from his Spanish past. *Al-Andaluz* was the Arabic name for Spain and the root of "Andalusia," the name of the province in which Williams was reborn, where he had seen the Alhambra. The "cure" also came to him through Dürer, Da Vinci, Bosch, Freud, Picasso, and Gris, all alter images in which Williams identified a sense of "line," i.e., those who saw "it— / the shattered masonry." Dürer passed on the discoveries of the Italian Renaissance to Northern European sensibilities; his "*Melancholy* / was aware of it— / the shattered masonry." Da Vinci "saw it, / the obsession, / and ridiculed it / in *La Gioconda.*" Bosch painted "congeries of tortured souls and devils / who prey on them / fish / swallowing / their own entrails." Freud, an artist whose medium was the mind, destroyed our reliance on surface perception, revealing a more powerful hidden self. Picasso similarly discovered an art that sees not as the eye sees reality but as the mind knows it to be. He redirected art away from the traditional Western emotional stimulus and toward the intellect, receiving tributaries from Andalusian Arabic art and African sculpture. Gris synthesized the two traditions by returning color and form to cubist art; he also best articulated the implications of cubism's discoveries to both the art world and Williams. In sum, each possessed the *duende;* each celebrated "deformities" of conventions and the logical, thus opening the imagination so Gertrude Stein could write poetry beyond the limitations of linear thought, of words as words:

> Satyrs dance!
> all the deformities take wing
> centaurs
> leading to the rout of the vocables
> in the writings
> of Gertrude
> Stein . . .
>
> (*CPII* 296)

Thus, in being a breaker of molds, icons, or expectations, each in his way also imaged Williams himself and in so doing contributed to his "cure," a therapeutic calm, a stasis, "without / liquor or dope of any sort":

> We know
> that a stasis
> from a chrysalis
> has stretched its wings
>
> (*CPII* 297)

This stasis comes to his female-poet soul, sensually and violently "like a bull / or the Minotaur," or as music, "Beethoven / in the scherzo / of his 5th Symphony / stomped / his heavy feet," in the sexual way that poetry affects him.

The painters' cure for Williams was to treat the mind's fragmentation as normal, as if thoughts were a dance in the imagination. "Dreams possess me / and the dance of / my thoughts," he proceeds, referring to that aforementioned simile "involving animals / the blameless beasts." But, reflecting on his own need to resort to an image, he becomes aware of "the tyranny of the image" and how "men / in their designs," i.e., the painters, "have learned / to shatter it":

> And there came to me
>   just now
>   the knowledge of
> the tyranny of the image
>   and how
>   men
> in their designs
>   have learned
>   to shatter it
> whatever it may be,
>   that the trouble
>   in their minds
> shall be quieted,
>   put to bed
>   again.

                                                                    (*CPII* 298)

Williams expresses his awareness of the ambiguous "it" in "to shatter it" (the tyranny or the image), but clarifies by adding an ambiguity, "whatever it may be," which also suggests "whatever [important icon] it may be" that is being shattered. The new designs shatter the false picture that images give us of an ordered, mirrored reality; the painters have allowed "men's minds," actually Williams', to feel stasis in accepting the natural fragmentation, confusion, and illogic. The "trouble" in the mind is cured, "quieted, / put to bed / again."

This image is actually a recycling of an earlier image found in a vignette in *Kora in Hell,* in which Williams described a murdered corpse on the county physician's table: "All the troubled stars are put to bed now" (*I* 38), the stars being literally the bullet holes and figuratively the person's misfortunes in life. The death here is an ultimate relief, demonstrating that in "Tribute to Painters" Williams is expressing gratitude for a *personal* cure. As the death of that troubled life cured that corpse of its misery, in opening his generation's locked mind and allowing him to feel normal the painters permitted him to be at peace with himself.

The "cure" in "Tribute to Painters," therefore, joins the chain of "cure" usages, all hinging on his imaginary translation from the Spanish *remedio,* which highlights the combined nuances of "solution" and "remedy." In the poem "The Cure," the word referred to both the *remedy* to being sick from not writing, and the *solution* to his foreignness by "interknit[ting]" his secret sources with the familiar. In the play "The Cure," modeling the lost prince after Prospero in *The Tempest,* Williams psychodramatically represents the crisis of his condition. Prospero, victim of a motorcycle accident, seeks a "cure" (remedy) as well as rebirth in the hands of the nurse (Anglo America) with whom he wants to be sexually united (solution), but who turns him down, faithful to her husband George. Thus "cure" in any of Williams' usages has to be understood according to the ambiguous usages in his stylistic lexicon; so the painters' "cure" was both a solution to the poet's problem and a remedy for the stressful conditions of the man. Grateful for this, he wrote his tribute.

The protean possibilities of the tribute device is illustrated in changes that Williams made to "Tribute to Painters" (1955) when he later imbedded most of that poem into Book Five of *Paterson* (1958). There the catalog of the painters is preceded by a sequence of poems and prose, each reflecting some facet of Williams' multiplicity: a letter from Pound; a lesbian to whom he was attracted on the street (who evokes Sappho and Williams' own female principle); a passage from Mezz Mezzrow's (and Bernard Wolfe's) *Really the Blues* (*NW* 716) on listening to Bessie Smith and the mistake of whitening and deadening jazz, the only "honest" music to come out of America. Then what was originally "Tribute" begins with its allusion to painters, followed by a CBS television transcript, in which the military-industrial culture puts the relevance of poetry into question. This ends Part II.

"Tribute," in other words, was made part of a potpourri of Williams' life experiences, making the section on painters now highlight a stasis between life and art, the same illogical balance evoked by juxtaposing ostensibly unrelated prose and poetry in *Paterson.* Different from the original poem, this new version ends with "blameless beasts" and lacks the original ending with its imagery on the troubled mind and its "cure," leaving that semantic layer to be decoded merely from the nuances of the words "cure" and "Freud." Without the original "Tribute to Painters" to help us, the therapeutic value that Williams ascribed to the image of the painters and "Freud" would seem farfetched. His compressing that personal theme into simple allusion, in this case, "Freud," demonstrates how other allusions, such as "Gris" or "Shakespeare," were intended to say much more than might appear.

By means of diverse "tribute" devices, Williams imaged in structure the spiritual stasis that was his life's obsession. For that stasis—between his two spirits, between his two selves—was attained only in the aesthetic balance of his diverse tributaries, which is to say their harmony in the illogic of the poem, a "Satyr's dance" (*CPII* 296), a dance "satyric when . . . most devout" (*P* 221). His life was "a mass of detail / to interrelate" (interconnect/internarrate) (*P* 20), and only the poem in its dance was capable of giving form to his signature of mingling, unity, fierce singleness. Only the poem composed stasis, whose music Williams needed to hear in the structure of his poem.

Chapter 7

The Music of Stasis

My furious wish was to be normal, undrunk, balanced in
everything.

(*The Autobiography* 51)

Where am I to go, whither?
The road's there, the road to Two-Gods.

(from "Three Nahuatl Poems," *CPII* 429)

Williams' wanderings, rebirths, and all other motifs of his "struggle" translated into structure, converge in the current that was his lifelong desire for stasis. In his earliest books, he celebrated stasis in balance: "The Wanderer" responds to "Philip and Oradie"; *The Tempers* is self-explanatory; *Kora in Hell* answers the poor reaction to his Spanish phase that produced *Al Que Quiere* and *The Tempers,* Kore intended as an ideal midpoint between his cultural "weathers" and temperatures. By *Kora,* however, he had also discovered stasis in structural and imagistic synthesis, the stylistic maturity that eventually led to *Paterson.* Following the current of his work back to his first poems, then, from the day Williams chose his three-part writer's name, stasis became his signature, a stasis in literary symbols that synthesized his quest for balanced personal identity; the cubist self-portrait one can extrapolate from his works forms a "fierce singleness" of rectifications and adjustments to approximate stasis.

Williams' account of how he chose the title of *Al Que Quiere* gives us a glimpse into his struggle to arrive at the precise words that would both serve as a revealing title and a proper encoding of his personal conflict. In a 1917 letter to Marianne Moore, he tells of his book's as yet lacking a title:

But the title bothers me. You see I am a mixture of two bloods, neither
of them particularly pure. Yet there is always in me harking back to

*some sort of aristocracy—probably of the gallows or worse—that will
have a hand in all my democratic impulses. Then again there is a certain strain in me that will always be handling an axe for budding
King Charles Firsts. So I torture myself through life. But there are acute
moments that seem distillations of agony and this is one of them.*

(*SL* 40)

Williams was confessing to Moore that all his life he aspired for a spiritual
balance, which at times resulted in a "torture" and "distillations of
agony." His explanation is just another case of his translating his autobiographical dilemma into symbols. Here, using historical symbols, he offers
an *apologia* for his feeling compelled to use Spanish in the title:

I want to call my book:
    A Book of Poems:
    al que quiere!

(*SL* 40)

Also characteristically, Williams camouflages the seriousness of his
choice with feigned whimsical motivation:

*—which means: To him who wants it—but I like the Spanish just as
I like a Chinese image cut out of stone: it is decorative and has a certain charm.*

(*SL* 40)

The "decorative" justification, of course, falls back on Bill's ingratiating
angle of view, already assumed in his symbolism of Spanish as synonymous with an aristocratic tendency and English as the equal of democratic tendencies.

This symbolism would appear to have been derived simply enough
from Williams' contrasting ideas that he associated with his Anglo American self with ideas conjured up by his mother's genteel life ("All the Fancy
Things") in Puerto Rico under monarchic Spain, but his heightened
awareness of contrasting civilizations was more likely prompted by the
historic events taking place during that time. The United States was entering a war against the German Kaiser. Anti-German feelings ran high
in his Rutherford community, which began spying on them. Williams, of
course, took to defending his oppressed fellow citizens, his father-in-law
among them, and was condemned by another Rutherford doctor in the
town newspaper (*NW* 120).

At the same time, and connected to the protection of U.S. merchant boats, there was talk of an amendment to the Jones Shipping Act, eventually enacted in 1917, that would impose citizenship on the United States' noncontiguous territories. The public debate over this Jones Act was laced with bitter words over opening the doors to a population of racially inferior types. Surely the Monsantos or the Enriquezes must have shared with Elena their thoughts over the changes that would take place in Puerto Rico. And wouldn't Williams have been drawn to the symbols of that discussion, whether at his parents' home or in the newspapers? Citizenship was the patrimony that Williams felt his parents had denied him by refusing to become citizens. Additionally, even though in his eyes citizenship would not have affected Elena's being Latin and therefore congenitally foreign, this impending act of Congress signified the final violence that history could perform on her: her being wedded involuntarily to her barbarian captors.

The Jones Act, then, promised to do for Williams what his parents had refused to do for him: integrate their backgrounds with his immediate culture. And the public justification for this undemocratic granting of citizenship was the same one invoked to start the war with Spain in 1898 and now with Germany: to defend democracy, an argument Williams surely had heard since he was young, from conversations his parents had with Henna, who had lobbied Teddy Roosevelt for citizenship to Puerto Rico. (Democracy, more than populist nationalism, was often the ideal of nineteenth-century Latin American liberal separatists. In this Henna betrayed Betances.) Williams, who in those years was personally declaring his own independence from his mother's nostalgia for her former aristocracy in colonial Puerto Rico, surely borrowed from the rationale for the Jones Act, i.e., celebrating democracy. Thus, beneath that academic historical explanation that Williams condensed for Moore to justify Spanish in the title seethed many more unsaid words about his cultural background, words that Williams needed to say but that he was encoding in Spanish. The "decorative" reasons he gave for using Spanish also camouflaged the point that all that historical talk on his democratic versus aristocratic tendencies was really a symbolic code through which he expressed his biculturalism.

Years later, as we recall from Chapter 4, Williams told Edith Heal that he used Spanish as a tribute to a student named "Suares" in Switzerland, who had taken Williams under his wing and who on the soccer field would shout to Williams that he should pass the ball. His friend probably shouted "*¡Al que quieras!*" ("to whomever you want"), but Williams either mistranslated the Spaniard's words, arriving at "To Him Who Wants It," or was simply giving Heal a mythical explanation for his extending an invitation to whoever wanted to read his poems. Whether factual or improvised, this explanation confirms Williams' concern over being accepted for being bicultural. In his previous book *The Tempers,* he had included some translations from "El Romancero." Williams doesn't explicitly make the connection to that book or his biculturalism, but one infers that he was worried that no one would receive his new poems because of his foreign component:

> *The phrase made me think of him, wanting the ball on the soccer field, and of myself. I was convinced nobody in the world of poetry wanted me but I was there willing to pass the ball if anyone did want it.*

> (*IWW* 19)

In the context of the impending Jones Act and the major change it augured to his Puerto Rican half, Williams' radical use of Spanish in an English-language book strongly suggests that he was taking the offensive against the "catalogue." The public rhetoric surrounding the citizenship question doubtless encouraged Williams to force the issue, for once and for all, to openly inject his bloodline into the mainstream as the Jones Act was about to violate Elena's homeland and force a mingling. This was another ritualized violence in the American grain. Then one had to consider the implications for Pound's Puritan attitude toward Elena and Carlos. If Elena's tribe was to have citizenship thrust upon it, then her Spanish henceforth also symbolized this Anglo America and democracy, a message to stuff into Pound's pipe. Thus, symbolizing both rebellion against the "catalogue" and a personal balance, the title had to contain Spanish—but only if his intended symbolism was to be clearly understood, which explains the first tentative title that he tested on Moore:

> *A Book of Poems:*
> *al que quiere!*
>   *or*
> *The pleasures of democracy.*

> (*SL* 40)

The *Pleasures of Democracy* served as much more than a counter-weight to the figuratively aristocratic background; the message also was directed at that other aristocracy that would question Williams' standing as an American and his right to choose a Spanish title, i.e., question his right to be both an American and bicultural. The "pleasures" of opening up to pluralism await those readers who would want his poems. With all those nuances covered, the title spoke for him, as "seen from the inside," which ambiguously means as he sees himself or, appropriately said parenthetically, in a way that he secretly understands:

> *Now I like this conglomerate title! It is nearly a perfect image of my own grinning mug (seen from the inside), . . .*

(SL 40)

The tentative longer title also reflects the lack of finesse in Williams' early "insisting upon a dichotomy between the ephemeral particulars and the timeless universal," which he eventually came to unify with "an un-flinching focus upon the particular" (MacGowan 5). A step in the direction of that maturity was his dropping the didactic "or the PLEASURES OF DEMOCRACY" and letting the Spanish stand alone. By so doing he both flaunted the language and turned its meaninglessness to the average reader into a cryptic sound image (as in "Yonolaquierobeber"), infusing his message of democracy into the simple symbolism of a title in two languages in perfect balance, as perhaps suggested by Al Kreymborg, giving the homonymic dedication "Al K Wants: A Book of Poems": *Al Que Quiere: A Book of Poems* (*NW* 145).

Williams' coming to stylistic maturity was signaled by his subsequent book *Kora in Hell,* in which balance finds another mode of expressing itself in a new aesthetics that weaves his obsessions more tightly into structure so that stasis, no longer a binary balance, is attained illogically and fluidly. One of the most revealing illustrations of this weaving, however, is found in the "Prologue," in Williams' answers to letters written to him by Ezra Pound, H.D. (Hilda Doolittle), and Wallace Stevens. The letters by Pound and Stevens had been written in reaction to *Al Que Quiere;* H.D.'s, even though commenting on a poem from an unfinished book, shares with the other two a common subterranean message. Like the objects in Gris' paintings, each letter is a distinct object, engaged in its particular discourse, and at the same time each becomes part of another two-tiered discourse, Williams' monologue on the aesthetics of his "improvisations" and his stylistic "cure" that would "interknit" into this introduction a cultural stasis.

Pound's letter, from which Williams quotes selectively, gnaws at Williams' Achilles' heel, questioning his identity as an American:

> *What the h—l do you a bloomin' foreigner know about the place. Your*
> pere *only penetrated the edge, and you've never been west of Upper*
> *Darby, or the Maunchunk. . . . But I have the virus . . . , the bacillus of*
> *the land in my blood, for nearly three bleating centuries.*

(I 11)

This was the hurtful letter that provoked Williams to answer Pound again in *Spring and All* (1923) and in *The Great American Novel* (1923). By referring only to Williams' *pere,* Pound had eliminated the participation of Mrs. Williams. Her contribution to him, of course, foreignized Williams, an effect that Pound praises ironically:

> *You thank your bloomin' gawd you've got enough Spanish blood to*
> *muddy up your mind, and prevent the current American ideation from*
> *going through it like a blighted colander.*

(I 8)

Pound's quoting from the French near the end of his letter, about the "L'amour excessif d'une patrie," is another sarcasm: French was the other culture toward which Williams' family aspired and fell short. The letter's final punning words reveal Pound's cynical awareness of the abusive punches he had been aiming at the bleeding gash in Williams' personal dichotomy: "Lie down and compose yourself." Pound obviously took "Bill" to be a mask and advised Williams to "lie" less to himself about it and "compose" his true self.

By citing Pound's words, however, Williams puts under scrutiny their flaw, and through them the mainstream's poor understanding of "America." Before quoting the letter, Williams had set up a subversive context by relating a pair of anecdotes that describe Pound's behavior during visits to the Williams home. On one occasion Pound said to Williams that "It is not necessary to read everything in a book in order to speak intelligently of it," adding quickly "Don't tell everybody I said so." Here Williams both tells everybody and turns Pound's off-the-record remark into a metaphor: if it was not necessary to read everything in a book to speak intelligently of it, then Williams didn't have to travel west of "Upper Darby" to speak intelligently of the United States.

At another time Pound read a poem in which his use of the metaphor "jewels" annoyed William George:

> *These jewels,—rubies, sapphires, amethysts and whatnot, Pound went on to explain with great determination and care, were the backs of books as they stood on a man's shelf. "But why in heaven's name don't you say so then?" was my father's triumphant and crushing rejoinder.*
>
> (*I* 8)

This story underscores Pound's pomposity and sense of inflating those things that he values.

Combined, the two accounts expose Pound's backhanded, pretentious, and elitist posture, which Williams had to suffer. Despite their friendship, Pound refused to mingle with or ingratiate himself to what was most important to Williams, and so between them ran an undercurrent of profound ethnic tensions, mainly because Pound never did get Williams' point. Williams' *pere* hadn't ventured west, but he had explored the America to the south. And his maternal blood had explored the whole of North America, from sea to shining sea. That Spanish blood had possessed the American virus for over a century longer than English blood had. But, as Pound demonstrated in his self-serving review of *A Voyage to Pagany,* "Dr. Williams' Position" (*Literary Essays* 398), he closed his eyes to Williams' real position and rationalized base prejudices with erudition and wit.

The paragraph that immediately follows Pound's letter in *Kora* is an ambiguous transition that both answers Pound and establishes the context for H.D.'s letter. Responding to Pound's high-toned observation about preferring the "Greeks as setting out for the colonies" to the (heat) of Sicily and the Italian peninsula (an obvious contradiction, given where Pound lived), Williams describes the balance and symmetry of Greek poetry and sculpture as important, but the wrong kind of balance, being too spiritually one-sided, on the "chilly" side:

> *The ferment was always richer in Rome, the dispersive explosion was always nearer, the influence carried further and remained hot longer.*

Hellenism, especially the modern sort, is too staid, too chilly, too little
fecundative to impregnate my world.

(*I* 12)

Williams, of course, was replaying his customary balance of dichotomies
in contrasting "chilly" Greek and "hot" Roman—a restructuring of heat/
cold and sexual/unsexual alter images that he associated with his Span-
ish/English dualism. None of this really answers Pound head-on, but it
subverts Pound's intentions by associating his "unamerican," "foreign,"
and Spanish-muddied mind with a fecund imagination. This interpretation is supported by the paragraph's concluding sentence, which complains about Hellenism's being "too little fecundative to impregnate my
world" and establishes the sexual context in which we should read the
subsequent paragraph:

Hilda Doolittle before she began to write poetry at least before she
began to show it to anyone would say: "You're not satisfied with me,
are you Billy? There's something lacking, isn't there?" When I was with
her my feet always seemed to be sticking to the ground while she would
be walking on the tips of the grass stems.

(*I* 12)

What was "missing" is implied by the juxtaposition of paragraphs. Coming right after "too little fecundative to impregnate my world," his description of H.D.'s walking on the tips of the grass stems suggests a lack
of physical intensity.

Continuing with that "lack" theme, Williams quotes H.D.'s 1914 letter,
in which she ironically complains about something missing in his poem
"March":

I don't know what you think but I consider this business of writing
a very sacred thing!—I think you have the "spark"—am sure of it, and
when you speak direct *are a poet. I feel in the hey-ding-ding touch run-*
ning through your poem a derivative tendency which, to me is not
you—*not your very self. It is as if you were* ashamed *of your Spirit,*
ashamed of your inspiration!—as if you mocked your own song. It's
very well to mock *at yourself—it is a spiritual sin to mock at your*
inspiration—[1]

H.D. had caught on to Bill's posturing, and alludes to a "shame" that, for us, evokes the shame that twenty years later, in "Eve," Williams himself confessed that he felt toward Elena. But Williams owns up to that defect in the poem, explaining that his mask was a literary phase that he went through:

> *But in any case H.D. misses the entire intent of what I am doing no matter how just her remarks concerning that particular poem happen to be. The hey-ding-ding touch was derivative, but it filled a gap that I did not know how better to fill at the time. It might be said that touch is the prototype of the improvisations.*

> *(I* 13)

The year of the letter, 1914, tells us that Williams was still in his secret Spanish phase when he wrote "March," which explains the attention to detail in the line "you remind me of / the pyramids, our pyramids" (*CPI* 137). Understanding that part of him was steeped in the heat of Spanish "hell," we must recall that the "hey-ding-ding touch" has always been a hallmark of Bill's "relief" against that heat and passion that he associated with his other interfering spirit. "What else, Latins, do you yourselves / seek but relief" from the heat and "lying" of their love songs, he scolds in "The Desert Music" (*CPII* 283). The "gap" that he claimed not to know how to fill at the time, therefore, was really the balance between the two personae.

But his "cure" was the very thing that H.D. disliked, indeed the "prototype of the improvisations," which was a breaking up of defining lines and a mixing up of binary parts. H.D.'s letter accurately described his courage to mock his spirit, if need be, to break new ground, but served it up as critique. Despite appearances, the improvisations were acts of balance, but H.D. could not see this stability, harboring as she did a conventional idea of balance, especially between what is profane and what is "sacred":

> *Oh well, all this might be very disquieting were it not that "sacred" has lately been discovered to apply to a point of arrest where stabilization has gone on past the time. There is nothing sacred about literature, it is damned from one end to the other. There is nothing in literature but change and change is mockery.*

> *(I* 13)

In sum, without getting explicitly biographical, Williams explains to H.D. that he wandered through his imagination looking for a balanced voice and style that would deliver him away from the wrong kind of stasis, be it Pound's ("a flat Hellenic perfection of style") or the deadening stability that nourishes the (here unmentioned but implied) "catalogue": "I'll write whatever I damn please, whenever I damn please and as I damn please and it'll be good if the authentic spirit of change is on it" (*I* 13), i.e., *duende*, the spirit of Carlos.

Wallace Stevens' letter, which contributes to this balance theme in subtler ways, reflects its author's cooly professional relationship with Williams. This quality comes through in the "Foreword" to *The Autobiography*, in which Williams stroked Stevens by reassuring him that, even though he was "scarcely mentioned," he was "constantly in my thoughts." The two other occasions that Stevens' name came up in that book were tangential, once beside Cummings', not especially a Williams favorite, and the other time in the summary remark that in a given year Auden, Cummings, and Stevens "were alive and writing." Stevens, for his part, addresses Williams with the same cordiality, while his letters to Moore make it plain that Williams was not his favorite either. Stevens demurred on reviewing *In the American Grain:* "And I feel sure that one of the things I ought not to do is to review Williams' book" (Stevens 246). He felt that Williams represented "a somewhat exhausted phase of the romantics" (Stevens 279). He was also too busy, he answered Marianne Moore in a letter, to write the announcement for the *Dial* award that Williams had won in 1926. More telling, perhaps, he appended that Moore pass on his "salutations to Carlos the Fortunate," then proceeds to end the single-paragraph letter with the underscored sentence, addressed to Moore, "*I wish I had an inscribed copy of your poems.*" When Stevens did write to Carlos the Fortunate to congratulate him on the award, his words were tinged with irony: "Your townspeople must whisper about you and, as you pass the girls, they surely nudge each other and say 'The golden boy!'"[2]

Stevens' letter, from which Williams quotes, criticizes a lack of consistency in *Al Que Quiere:*

> *My idea is that in order to carry a thing to the extreme necessity to convey it one has to stick to it; . . . Given a fixed point of view, realistic, imagistic or what you will, everything adjusts itself to that point of*

view; and the process of adjustment is a world in flux, as it should be
for a poet. But to fidget with points of view leads always to new begin-
nings and incessant new beginnings lead to sterility.

(*I* 15)

Stevens goes on to praise the talent evident throughout the book, but laments its being "dissipated and obscured." Like H.D., he took the high moralistic road in admonishing that a book is "a damned serious affair." But at best Stevens is oblique about what Williams was actually guilty of:

I am only objecting that a book that contains your particular quality
should contain anything else and suggesting that if the quality should
contain a communicable extreme, in intensity and volume, etc. . . . [Wil-
liams' ellipses] I see it all over the book, in your landscapes and por-
traits, but dissipated and obscured.

(*I* 15)

Exactly what was Stevens getting at? Indeed, *Al Que Quiere* was a salad of a book. It had its Spanish-language images of rebellion, the title and Arévalo Martínez epigraph being only two examples. A few poems have Spanish titles. The selection itself can be classified under two rubrics: poems with the "weather" and those against the "weather." The poem "Apology" epitomizes this counterpoint, addressing those entities who belong to the "weather" and giving Williams' reason for preferring to write about "our non-entities," those against the "weather": "the set pieces / of your faces stir me / —leading citizens— / but not / in the same way" (*CPI* 70). This is a glaring example of how Williams "fidget[s] with point of view" (*I* 15). The inclusion of "The Wanderer," with its twisted syntax and its mythic birth of Bill, is another kind of shift.

But in tiptoeing around his point, Stevens' words take on a life of their own, and Williams milks them for their design. *Kora,* the book being in-troduced, celebrated illogic and conflicting consciousness, so the impro-visations, deserving the same *words* Stevens had for *Al Que Quiere,* if not the same meaning, are effectively explained by the letter (the same trick Williams would pull, sixteen years later, on Quintana's critique of Gón-gora), which Williams quotes with the net effect of putting Stevens' own preconceptions in doubt. The traits in *Al Que Quiere* that Stevens saw as bad things—inconsistency of consciousness, new beginnings, and a lack of a "single manner or mood thoroughly matured and exploited"— Williams transforms into good. Thus he proclaims that Stevens' "criticism . . . holds good for each of the improvisations" (*I* 14–15).

Williams also used the *ad hominem* argument of characterizing Stevens as conformist, adding parenthetically that Stevens was someone whom the poet Skipwith Cannell had "likened to a Pennsylvania Dutchman who has suddenly become aware of his habits and taken to 'society' in self-defense. . . . He is always immaculately dressed" (*I* 15). So interpreted for the reader, Stevens' own words on Williams' "fidget[ing] with points of view" characterize him as a social conformist. And this subversion was on top of the general context in which Williams segued to Stevens' letter, by expounding on the imagination's ability to fuse divergent views. This previous discussion answered Stevens even before we read his complaint:

> *The imagination goes from one thing to another. Given many things of nearly totally divergent natures but possessing one-thousandth part of a quality in common, provided that be new, distinguished, these things belong in an imaginative category and not in a gross natural array.*
>
> (*I* 14)

Of their "totally divergent natures," the two men possessed the "one-thousandth part of a quality in common" as poets. Whatever Stevens thought of Williams personally, Williams was saying, the freshness of his offerings warranted that their mutual point of convergence remain "in an imaginative category" and not in the "gross natural array." In other words, whatever Stevens' real gripe behind his "point of view" remarks, Williams was just as obliquely putting him straight to keep his eye on the vein that runs throughout his work: poetry and what is poetically new. He then takes a swipe at Stevens' characteristic retreat from the physical to the metaphysical, suggesting that Stevens' focus on the latter results from his inability to confront reality, which would explain Stevens' failure to appreciate how Williams the poet lifts to the imagination and poetry those things that Stevens' senses can't handle:

> . . . *But the thing that stands eternally in the way of really good writing is always one: the virtual impossibility of lifting to the imagination*

> *those things which lie under the direct scrutiny of the senses, close to*
> *the nose.*
>
> (*I* 14)

The reference to the nose suggests that Williams' Quevedo-esque poem "Smell!" in *Al Que Quiere* was a swipe at Stevens' eschewing of gross physical reality for metaphysical reflection (as well as a swipe at Stevens' nose):

> Can you not be decent? Can you not reserve your ardors
> for something less unlovely? . . .
> Must you taste everything? Must you know everything?
> Must you have a part in everything?
>
> (*CPI* 92)

The nose is "indiscriminate" while, of course, Stevens was discriminating about many things, which included, Williams doubtless suspected, his "unlovely" half.

It would be simplistic and contrary to the facts to infer from the disagreement between them that Stevens was put off by Williams for ethnic reasons. Stevens was no xenophobe, as is evident from the effusive and substantive dialogue in letters between him and the editor José Rodríguez Feo, whom he patently respected. Another convention, however, does appear to play itself out here: the customary affection Anglos more readily display for the courtesy-buffered contact with imported Latins over the familiarity, stridency, and offensive implications of the domestic variety. That convention appears to explain Stevens' inability to communicate with either Williams' style or cultural vision. Stevens' *quality* argument is the same proffered today by Eurocentric critics to justify their disregard of non-mainstream writing ("if the quality should contain a communicable extreme, in intensity and volume"). As with those latter-day critics, the "quality" rationalization also appears to be an expression of Stevens' resistance to having his own sense of stasis disrupted.

To test this intepretation one need only compare Stevens' letter to Williams with his letter to Moore on *In the American Grain.* Stevens' declaration on the inconsistency of style in *Al Que Quiere* and his perceiving quality "over the book, in your landscapes and portraits, but dissipated

and obscured," parallels how, eight years later, he worded his objection
to *In the American Grain:*

> *What Columbus discovered is nothing to what Williams is looked for.*
> *However much I might like to try to make that out—evolve a main-*
> *land from his leaves, scents and floating bottles and boxes—there is a*
> *baby at home.*

(Stevens 246)

Again Stevens didn't question or counter, and simply pleaded that he was
unable to "make . . . out" what Williams is after, which reveals less an
inability and more a lack of interest in doing so: "However much I might
like to try. . . ." The casual-sounding remark about "a baby at home" was
either part of Stevens' retort or a felicitous irony. The spiritual site of Williams' stasis, in a maelstrom of landscape, cultures, and other figurative
flotsam, was a place that Stevens could not identify as home.

In summary, Williams quoted from these three letters to weave their
perspectives into the prologue in the same way that contrary viewpoints
are juxtaposed and aesthetically balanced in the body of *Kora:*

> *A young woman who had excelled at the intellectual pursuits, a person*
> *of great power in her sphere, died on the same night that a man was*
> *murdered in the next street, a fellow of very gross behavior. The poet*
> *takes advantage of this to send them on their way side by side without*
> *making the usual unhappy moral distinctions.*

(*I* 38)

A second justification for quoting those letters was that they too were improvisations, examples of spontaneous subjective writing charged with
their own sublimations. Finally, all three letters invoked Carlos and thus
helped Williams encode the stasis at the core of the aesthetics of *Kora.*
For *Kora* was doubtless the first book in which Williams came to realize
that he "was lost / failing the poem," as he would write years later in
"Asphodel." Writing the poem and *being* became one, motivated by the
same "agony of self-realization" about which he wrote in "The Desert
Music," his masterpiece on the music of stasis.

"The Desert Music" captures Williams' moment of discovering the stabi-
lizing triumph of poetry over the agony of possessing a divided soul.
Throughout the poem a catalog of antagonistic cultural symbols—Juárez

and El Paso, the man-embryo and the poet-doctor, Mexican popular music and Casals' music, empty gestures and meaningful form, the lying and the genuine, English and Spanish, "us" and "them"—haunt Williams, competing, contradicting each other, transforming him constantly while collectively composing him. Inhabiting these cultural symbols (tributes/tributaries), his different spirits "dance" to the music of his poem that, on another semantic level, also carries on an argument on the nature of literature and art.

The poem opens with an imagistic reiteration of the border between Mexico and the United States:

> —the dance begins: to end about a form
> propped motionless—on the bridge
> between Juárez and El Paso—unrecognizable
> in the semi-dark

(*CPII* 273)

Between dashes, with no upper-case to signal a beginning, the "dance" of the poem is already in process and indicates where it will end "about a form / propped motionless." Meanwhile, the dominant image is the middle, with the first line interrupted with a colon and again the second line with a dash, which marks the middle of the stanza, where like a hinge between four lines is the bridge image, "bridge / between." The bridge spans a divided city and, symbolically at least, two cultures: Juárez, which, although an image in an English-language poem, Williams makes a point of writing with its accent, and El Paso, which although ostensibly Spanish is now English.

By itself the border bridge was charged with Williams' favorite themes. But, as was discussed in Chapter 2, during the time of the writing of this poem (1951), Williams would have already read or heard the image in the propaganda describing the Commonwealth plan for Puerto Rico before the UN as a valid decolonization formula that would make the island "A Bridge between Two Cultures." He later repeated this image in *Yes, Mrs. Williams,* in his description of Elena as a "grotesque" because she "bridged" two cultures. The Commonwealth propaganda doubtless provided the precise visual image beneath a picture he had of himself early on as a "grotesque" who looked for others to play in his "band," as he wrote in "Sub Terra" (*CPI* 63), the opening poem in *Al Que Quiere.* That unchanged, original "grotesque" image—concretized by the embryonic form—is what the first stanza abstractly reiterates in midpoints, halves, borderlines, "semi-dark," and the "dance," which itself implies a bridging, of dancer and dance, dancer and music, or two dancers. That the poem as dance indeed suggested a dichotomy to Williams, had been stated in *Kora:*

> *It is the music that dances but if there are words then there are two dancers, the words pirouetting with the music.*

(I 47)

The bridge/midpoint conceit is graphically sustained in subsequent lines, as whoever saw the mysterious figure first cried out "Wait!," and the word appears centered on the otherwise blank line.

The "form" on the bridge was not a "sack of rags someone / had abandoned," but a living "Egg-shaped" thing propped against the bridge's "supporting girder." What irony, this embryo/form "propped up" against the bridge's most vital point. "What a place to sleep! / on the International Boundary," Williams privately jokes, then proceeds to embellish his *conceptista* image:

> Where else,
> interjurisdictional, not to be disturbed?
>
> How shall we get said what must be said?
>
> Only the poem.

(CPII 274)

How to be inter-juris-dictional, or "say between laws," of languages, of societies, of formal poetry, of literary "catalogues." On the international border one is free from all rules. That interjurisdictional midpoint, to say "what must be said," can be reached only by the poem:

> Only the counted poem, to an exact measure:
> to imitate, not to copy nature, not
> to copy nature
>
> NOT, prostrate, to copy nature
>
>   but a dance! to dance
> two and two with him—

> sequestered there asleep,
> right end up!
>
> (*CPII* 274)

To copy nature is to repeat and not create. To imitate nature would be to create as it does, using its illogical idea of order, identifiable patterns yet with spontaneous, unexplained variations that justify themselves in the total harmony, a mixture of counted measures and breaks from the pattern, a dance. The poem is also a dance, awakened in Williams when he hears a certain music:

> A music
> supersedes his composure, hallooing to us
> across a great distance
>
>   Awakens the dance
> who blows upon his benumbed fingers!
>
> (*CPII* 274)

Williams, aroused to poetry, embodies the dance, which is referred to as "who," it now being the form on the bridge. The composition that begins to take shape in Williams' mind supersedes the form's "composure," a different way of being composed.

The poem taking shape is therefore an "interjurisdictional" dance with the embryo/form, who in the middle of the bridge on the international border is reborn in being free from rigid laws. The law would see in the embryo/form not an image but a dirty vagrant or a corpse:

> The law? The law gives us nothing
> but a corpse, wrapped in a dirty mantle.
> The law is based on murder and confinement,
> long delayed, . . .
>
> (*CPII* 275)

These lines evoke the poem "At Kenneth Burke's Place," in which Williams reminds us that "catalogues" are not the business of earth, that in being respectful of the "catalogue"'s rules anthologies practice an "orthodoxy of plotted murders." In that poem, Williams offers "the green apple smudged with / a sooty life that clings, also, / with the skin" (*CPII* 107), one of many "half rotted" in a basket, as the image of the fruitful outcast with something to offer. In "The Desert Music" that role is played by the "form" that the law would see as a corpse, but that the poet sees as an embryo, promising because of its unheard inner music that had awakened in him the dance. The form's "insensate music" produced this poem, an event "based on the dance":

> but this, following the insensate music,
> is based on the dance:
>> an agony of self-realization
> bound into a whole
> by that which surrounds us
>
> (*CPII* 275)

And what surrounds them are Mexico and the United States, grand operatic symbols of Spanish and English. So that the "agony of self-realization" will not be just that of the embryonic form on the bridge, but of Williams who sees himself in that alter image:

>> I cannot escape
>
> I cannot vomit it up
>
> (*CPII* 275)

The "it" is his own chronic spiritual embryo, ever in "agony of self-realization," which will always be there, and which only the poem brings to full gestation:

> Only the poem!
>
> Only the made poem, the verb calls it
>> into being.
>
> (*CPII* 275)

The "verb" is translated from the Spanish usage of *el verbo,* from the Latin root *verbum,* which also means "word," evoking all creation and also epitomizing the act, doing. A voice—maybe Bill's—says "Heave it into the river." But a Carlos consciousness seems to subvert the literal meaning of that line. The Rio Grande (where the United States and Mexico fuse) can be the perfect symbol where this embryo can be born. The line that follows, then, both works to approve of the dumping and echoes the affirmation of the mingling in *In the American Grain:* "A good thing."

Although the poem had opened with the discovery of the "form" on the bridge, the narrative's chronology began with the trip from California, and the greater portion of the poem is recounted from memory as what "subsequently I saw and what heard" after stopping at El Paso. The second section therefore regresses to describe how they got to the desert.

Returning east by rail, they had crossed a "fertile desert," which as an image of the imagination was fertile, but as a real desert was fertile only "(were it to get water)." This oxymoron harmonizes with other (Gongorine) juxtapositions of contrary viewpoints and counterpoints throughout the poem. The desert is also that plane over which he "half / heard" a music that was a "music of survival," which superficially evokes the explorers and pioneers who ventured out West. Ultimately, we discover, that desert music is the existential plane, a page of his imagination, poetry. Over that desert, passing Yuma on his way to El Paso, Williams' mind was full of his tributaries, Native American, Spanish, an experience that allowed him to sleep "fitfully." "Thinking of Paris," which was, of course, how Elena survived, and an allusion that complements his other tributes, he awoke hearing "the tick / of the rails," suggesting a clock (perhaps of home), and seeing the "jagged desert" upon whose plane he was ready to "lay" himself down:

> —to tell
> what subsequently I saw and what heard
>
> —to place myself (in
> my nature) beside nature
>
> —to imitate
> nature (for to copy nature would be a shameful thing)
>
> I lay myself down:
>
> (*CPII* 275–276)

The poem then originated with his urge to "lay myself down," as if to say laying down the colors and textures of his words on the jagged (cubist) desert-canvas now made fertile by his memory and imagination.

After that digression, the poem takes us back to the Old Market in Juárez. The market has side streets, with "joints" that sell tequila at "a nickel a slug." But in these places one is in danger of getting "beaten up."

This evokes the involvement of De Soto, of consuming and being consumed, of coming into contact with America. But, as he did the last time he visited Mexico, with the Gonzales family, Bill postures that he is there as an Anglo:

I do
my drinking on the main drag

(*CPII* 276)

As Williams and Flossie take in the market's colors and bustle, they pass a bull ring. The entire scene comprises a layering of opposites, the "few squatted Indians" and the Mexican crafts contrasted to a six-foot Texan woman and her mink cape. The bull ring has a second tier, from where he sees another counterpoint, this time of nature and human hands: "about a million / sparrows" in the trees of a park where the buses stop. The park, Williams supposes, is a sanctuary from a "driving sand" called "Texas rain." Lastly, they pass a fountain (a source, a spring) in which Williams sees only two alligators, which Flossie insists were four and that they looked at Williams "all the time." Except for the importance of Williams' seeing two, the significance of the alligators is unclear.

While they walk through that marketplace, Williams is approached by children who ask for a penny. Bill responds "instinctively" but also divided:

instinctively
one has already drawn one's naked
wrist away from those obscene fingers
as in the mind a vague apprehension speaks
and the music rouses

(*CPII* 277)

Using the pronoun "one," assuming a neutral stance, his instinctive reaction is the Puritan's ingrained refusal to touch: the "obscene fingers" belong to the *other*, the demon. Bill draws his wrist away, but not cleanly, not without Carlos' consciousness adulterating his gesture with "a vague apprehension." The dramatic conflict of spirits, which had already taken place in subtle ways around him, now consciously rouses the music of poetry.

Williams and Flossie pass by a bar and hear another music. They are surrounded by crafts ("hats, / riding boots, blankets") and the *others*, whose imagistic presence is "a stream of Spanish," spoken by a "she," without antecedent, who "brushes by, intense, wide / -eyed in eager talk with her boy husband," what he was to Elena. The "she" with her boy husband is either one of four or followed by "three half-grown girls, one of them eating a / pomegranate." That girl with the pomegranate is an image of his dark muse, his Kore, symbolized here by the pomegranate Persephone ate in hell. The girl also evokes his experience in Granada, recounted in "Asphodel," when he came down the hill and found himself "surrounded / by gypsy women," and a young girl guided him on his way: "pomegranate" is one of the several English meanings of the Spanish word *granada.*

The poem briefly changes its viewpoint to that of the *others* who look upon a Midwestern man and wife, who are tourists in search of bargains and also conniving looters:

> and the serious tourist,
> man and wife, middle-aged, middle-western,
> their arms loaded with loot, whispering
> together—still looking for bargains

> (*CPII* 278)

They are takers from America, who don't even allow their words to mingle with the environs and whose spiritual attitude is echoed by a voice heard as it passes a candy booth, which expresses doubt that any tourist would ingest Mexico: "Do you suppose anyone actually / buys—and eats that stuff?" (*CPII* 278)

The next section returns to Bill's viewpoint and relates his experience in the strip joint. The Anglo striptease dancer, an appropriate metaphor for this poem, teases with her own personae, an image of Williams himself. Williams and Flossie had stopped in a place that plays "the usual local / jing-a-jing," as a singer crooned with her heart fixed on someone offstage. When the stripper comes out, Bill makes fun of the "worn-out trouper," who is not Mexican. But Carlos, appreciating her sensuality, does not see her as funny:

> There is a fascination
> seeing her shake

> the beaded sequins from
> a string about her hips
>
> She gyrates but it's
> not what you think,
> one does not laugh
> to watch her belly.

(CPII 279)

"One" is moved by something that transcends her tawdriness. Her belly is the altar of her female principle, her poetic faculties. Her gyrating belly is simultaneously both sensual and serious, anatomy and spiritual site. Her eyes have a certain "candor," which is used bilingually to signify *frankness* as English (to please Bill) and *white heat* as Spanish (to satisfy Carlos). While she dances to an unacceptable public music, she concurrently dances to his inner music because she knows that her performance is a deception, an act—as Williams too is aware of his Bill persona for the sake of art. Like him, she performs duplicitously, making herself naked and yet not truly baring herself.

Carlos' admiration of her sensuality is interrupted by Bill's contemplating the Latin music that had been playing before:

> *Why don't these Indians get over this nauseating prattle about their souls and their loves and sing us something else for a change?*

(CPII 280)

Here Williams gets his Bill and Carlos personae confused in his demand that the "Indians," actually Mexicans, sing "[to] us": that music in Spanish is not directed at Bill's world. Nevertheless, Bill calls that earlier music a "lying music." Appreciating the stripper as an alter image of his own duplicity, he understands that she is "part of another tune," which is not that of her Latin audience:

> She
> at least knows she's
> part of another tune,
> knows her customers,
> has the same

> opinion of them as I
> have.
>
> (*CPII* 280)

While Carlos admires her sensuality and Bill embraces her as having her own tune more honest than the Latins', these unbridged selves do not communicate, and that contradiction elicits the sweet tune of poetry in him, a situation that prompts Bill to question himself as to what he finds "so refreshing" about that stripper.

> What in the form of an old whore in
> a cheap Mexican joint in Juárez, her bare
> can waggling crazily can be
> so refreshing to me, raise to my ear
> so sweet a tune, built on such slime?
>
> (*CPII* 281)

(This question parallels the one asked in "A Portrait in Greys" of his other spirit: "Must I be always / moving counter to you?") Significant here is the use of the word "joint," where Americans and Mexicans join, as Juárez/El Paso form a joint between the two countries. For in this joint, Bill and Carlos are also being joined in the sweet tune he is hearing. Of course, while Bill at first was admiring that she was holding back something of herself, Carlos perceived that what was so refreshing was that she was willing to mingle her nakedness, her sensuality, with the Mexicans. Her spirit, as Carlos would have said, is good. But Williams only hints at that saving grace in his questioning what he found so refreshing, refusing to step out of Bill's character, as if Bill were unaware that Carlos had long ago answered his question in *In the American Grain*. Instead, Bill's attention has all along been fixed on his ability to hear another tune, questioning himself about whether those thoughts about the stripper were his "merely playing the poet" or his inventing "it out of whole cloth."

The poem passes from the "joint" to the restaurant, whose Latin root means "restore." There Bill is restored to an environment without a lying music, while the poem enjoys a stasis in a shift in viewpoint. In contrast to the joint, in the restaurant's kitchen the presumably Mexican cook is well-dressed. Here the "lying" is being done by Americans:

> A foursome, two oversize Americans, no
> longer young, got up as cowboys,
> hats and all, are drunk and carrying on
> with their gals, drunk also, . . .
>
> (*CPII* 281)

One of the women is trying to incite her man to dance, but he can't keep up with her. She is "insatiable" and he is exhorted to "Give it the gun, pardner!" Behaving sensually, like Carlos and thus truly American, the cowboys and their gals consume the tequila (consume America) and evoke Morton and not Mather. On the other hand, they are boisterous, while around them are families, presumably Mexican, "some with children, eating. Rather a better / class than you notice / on the streets." Similarly balancing, the Mexican cook embodies honesty:

> his shirt sleeves
> rolled up, an apron over
> the well-pressed pants of a street
>
> suit, black hair neatly parted,
> a tall
> good-looking man, is working
> absorbed, before a chopping block
>
> (*CPII* 281–282)

This is a far cry from the world outside with its market and joints; in this restaurant, Bill is home: "Old fashioneds all around?"

But the dinner conversation makes him reflect on his identity:

> So this is William
> Carlos Williams, the poet
>
> Floss and I had half consumed
> our quartered hearts of lettuce before
> we noticed the others hadn't touched theirs
>
> (*CPII* 282)

Subtly, the agony of self-realization is represented in the motif of twos: "William / Carlos," "Floss and I," "half consumed," "quartered hearts," "the others . . . theirs," and if one is permitted a *conceptista* pun, "lettuce" homonymously split into "let us." Also the "touch" theme arises: the others would not consume Mexican produce as Flossie and he did, "even though you get typhoid," as he notes further on.

After being asked why he writes poetry, Williams answers that he writes "Of necessity." His response to the question of what sets a poem off is itself set off in the center:

Oh. But what sets it off?

> I am that he whose brains
> are scattered
> aimlessly

(*CPII* 282)

His answer captures in its syntax the complexity of Williams, man and poet. His "I" is a "he," a persona, that is a composite of fragments "scattered / aimlessly." Only the poetic syntax composes the image that composes the "I."

Williams and Flossie walk back to El Paso, whose name means both step and passage, and he again feels the children's fingers "on the naked wrist." This time, succumbing to the "vague apprehension" mentioned earlier, he gives them money: "Here! now go away." This symbolic gesture of exchange is consistent with the consumption of the lettuce and quail, the mingling with America. But on a personal, encoded level, something else was intended, as revealed in a draft:

An insistent
—penny please. The ~~delicate~~ touch upon

Here! now go away.

Go away! [In pencil:] no come back I am you[3]

Clearly Carlos and Bill disagreed over whether the touch was "delicate" or "insistent." Williams also debated with himself over whether he should order the children to "go away" or, as he penciled in, call them back, embrace them: "no come back I am you." In the final version, the "Here! now go away" is left to stand alone, a capitulation to Bill despite, in the previous scene with the children, Carlos' intrusion, which left him with a "vague apprehension."

The earlier draft, then, renders explicit the encoded identity theme in this complex poem and is yet another confirmation that one has to read

Williams presupposing a "conceptualist" enciphered style. Only after we decipher his dual Anglo/Latin usage of "apprehension," for example, do we better understand that the first time that he sent those children off and in his mind he heard an ambiguous impulse of uneasiness and understanding, "a vague apprehension," he also felt the contrary impulse to *apprehendere,* or "seize" them, which is what the draft confirms: the word "apprehension" itself is an emblematic image of balance between Bill's impulse and Carlos'. Similarly, in requesting a penny the children are really asking him for *currency,* money, intercourse and, ultimately, touch. What Bill gives them is a symbolic representation of the best his culture had to offer, Abraham Lincoln, in whom among his army "the least private would find a woman to caress him" (*AG* 234). In the final version, the draft's "no come back I am you" and the *prendere* ("grab") encoded in "apprehension" were translated in the later scene into the gesture of giving, the currency, the penny.

Nevertheless, the inner conflicts involved in his giving that penny cause him to hear the inner music again, and Williams figures that it was prompted by the "annoyance" of the children's fingers. This thought is immediately juxtaposed with the idea of Bill's having given his time to the host at dinner:

> so that's
> where the incentive lay, with the annoyance
> of those surprising fingers.
>
> So you're a poet?
> a good thing to be got rid of—half drunk,
> a free dinner under your belt, even though you
> get typhoid—and to have met people you
> can at least talk to
>
> relief from that changeless, endless
> inescapable and insistent music

(*CPII* 283)

Bill's evening was full of contradictions: he was the guest poet even if a good thing to get rid of, and he received a free dinner but a meal that can kill you with typhoid. But Bill saw the true reward as that of having met "people you / can at least talk to," a "relief" from the lying music outside the restaurant. That music is called "insistent," as had been the Mexican children's fingers. By crying out for relief from the Latin music, Bill reveals his compulsion to reject it and Latins, with whom he associated Elena's immoral escapism in romance:

> What else, Latins, do you yourselves
> seek but relief!
> with the expressionless ding dong you dish up
> to us of your souls and your loves, which
> we swallow. Spaniards!

(CPII 283)

Getting carried away with his tirade, Bill again complains that Latin music dishes up its "ding dong" to Anglo Americans, "to us," the "us" being Bill's rhetorical solidarity device, used to characterize his experiences as shared American experiences. In "Two Pendants: For the Ears," he clarifies: "I / say 'us' but I mean, alas, only me" (*CPII* 207).

Additionally, in his passionate tongue-lashing against the Mexicans, Bill employs the same misnomer he often used to describe Spanish-speakers in his life, "Spaniards." Then, balancing by contradicting Bill, Carlos who knows better whispers from out of a parenthesis:

> (though these are mostly
> Indians who chase the white bastards
> through the streets on their Independence Day
> and try to kill them)

(CPII 283)

Again, the conflict between his personae arouses "the music":

> What's that?
> Oh, come on.
> But what's THAT?
> the music! the
> *music!* as when Casals struck
> and held a deep cello tone
> and I am speechless

(CPII 283–284)

In one of the drafts, this scene is revealingly different. In a lined-out stanza, Bill makes the same complaint of Mexicans, whom he calls "Spaniards," but the musical imagery is more detailed, quoting the singer's refrained "Ai,ai,ai,ai,ai!," which identified the "lying music" as Mexican *rancheras:*

> . . . I am sick of such stuff you call music
> When will you remember el Cid again
> —not this everlasting prattle of *amor*
> Have you turned women with your silly
>   Ai,ai,ai,ai,ai![4]

As he had often celebrated the woman in himself, inevitably that stanza was destined to be changed. Also in his summoning "el Cid" as a high-brow response to the *ranchera,* Bill would have played the Europhile Eliot before America, a contradiction the poem ultimately avoided.

The final version offers the music of Pablo Casals as a counterweight to the "prattle" of romantic *rancheras.* Listening to his inner music in counterpoint with the "lying music," Williams' composite "I" becomes speechless in stasis, as when he listens to Casals. But why Casals? Because, offspring of both America and Europe, Casals too was born of a mother from Puerto Rico, the land in which he lived and worked after the Spanish Civil War, and where he died. Being Puerto Rican and his mother's favorite musician, Casals was another Williams alter image and a tributary, the musician always evoked by Williams' reference to the cello. In the poem "Wide Awake, Full of Love," he implicitly compares Casals' playing with Elena's voice, the instrument whose "cello notes" led him "to the music":

> Your voice
> whose cello notes
> upon the theme have led
> me to the music?

                                                          (*CPII* 197)

Casals also aroused in Williams angry memories of the defeated Loyalists, which explains why a version of "The Desert Music" published in 1951 included a reference to Franco:

>   the music! the
> *music!* as when Casals struck

> and held a deep cello tone across Franco's
> lying chatter and I am speechless

(CPII 493)

The reference to Franco, had it remained, would have limited Casals to a symbol of Spain, overshadowing his Puerto Rican half, and also turned his music into a protest against Fascism, diminishing its breadth as image, which here encompasses poetry itself.

That music-poetry incarnate is also what Williams perceived in the "form" propped up on the bridge. Like the Spanish *pícaro* protagonist from *Lazarillo de Tormes,* who was born in the middle of a river, and thus in no land, Williams the wanderer sees himself symbolized on the Río Grande. (And who can say that Williams did not have in mind that image of Lazarillo's birth from this most famous paradigm of picaresque novels?) The "form" was visible in "half-light" and regressing to an even earlier state of gestation. Frozen in his *unformed* state, protected by the music of poetry, the embryo/"form" can evolve eternally in the possibility of never having to become a fish to swim "against the stream," as Williams had to, against the mainstream, or be born a child-artist like himself prepared "to imitate life":

> The music
> guards it, a mucus, a film that surrounds it,
> a benumbing ink that stains the
> sea of our minds—to hold us off—shed
> of a shape close as it can get to no shape,
> a music! a protecting music

(CPII 284)

The music spreads over the mind in the way that a spill darkens the water, obscuring thoughts so the mind doesn't think too much, and thus protecting the mind from the logic that would force a decision as to what that embryo is to become. Torn by incompatible Anglo and Latin animi, Williams sees himself resolved in this fish/child swimming in its sack of music, on no land. The "grotesque" does not have to choose or evolve, and only to a logical mind does this reluctant primal mass seem undefined or unformed; for Williams it is "form," a work of art, a poet. As were those children whom he wanted to call back, that "form" on the bridge is "I":

> I *am* a poet! I
am. I am. I am a poet, I reaffirmed, ashamed

> (*CPII* 284)

If we trace the chronology of that word "ashamed" in Williams' lexicon, we recall that shame was what Elena's spiritualism made him feel. The pairing of "reaffirmed" and "ashamed" corresponds to his public and private personae, his Bill and Carlos, his being both Anglo and Latin American. Only now he hears the music of his unified identity as poet, an identity defined by the dance of images that now surround him "as in a lonely moment," when he writes a poem. The "verb" therefore wants to "become articulate," which also means to form a joint, extend a bridge between his disjoined parts:

> Now the music volleys through as in
> a lonely moment I hear it. Now it is all
> about me. The dance! The verb detaches itself
> seeking to become articulate

> (*CPII* 284)

The final stanza comments on the improvisational, fragmented appearance of his poem, reflecting on "the wonders of the brain" that can hear the music and of the possibility to record it, as in "The Desert Music" itself. The brain image sustains the motif of body parts (embryo, fingers, wrists, hips, breasts), which reinforces the concomitant theme of joints, composition, articulation. In summary, this poem paints yet another cubist self-portrait, a form that becomes visible in a design that juxtaposes images of contradiction and counterpoints so they all dance to the music of his stasis.

Epilogue:
Conversation on the "Weather"

During the early stages of writing this book, I described its subject to an editor acquaintance, who after evincing excitement paused, his tone suddenly reversed: "They'll never forgive you for this." Because a feature of being unforgiven is being unforgotten, I took the warning as a sign that I was doing the right thing. Actually, how "they" would react was the first distraction against which I had plugged my mental ears in order to write my book my way. ("They" had also told Williams that he couldn't retrieve "roses from dead briars.") On nearing its completion, however, as I allowed myself to imagine it in the real world, that editor's words came back, and this time they seemed more justified than in the seventies when he said them. They helped me to see that by writing this book I myself had been responding to a condition of time and place that he called "they" and Williams likened to the "weather": that combination of social and institutional forces in the face of which an artist discovers self-realization. Comfort with the prevailing vectors inevitably produces work that is *with* the "weather," but if the surrounding atmosphere irks or represses, then the work will turn *against* the "weather," a definitive stand taken, whatever the content may say, in its structure. Williams' confrontation with his "weather" is examined at length in this study, but the increasing applicability of that editor's warning of two decades ago warrants some reflection on the "weather" in which this book endeavors to restore the visibility of Carlos.

Williams' stance "Against the Weather" emanated from his disagreement with his country's self-understanding. His aesthetic and cultural shocks to the national organism aroused a deeper-rooted consciousness that flourished in the Beat Generation, the literary revolts of the sixties and seventies and, in the nineties, the questioning of the canon. Unsurprisingly, the cultural nuances epitomized in Williams' Bill/Carlos dichotomy generally parallel the divers cultural underpinnings of today's academic factions. But the impetus to write this book actually came to me from the earlier, sixties consciousness. It was Williams' lineage that first provoked me to reread him, which I did with very modest expectations, never anticipating an extensive and vital connection between his Puerto Rican background and his work. As I stated in the introduction, I did not have to play detective. Besides his numerous encodings, Williams himself provided glosses on his ethnic consciousness, which gained importance in exact proportion to the intensity with which he attacked his "weather"; his critics simply tuned out what they had no use for. Nor did today's polemic persuade my critical approach. While my book naturally lends itself to being conscripted for the left side of the controversy, my critical method, which some might call unfashionable, was not intended to reflect solidarity with that friendly faction. I fortuitously followed Williams' dictum on the subject of what artists must do whatever the "weather" conditions: remain true to themselves. This meant concentrating on Williams as man and poet, putting aside his attributes as icon in the counterattack by the new formalists or in the tempest over the canon.

The underlying issue in both discourses is, of course, whether the national culture that once responded to traditional poetic forms still exists, and if its form and character correspond to the culture imaged by the canon: What is the "America" in American literature? Personally, as the mainstream has long carried itself as a mythic ethnicity, I have had no quarrels with the canon understood as a compendium of a great ethnic literature. But one need not possess a non-mainstream soul to deduce that the canon embodies the "weather"'s ignoble flaw, operative throughout American literary history but especially questionable in modern times. That flaw is its clinging to the assumption that only the fort or settlement will harvest important ideas and aesthetic innovations, so that writings from a different ethnocentricity on the Great Plains of the American experience are presumed unfit for the *universal* literary feast, with "universal" frequently being an alternately naive or duplicitous substitute for "our."

Similarly, implicit in the new formalism is an understandable nostalgia for a lost craftsmanship, a sentiment that suffers great pains to express itself dissociated from an implicit ethnic pride in one's literary roots in Europe—a characterizing feature that is explicitly ascribed to identify cultural "others." Against this hypocrisy, I would like to believe that this book will provoke some thought on the abusive use of identifiers such as "ethnic," "non-mainstream," and "minority," whose original denotations have deferred to their connotative usages, making them interchangeable. Socially, they have come to signify the powerlessness to demythicize the centricity of those in power. In a literary context, they have become codes with which to describe content that is predictable and intended to be read with no expectation of mature aesthetic, philosophical, or stylistic originality or merit. Moreover, because those identifiers all connote "social" or "socially committed," they also imply a simplicity of language that makes it accessible to an unsophisticated readership, a style that addresses the least educated members of the "weather"'s low preconception of that group. Codification of this sort is not distant from the pattern used to disqualify and therefore manage ideation in colonies.

This connotative culling also distorts by implying that a writing exists that never began from a localized, ostensibly small, human experience. We all hold the contrary to be self-evident, of course, but sophistication behooves that in practice we disregard that truth: some writers are just too good to be "ethnic." In the still-revolutionary seventies, young writers from diverse communities intentionally labeled themselves "ethnic" or "minority" or "non-mainstream" as their way of turning the table on the "weather" and undermining its haughtiness toward their respective groups. Arguably, this countercultural labeling also provided a shield against being subjected to what they considered "elitist" critical standards, but the movement's altogether valid argument was that their writings restored to American letters dimensions of the national pluralism that the "weather" habitually marginalizes. Soon it became apparent that this young writing was part of a broader program against the "weather": critics and marginalized literary communities in a joint campaign to expose the political deep structure of hallowed assumptions of what constitutes literary excellence, what in fact is the ethnocentric message of tradition and the canon.

Liberated by new critical theories, academic revolutionaries began to eschew the traditional emphasis on artistic execution in favor of inquiries into pluralistic representation and egalitarian ethnocentricities, a perspective that, at an extreme, has led to the dismissal of writing too preoccupied with aesthetic novelty as that which betrays the writer's secret desire to collaborate with the white male power structure, otherwise known as tradition. That power is what conservatives are accused of defending, in their pride in tradition and a total disregard of writing that does not originate from the cultural center. But conservatives are not so homogeneous, ranging from those who plainly concede to having no sympathy with pluralism or egalitarian notions to those who, appealing to an unbiased objectivity, defend the traditionalist's discrimination as being based on proven quality and the highest aesthetic and intellectual standards—although the measure continues to be the syllabus of the Great Works, the canon.

The ongoing dialectic notwithstanding, both Right and Left share the same preconceptions about writing from outside the "catalogue"; for both, writing with a social consciousness is antagonistic to writing whose objective is aesthetic and intellectual truth. If one adheres too puristically to the preachings of either camp, Ellison's existentialist motif in *Invisible Man* remains disconnected from the theme of racial consciousness. Similarly, the use of point of view in "Benito Cereno," as well as the brilliant tropes whose effects allow Melville to deliver his story/message in its fullness, could be exploited to focus on literary technique and distract from his uncompromising examination of ethnocentricity, racial injustice, and the corruption of white civilization. In other words, the literary clash taking place is between irreconcilable sides that are entrenching their particular applications of a very old convention about, on the one hand, the parameters evoked by "mainstream" and, on the other hand, marginalizing modifiers. Critics today may find the convention useful, but Ellison and Melville obviously didn't. Williams' tenet that, in the *structure* of a work the artist reveals, and thus takes, the truest stand against the social "weather" is predicated on the nonexistence of an antagonism that both camps take for granted.

Owing to the present condition, I am therefore compelled to advise the reader to think twice before summarizing this book as "an ethnic interpretation of Williams." To begin with, this book interprets *poems*, not Williams, whose identity as Carlos is incontrovertible. And yet ethnicity does figure in this book, which *can* be called an ethnic interpretation of Williams' work, but not to connotatively muffle the implications of his unique understanding of himself as an American poet so as to protect the nervous Anglo American consciousness. That Williams ambivalently kept Carlos in a blind spot of the culture was the consequence of his refusal to be marginalized as "foreign," the then equivalent of today's abusive usage of "ethnic" and "minority," or dismissed by being perceived as belonging to another race, as even more so than now "Hispanic" was popularly understood to denote in his day. But, as I demonstrate in this book, Williams only retreated to arm a better attack against narrowness; to keep from being straitjacketed as a writer, he invested all his prodigious ingenuity, to our lasting profit. In this way, Williams repeated a secret ceremony performed by many American writers, who out of fear of exclusion, simply in order to survive, have hidden from their country's view the true sources of their enriching contributions. Today the "weather" demonstrates a broader acceptance to seeing the world through exotic eyes, but selectively, as best illustrated by the prestigious status of literary translations.

Presently translations from any language, even of writings that are ethnic in the original sense, are endowed with a glow—apparently carried over from the time when translations were scarce and only the masterworks found their way into American markets. As implied by the convention, the act of translation bridges the distance between the foreignness of a culture and its universality in a way that ethnic writing in a common language does not. Thus, even though recent prospects of a new domestic commercial market—the non-mainstream reader—have improved the situation somewhat, many publishers are still prone to forecasting a general reception for translations while foreseeing only an ethnic audience for ethnic authors in English. A nuance of this preconception is the practice of inviting to academic conferences Latin American or African authors as surrogate minority keynote speakers who would attract a greater number of conferees.

Translation's relatively new marketability, to which the sixties' and seventies' "boom" in Latin American writing contributed significantly, reveals an important shift in "weather" patterns toward the "other," contrasting with the view in Williams' time, when translated works had constrained commercial possibilities, although even then translations had a greater life expectancy than writing completely from outside the "catalogue." That's why Williams assumed the posture of translator as part of his "cure," a writing that secretly, conceptually, structurally "interknit" his Anglo American idiom with his true bicultural person. Williams' technique subverted his biased "weather" by encoding in "imaginary translation" those elements that the dominant culture deemed outside the "catalogue" of its possible representative voices and roots. The culture's ignorance became his gain, an unmapped mother lode of novelty.

Additionally, in his going as far as titling two original poems as "Translations," he was making a statement about a universal process of sign manipulation in the psyche. Labeling a poem as a translation alters the language by changing the ethnocentricity from which we read it. In Williams' case, ostensible English becomes Spanish and furthermore conveys the lesson that a writer's experience is always foreign, isolated, and unique, always needing to be translated into the local currency; in other words, the truth carrying over to collective literary expression, there is no such thing as a nonethnic writing. This remedy for his condition of being a bicultural member of a xenophobic society leveled the playing field. Seeing others as no different than himself, part American and part foreigner, gave him the confidence, the "strange courage," that today should encourage others who write in English translating from any foreign heart.

Williams' remedy of translating himself was destined, if not planned, to subvert the canon, in which he as Bill now shines, albeit ironically and, as already noted, not with uniform brightness to all eyes in today's "weather." In fact, my positing Carlos' centrality in Williams' work only aggravates his already ambiguous position in the canon. His career adversary had been the "catalogue," whose pantheon is the canon, so that his being inducted into it had already implied a customization, a censoring by omission, the downplaying of Carlos by his admirers. On the other hand, Williams' becoming the patron saint of free verse, spontaneity, automatic writing, and even language poetry has prompted disbelievers to ascribe to him the start of literary pulmonary plague. This dichotomous "weather" report is what Carlos has to look forward to on publication day, a reception that propelled half-facetious questions across my mind. In revealing that the "weather" ambivalently preserves Bill in its own image and likeness, does this book put Williams' immortality at risk? Are there provisions for decanonization? Now that his "spontaneity" proves to be the result of deliberation and fluid craftsmanship, do his detractors turn around, disassociate him from the free versers who felt inspired by the easy-rolling Williams everyone thought he was? Do these movements now continue to accept the baroque Williams, or is he now of less value to them? Unanswerable all, those inquiries yielded to a final one, tangentially related but at least manageable: How would Williams have received this book?

Bill, who waited for the end of his career to write about "what has concerned him most in the past," his mother and her Puerto Rican background, would probably have been pleased, secretly of course. In his own way, to the extent that he understood them, Williams remained true to and forthright about his Latin American roots. The cultural and spiritual balance he pursued in his writings was a solution for offering his country the gift of his composite genius while allowing him to remain true to his bicultural self. Balance also meant that his posturings, personae, and contradictions form an existential whole that should be judged like a work by Juan Gris, all of a piece, with each element distinctly its own yet contributing to a singleness, a continuity of spirit. Spirits are the one permanent thing, Williams celebrated, and of his two selves Carlos was his Dionysian *duende*. In the same way that spirits returned to possess his medium mother, through Bill's words Carlos would perpetually haunt posterity's "weather" with his message that unless it turns a deaf ear to Puritan ghosts and listens to those in his "line," expanding the imagination to do the "mingling," the good thing, any reading of America or William Carlos Williams would only be a Eurocentered misreading. In sum, he would not be offended that my book invites Carlos to walk unencodedly among us in his poems and understands those poems as Bill's words with Carlos' soul—Carlos, from the grave, getting the last laugh on Pound.

Abbreviations Used

The following abbreviations for works by or about Williams Carlos Williams are used throughout this book:

A	*The Autobiography of William Carlos Williams*
AG	*In the American Grain*
CPI	*The Collected Poems, Vol. I*, ed. A. Walton Litz and Christopher MacGowan
CPII	*The Collected Poems, Vol. II*, ed. Christopher MacGowan
EK	*The Embodiment of Knowledge*, ed. Ron Loewinsohn
FD	*The Farmer's Daughters*
I	*Imaginations*
IWW	*I Wanted to Write a Poem: The Autobiography of the Works of a Poet*, ed. Edith Heal
ML	*Many Loves and Other Plays*
MM	*William Carlos Williams and the Maternal Muse*, by Kerry Driscoll
NW	*William Carlos Williams: A New World Naked*, by Paul Mariani
P	*Paterson*
SE	*Selected Essays*
SL	*Selected Letters*, ed. John C. Thirlwall
VP	*A Voyage to Pagany*
Y	*William Carlos Williams Papers*, Beinecke Library, Yale University
YM	*Yes, Mrs. Williams*

Notes

INTRODUCTION
1. Ginsberg was reading Williams' poem XVIII from *Spring and All* (*CPII* 217).
2. John Richardson, *A Life of Picasso*, vol. 1, 11.

CHAPTER 1. A CUBIST PORTRAIT
1. Quoted in Emily Farnham, *Charles Demuth: Behind the Laughing Mask*, 52.
2. From an interview. Farnham 47.
3. Felicity Barringer, "Ethnic Pride Confounds the Census," *New York Times*, 9 May 1993, late ed., sec. 4: 3.
4. Rod Townley, *The Early Poetry of William Carlos Williams*, 65.
5. Harry Levin, "Introduction," *A Voyage to Pagany*, by William Carlos Williams, x.
6. William Carlos Williams, *The Collected Poems, Vol. I,* ed. A. Walton Litz and Christopher MacGowan, 409. (In subsequent notes, Williams should be assumed to be the author, if not otherwise stated.) Williams' phonetic Spanish is often misspelled and ungrammatical, which raises some questions touched upon later. Here "tenia" only lacks an accent, but *The Collected Earlier Poems* has this line read: *desde que avia cinco años,* with "avia" for "había," which even if correctly spelled incorrectly used the auxiliary verb "to have."
7. "Philip and Oradie," handwritten manuscript, in Beinecke Library, Yale University, Za Williams 297x.
8. Reed Whittemore, *William Carlos Williams: Poet from New Jersey,* 13.
9. Flores was incensed at Williams' treatment of him in *The Autobiography* and countered by publishing a short piece in Spanish in a Mexican journal. In a conversation at the Edna St. Vincent Millay Colony in June 1990, Flores said that he didn't publish Williams' poetry because he didn't care for it, adding "To my regret, of course."
10. Flores, it should be noted, was of a character that is readily and unpredictably poisoned. A poet in Puerto Rico, who had dined and conversed with Flores in San Juan on several occasions over a

few weeks, had an experience that left him perplexed. After a two week lapse of contact, during which the poet had to resolve some personal affairs, he telephoned Flores only to be promptly told that he was exactly the person with whom Flores did not want to speak.

11. Dated 7 January 1933, in John Sanford (Julian Shapiro) and William Carlos Williams, *A Correspondence*, 37. The relationship between Shapiro and Williams is laden with thematic coincidences. As Shapiro felt that his Jewish name was an obstacle, he changed it to Sanford. Williams congratulated him on his "new role." Shapiro, now John Sanford, gave this account: "By 'new role' Dr. Williams meant my new name: John Sanford. I had become in fact my own character of *The Water Wheel*, and from *Old Man's Place* onward, I have been so known. The change had long been urged on me by [Nathaniel] West, whose name had once been Weinstein. For me, he proposed that Shapiro be abandoned for Starbuck (why not Quee-queg?, I wonder), but I settled for something from a lesser work" (44).

12. Sources disagree over whether his name was José Julio or Julio José.

13. Loida Figueroa, *Breve Historia de Puerto Rico*, vol. 2, 192. In footnote 318 Figueroa cites Henna's name among those of others arrested, from a set of documents originally published in *Caribbean Studies* 5.3 (October 1965).

14. *Memoirs of Bernardo Vega*, trans. Juan Flores, 138–139.

15. ". . . somewhat better than blacks." Unless noted otherwise, all translations in this book are by the author.

16. Paul Mariani, *William Carlos Williams: A New World Naked*, 729. In *Yes, Mrs. Williams* Williams says he found his maternal *grandmother's* license. This is the only time Williams refers to Elena's mother as his grandmother.

17. In Mayagüez Williams read with poet Luis Hernández Aquinó and University of Puerto Rico professors of English, the poets Charles Bell and Irving Feldman.

18. *Alma Latina*, 22 March 1941: 51.

19. *NW* 54. Mariani quotes the first eleven lines, which open with the couplet: "Within the lofty hall is gay with flags / In battle won and many bristling antlers." The handwritten manuscript opens with "When chivalry like summer's crimson fruit / From blossom, April's flimsy pride and all. . . . "

20. Mariani's version has "kingdom's" misspelled.

21. Ann Fisher-Wirth, *William Carlos Williams and Autobiography: The Woods of His Own Nature*, 82.

22. Stieglitz Archive, Yale University, quoted in William Marling, *William Carlos Williams and the Painters, 1909–1923*, 9.

CHAPTER 2. THE FEMALE TOTEM

1. William Eric Williams, "Foreword" to *Yes, Mrs. Williams,* xvi.
2. Linda Welshimer Wagner, ed., *Interviews with William Carlos Williams: Speaking Straight Ahead,* 24.
3. From a letter to Bob Brown, *NW* 17.
4. *The Build-Up,* 330–331.
5. "From Notes about My Mother," *Literary Review* 1.1 (Autumn 1957): 7.
6. "... no se atreven [los puertorriqueños] a salir a pescar en un barco, porque luego los coge el holandés." From Antonio S. Pedreira, *Obras de Antonio S. Pedreira,* vol. 1, ed. Concha Meléndez, 130.
7. "Commonwealth" was the loose translation of the Spanish name *Estado Libre Asociado,* literally "Associated Free State," and often taken one step further in the U.S. press to the more positive "Free Associated State." The word "Commonwealth" was chosen to suggest to the UN delegates that, as the English Commonwealth nations were independent, so too would Puerto Rico be a separate nation. So this was explained, in conversation, by a former UN diplomat from Ceylon. The ploy succeeded, with the semiautonomous government still calling itself a "Commonwealth."
8. The original military rationale was to have an institution that would mold bicultural Latin American leaders, who would then facilitate the implementation of foreign policy to benefit the United States' hemispheric interests—all at the cost, extolled *The Congressional Record,* of "less than one battleship."
9. Cited from Concha Meléndez and Antonio S. Pedreira, "Luis Lloréns Torres, El Poeta de Puerto Rico," *El Imparcial* 30 June 1944, in Carmen Marrero, "Prólogo," Luis Lloréns Torres, *Obras Completas,* ciii.
10. Bryce Conrad, *Refiguring America: A Study of William Carlos Williams' In the American Grain,* 15.
11. Manuel Zeno Gandía, *La Charca,* 104.
12. Pedreira 63.
13. As the practice spread to other social classes, and especially Afro-Puerto Ricans, a commingling of spiritualism and *santería* (Afro-Cuban religion) took place, but that was considerably after Elena's time.
14. Unpublished manuscript, *Y,* Za Williams 269.
15. Ibid.
16. From an unpublished letter, William Carlos Williams to Louis Untermeyer, 8 March 1929, cited by Kerry Driscoll, *William Carlos Williams and the Maternal Muse,* 26.
17. Jerome Mazzaro, *William Carlos Williams: The Later Poems,* 135.
18. James E. Breslin, *William Carlos Williams: An American Artist,* 7.

19. *MM* 15.
20. This transcription of the sound of *Allá* (meaning "over there" or "out there" or "back then"), is ironically identical with the one meaning "High ya," said by his grandmother in "The Wanderer": "Haia! Here I am son."
21. Webster Schott, "Introduction," in *Imaginations*, 3.
22. From a 1939 letter to Horace Gregory, in *Selected Letters*, ed. John C. Thirlwall, 185.

CHAPTER 3. ALTER IMAGES

1. Jorge Luis Borges, *A Personal Anthology*, trans. and ed. Anthony Kerrigan, 115.
2. That Borges read Williams' posthumously published essay is unlikely and not at issue.
3. Letter dated 10 November 1930, quoted in *NW* 313.
4. These translations were part of the original London edition. The *Collected Early Poems* omitted those translations, which the 1991 *The Collected Poems, Vol. I* reinstated.
5. *I Wanted to Write a Poem: The Autobiography of the Works of a Poet*, ed. Edith Heal, 16. As was Williams' custom, speaking as Bill he distracts us from the significance of Elena's formation in Puerto Rico with her three years in Paris, which in *Yes, Mrs. Williams* and his writings is given relatively little space. It should also be noted that *I Wanted to Write a Poem* appears in 1958, well after the settling of the postwar immigration of Puerto Ricans. By then in the United States there had evolved a distinct, if negative, popular identity of Puerto Ricans, beyond the generic Spanish. This, along with Williams' having made another visit to Puerto Rico in 1956 appears to account for his referring, for the first time, to Elena's background not as "Spanish" but "Puerto Rican."

CHAPTER 4. TRANSLATIONS, IMAGINARY AND REAL

1. During a graduate lecture on *Moll Flanders* at a major university, the "picaresque" novel was discussed at length with no mention of the original *pícaro, Lazarillo de Tormes*. When subsequently asked in his office about the Spanish work's contribution to the genre, the professor waved it off with an "Oh, yes."
2. Updike's use of the preposition "by" in the phrase "drowned by the vitality" confirms Williams' thesis in *In the American Grain:* Wasps do not see themselves as drowning "in" the vitality of those other races, which would imply contact and interaction, so much as they are weighed down by them.
3. *NW* 112. This reference to his translating Lope de Vega comes from a 1914 letter to Viola Baxter Jordan, which Mariani cites. Nothing

else is said about this translation in *William Carlos Williams: A New World Naked.*

4. The two volumes are with Williams' papers in the Beinecke Library at Yale University. As the book is inscribed by Pound, adding "Ropallo," and *The Tempers* being published in 1913, we can place Williams' age at nearing thirty when he took an interest in translating.

5. After writing his autobiography, Williams also translated a poem by the Spaniard Jorge Guillén and works by the Latin Americans Alí Chumacero, Alfaro Figueredo, Pablo Neruda, Silvia Ocampo, Nicanor Parra, and Octavio Paz. With the exception of the translation of Guillén's poem, which is in the Beinecke Library at Yale, the translations of the Latin Americans' works were published and are found in *The Collected Poems of William Carlos Williams, Vol. II.*

6. Dated as "1937(?)" in *Selected Essays.*

7. My coming upon this poem was an invigorating confirmation: years before my trip to Passaic, the spark that eventually ignited the writing of this book, I had chosen to title my first poetry book, finally published in 1986, *Translations without Originals.*

8. Christopher J. MacGowan, *William Carlos Williams' Early Poetry: The Visual Arts Background,* 1.

9. Besides MacGowan, see also Bram Dijkstra, *The Hieroglyphics of New Speech: Cubism, Stieglitz and the Early Poetry of William Carlos Williams,* and William Marling, *William Carlos Williams and the Painters, 1909–1923.*

10. *Y, Za* Williams 202 n.p.

11. Ibid.

12. Reed Whittemore, *William Carlos Williams: Poet from New Jersey.*

13. Dijkstra 168.

14. *Y, Za* Williams 202 n.p.

CHAPTER 5. BLOODLINE, POETIC LINE

1. "An Informal Discussion of Poetic Form," *Revista de la Asociación de Mujeres Graduadas de la Universidad de Puerto Rico* (1941): 45.

2. Richardson 11.

3. John Russell, Introduction, *Góngora,* by Pablo Picasso, trans. Alan Trueblood, n.p.

4. R. O. Jones, Introduction, *Poems of Góngora,* by Luis de Góngora y Argote, 5.

5. Luis de Góngora y Argote, *Soledades,* ed. John Beverley, 84–85.

6. John Beverley's succinct and lucid annotations are paraphrased in this description, Góngora, *Soledades* 85.

7. Juan de Jáuregui, "Antídoto," in J. Jordán de Urríes, *Biografía y Estudio Crítico de Jáuregui* (Madrid: n.p., 1899), 167–168, cited in "Apéndice Tercero" in Luis de Góngora y Argote, *Poesía,* ed. José Manuel Blecua, 116–117.

8. Francisco de Quevedo, *Antología Poética*, ed. José María Balcells, 198.
9. Jorge Luis Borges, *Otras Inquisiciones*, 64.
10. This is not intended as an endorsement of Williams' alter image interpretation of Lorca, a poet who went through several literary phases in which he alternated between being a formalist and a surrealist poet.
11. Williams gives no source for his quoted translation of Unamuno, *SE* 224.
12. Federico García Lorca, *Poet in New York*, trans. Ben Belitt, 155. According to Belitt's notes, Silverio Franconetti was an Italian singer–song writer who went to Seville and cultivated the *cante jondo*, of which the *siguiriya* and *flamenco* are different forms.

CHAPTER 6. INHERITED SOULS

1. Conrad 105. The final quotation is cited by Conrad from William Carlos Williams, "Comment," *Contact* 4 (Summer 1921): 18.
2. José Martí, "Aboriginal American Authors," in *On Art and Literature: Critical Writings*, ed. Philip S. Foner, 202.
3. Martí, "Literary Matters," excerpted by Foner from a notebook written in 1881, translation by Elinor Randall, in *On Art*, 305–306.
4. José Martí, *Our America: Writings on Latin America and the Struggle for Cuban Independence*, ed. Philip S. Foner, 85.
5. Paul Laurence Dunbar, "The Party," *American Negro Poetry*, ed. Arna Bontemps, 8–9.
6. Note the wordplay on the etymology of *maneuver*, from the French for manual work, fusing that denotation with the current one of movement.
7. Luis Palés Matos, *Poesía Completa y Prosa Selecta*, ed. Margot Arce de Vázquez, 149.
8. The Guatemalan Miguel Angel Asturias, one of the forefathers of "magical realism," studied anthropology in Paris when he realized that surrealism was a vision that his native traditions had long known as something more than an artistic device. The Cuban Alejo Carpentier also noted that difference between adopting a new vision as artifice and that vision being one's conduit to the world, a difference summarized in his often-quoted statement: "Those who don't believe in saints cannot be cured by their miracles...." (*Tientas y diferencias* [Havana: Ediciones Unión, 1966] 97.)
9. Translated from "Plena del Menéalo," Palés Matos 183.
10. "Prelude in Boricua," *American Prefaces* 2.2 (Winter 1942): 155. In *CPII* "Prelude in Boricua" is printed without the note, which is quoted in an endnote that expunges Williams' description of the poet.

11. "Prelude," *American Prefaces* 156. Observe, as noted earlier, Williams' objectifying his interest in the poem, a celebration of Caribbean mingling, by using the term "nigger talk," to sound more like Bill than Carlos.

12. Williams' referring to the year 1941, in fact, prompted my investigation into this connection, as that year immediately suggested the parallels between the two works. I readily assumed that, in keeping with Williams' pattern, if he had received from Palés Matos he would encode a sign of gratitude and tribute, which I promptly found in Book One.

13. Louis Simpson, *Three on the Tower,* 22.

14. Why he chose to write about Neruda in the past tense is unclear. Williams, according to José Vázquez Amaral, had given the poem to him to pass on to Neruda. See *CPII* 500.

CHAPTER 7. THE MUSIC OF STASIS

1. *I* 13. Litz and MacGowan cite in a note the lines that Moore removed, in which "hey-ding-ding" is actually used.

2. Wallace Stevens, *Letters of Wallace Stevens,* ed. Holly Stevens, 248–249.

3. *Y,* Za Williams 60.

4. Ibid.

Bibliography

WORKS BY WILLIAM CARLOS WILLIAMS

Al Que Quiere: A Book of Poems. "Epigraph" by Rafael Arévalo Martínez. Boston: The Four Seas Company, 1917.

The Autobiography of William Carlos Williams. New York: New Directions, 1951.

The Build-Up. New York: New Directions, 1968.

The Collected Earlier Poems. New York: New Directions, 1966.

Collected Later Poems. New York: New Directions, 1967.

The Collected Poems of William Carlos Williams, Volume I, 1909–1939. Edited by A. Walton Litz and Christopher MacGowan. New York: New Directions, 1986.

The Collected Poems of William Carlos Williams, Volume II, 1939–1962. Edited by Christopher MacGowan. New York: New Directions, 1988.

Dear Ez: Letters from William Carlos Williams to Ezra Pound. Edited by Mary Ellen Solt. Bloomington, Ind.: Frederic Brewer Press, 1985.

The Dog and the Fever. Translated, with Raquel Helene Hoheb, from *El Perro y la Calentura* by Francisco Quevedo. n.p.: New Directions, 1954.

The Embodiment of Knowledge. Edited by Ron Loewinsohn. New York: New Directions, 1961.

The Farmer's Daughters. "Introduction" by Van Wyck Brooks. New York: New Directions, 1961.

"From Notes about My Mother." *Literary Review* 1.1 (Autumn 1957): 5–12.

Imaginations. New York: New Directions, 1970.

"An Informal Discussion of Poetic Form." *Revista de la Asociación de Mujeres Graduadas de la Universidad de Puerto Rico* (1941): 44–45.

In the American Grain. New York: New Directions, 1956.

In the Money. New York: New Directions, 1967.

I Wanted to Write a Poem: The Autobiography of the Works of a Poet. Edited by Edith Heal. New York: New Directions, 1978.

The Knife of the Times. n.p.: Dragon Press, 1932.

Many Loves and Other Plays. New York: New Directions, 1961.

Paterson. New York: New Directions, 1963.

Pictures from Brueghel. New York: New Directions, 1962.
"Prelude in Boricua." *American Prefaces* 2.2 (Winter 1942): 155–157.
A Recognizable Image: William Carlos Williams on Art and Artists. Edited
    by Bram Dijkstra. New York: New Directions, 1978.
Selected Essays. New York: New Directions, 1969.
Selected Letters. Edited by John C. Thirlwall. New York: McDowell, Obol-
    ensky, 1957.
Selected Poems. Edited by Charles Tomlinson. New York: New Directions,
    1985.
A Voyage to Pagany. New York: New Directions, 1970.
White Mule. New York: New Directions, 1967.
William Carlos Williams–John Sanford: A Correspondence. Foreword by
    Paul Mariani. Santa Barbara, Calif.: Oyster Press, 1984.
Yes, Mrs. Williams. "Foreword" by William Eric Williams. New York: New
    Directions, 1982.

SECONDARY SOURCES
Aiken, Edward A. "'I Saw the Figure Five in Gold': Charles Demuth's
    Emblematic Portrait of William Carlos Williams." *Art Journal*
    (1987): 178–184.
Atlas, James. "Updike's Version." [Interview with John Updike.] *Vanity
    Fair* 49 (September 1986): 90–91.
Barrett, Linton Lomas, ed. *Five Centuries of Spanish Literature: From the
    Cid through the Golden Age.* New York: Dodd, Mead and Company,
    1962.
Bontemps, Arna, ed. *American Negro Poetry.* New York: Hill and Wang,
    1968.
Borges, Jorge Luis. *Otras Inquisiciones.* Buenos Aires: Emecé Editores,
    1971.
———. *A Personal Anthology.* Translated and edited by Anthony Kerri-
    gan. New York: Grove Press, 1967.
Breslin, James E. *William Carlos Williams: An American Artist.* Chicago:
    University of Chicago Press, 1985.
Cabrera, Francisco Manrique. *Historia de la Literatura Puertorriqueña.*
    New York: Las Américas Publishing Co., 1956.
Conrad, Bryce. *Refiguring America: A Study of William Carlos Williams'
    "In the American Grain."* Urbana and Chicago: University of Illi-
    nois Press, 1990.
Dickran, Tashjian. *William Carlos Williams and the American Scene.* New
    York: Whitney Museum, 1979.
Dijkstra, Bram. *The Hieroglyphics of New Speech: Cubism, Stieglitz and
    the Early Poetry of William Carlos Williams.* Princeton: Princeton
    University Press, 1966.
Driscoll, Kerry. *William Carlos Williams and the Maternal Muse.* Ann Ar-
    bor: UMI Research Press, 1987.

Farnham, Emily. *Charles Demuth: Behind the Laughing Mask*. Norman: University of Oklahoma Press, 1971.

Figueroa, Loida. *Breve Historia de Puerto Rico*. Vol. 2. Río Piedras, Puerto Rico: Editorial Edil, 1970.

Fisher-Wirth, Ann W. *William Carlos Williams and Autobiography: The Woods of His Own Nature*. University Park and London: The Pennsylvania State University Press, 1989.

García Lorca, Federico. *Poet in New York*. Translated by Ben Belitt. New York: Grove Press, 1955.

Góngora y Argote, Luis de. *Poesía*. Edited by José Manuel Blecua. Zaragoza: Editorial Ebro, 1976.

———. *Soledades*. Edited by John Beverley. Madrid: Ediciones Cátedra, 1982.

Heal Berrien, Edith. "A Poet's Integrity." *The Literary Review* 9.1 (Autumn 1965): 115–119.

Jones, R. O., ed. *Poems of Góngora*. By Luis de Góngora y Argote. Cambridge: Cambridge University Press, 1966.

Lazarillo de Tormes. Edited by José Miguel Caso González. Barcelona: Ediciones B., 1989.

Liebowitz, Herbert. "You Can't Beat Innocence." *American Poetry Review* 10.2 (March/April 1981): 35–48.

Lloréns Torres, Luis. *Obras Completas*. "Prólogo" by Carmen Marrero. San Juan: Instituto de Cultura Puertorriqueña, 1967.

MacGowan, Christopher J. *William Carlos Williams' Early Poetry: The Visual Arts Background*. Ann Arbor: UMI Research Press, 1984.

Mariani, Paul. *William Carlos Williams: A New World Naked*. New York: McGraw-Hill, 1981.

Marling, William. *William Carlos Williams and the Painters, 1909–1923*. Athens: Ohio University Press, 1982.

Martí, José. *On Art and Literature: Critical Writings*. Edited by Philip S. Foner. New York: Monthly Review Press, 1982.

———. *Our America: Writings on Latin America and the Struggle for Cuban Independence*. Edited by Philip S. Foner. New York: Monthly Review Press, 1977.

Mazzaro, Jerome. *William Carlos Williams: The Later Poems*. Ithaca: Cornell University Press, 1973.

Meléndez, Concha. "Sobre los manuscritos presentados en la Conferencia Interamericana de Escritores." *Revista de la Asociación de Mujeres Graduadas de la Universidad de Puerto Rico* (1941): 58–59.

Palés Matos, Luis. *Poesía Completa y Prosa Selecta*. Edited by Margot Arce de Vázquez. Caracas: Biblioteca Ayacucho, 1978.

Pedreira, Antonio S. *Obras de Antonio S. Pedreira*. Vol. 1. Edited by Concha Meléndez. San Juan: Instituto de Cultura Puertorriqueña, 1970.

Pound, Ezra. *Literary Essays*. New York: New Directions, 1935.

———. *Selected Letters, 1904–1971.* New York: New Directions Books, 1971.

Quevedo, Francisco de. *Antología Poética.* Edited by José María Barcells. Madrid: Sociedad General Española de Librería, 1982.

Quintana, Manuel Josef. *Poesías Selectas Castellanas.* Madrid: Gómez Fuentenebro y Compañía, 1817.

Reeve, F. D. "What's the Matter with Poetry." *The Nation* 20 (1993): 708–713.

Richardson, John. *A Life of Picasso.* Vol 1. New York: Random House, 1991.

Rodó, José Enrique. *Ariel: Motivos de Proteo.* Edited by Angel Rama. Caracas: Biblioteca Ayacucho, 1976.

Ruiz, Juan. *Libro de Buen Amor.* Edited by Nicasio Salvador Miguel. Madrid: Alhambra, 1985.

Russell, John. Introduction. *Góngora.* By Pablo Picasso. Translated by Alan Trueblood. New York: Braziller, 1985.

Sanford, John (Julian Shapiro) and William Carlos Williams. *A Correspondence.* Santa Barbara, Calif.: Oyster Press, 1984.

Sarmiento, Domingo Faustino. *Facundo: Civilización y Barbarie.* Barcelona: Planeta, 1986.

Simpson, Louis. *Three on the Tower.* New York: William Morrow, 1975.

Stevens, Wallace. *Letters of Wallace Stevens.* Edited by Holly Stevens. New York: Alfred A. Knopf, 1966.

Townley, Rod. *The Early Poetry of William Carlos Williams.* Ithaca: Cornell University Press, 1975.

Vega, Bernardo. *Memoirs of Bernardo Vega.* Translated by Juan Flores. New York: Monthly Review Press, 1984.

Wagner, Linda Welshimer, ed. *Interviews with William Carlos Williams: Speaking Straight Ahead.* New York: New Directions, 1976.

Wallace, Emily. *A Bibliography of William Carlos Williams.* Middletown, Conn.: Wesleyan University Press, 1968.

Whittemore, Reed. *William Carlos Williams: Poet from New Jersey.* Boston: Houghton Mifflin, 1975.

Zeno Gandía, Manuel. *La Charca.* Río Piedras: Editorial Edil, 1973.

Index